THE AUTHOR'S ANNOTATED EDITION*

1001
Ways To Be
ROMANTIC®

Gregory Godek

*Includes Greg's handwritten notes.

D1537752

*Life is simply too short **not** to be romantic.*

A Handbook for Men ——•—— A Godsend to Women

SOURCEBOOKS CASABLANCA™
AN IMPRINT OF SOURCEBOOKS, INC.®
NAPERVILLE, ILLINOIS

Title Page Theme Song:
"Who Wrote the Book of Love,"
The Monotones

"Greg Godek should be nominated for the Nobel Peace Prize for teaching 1001 Ways To Be Romantic."

~ BOSTON MAGAZINE

"The book is a well-thumbed romantic Bible that I consult often."

~ B. WICKER, READER

❤

1001 Ways To Be Romantic® is a federally registered trademark of Gregory J.P. Godek, denoting a series of products and services including (but not limited to) books, newsletters, calendars, audio cassette tapes, videotapes, CDs, music collections, coupons, product kits, gift collections, catalogs, greeting cards, games, Internet services, speeches, seminars and workshops, documentaries and TV shows.

The following are trademarks of Gregory J.P. Godek:
"LoveStories," "LoveLetter," "America's Romance Coach," "America's Leading Authority on Romantic Love," "America's #1 Romantic," "365 Days of Romance," "LoveTalks," "A Little Romance," "Changing the world—one couple at a time," "Romance Across America," and "1001WaysToBeRomantic.com."

❤

❤

Published by the Casablanca Press Division of Sourcebooks, Inc.
P.O. Box 4410, Naperville, Illinois 60567 • 630-961-3900 • Fax: 630-961-2168

❤

Cover photo by Allen Hochman
Cover and internal design © 1999 Sourcebooks, Inc.
Author photo by Victor Avila: 619-232-5154

❤

Visit www.1001WaysToBeRomantic.com

❤

Library of Congress Cataloging-in-Publication Data:
Godek, Gregory J.P., 1955-
1001 Ways To Be Romantic / Gregory J.P. Godek—Author's Annotated Edition
p. cm.
ISBN 1-57071-481-9 (pbk.: alk. paper)
1. Courtship Miscellanea. 2. Dating (Social customs) Miscellanea. 3. Love Miscellanea.
I. Title.
HQ801.G554 1999 646.7'7—dc21 99-36946 CIP

❤

Printed in the United States of America.
BA 10 9 8 7

Dedications

"I like your book 1001 Ways To Be Romantic! It will fill your brain with all kinds of wonderful romantic ideas. I like number 584!"

~ OPRAH WINFREY

Dedication Page Theme Song:
"Dedicated to the One I Love,"
The Mamas & The Papas

Also by Greg Godek

* 10,000 Ways To Say I Love You
* Love—The Course They Forgot To Teach You In School
* Love Coupons
* I Love You Coupons
* The Portable Romantic
* The Lovers' Bedside Companion
* 1001 *More* Ways To Be Romantic
* Romantic Mischief: The Playful Side of Love
* Romantic Dates: Ways to Woo & Wow the One You Love
* Romantic Fantasies—And Other Sexy Ways of Expressing Your Love
* Romantic Questions: Growing Closer Through Intimate Conversation
* (Music CD): 1001 Ways To Be Romantic—The Music: The Most Romantic Classical Music of All Time

Page Theme Song:
"Paperback Writer," The Beatles

Acknowledgments

- Tracey
- Deborah Werksman
- Bruce Jones
- Kate Broughton
- Dale Koppel
- Mary Ann Sabia
- Mary-Lynne Bohn
- Bonnie Robak
- John & Jean
- Warren & Judy
- Steven Jobs
- Lou Rizzo & UPS
- Sam & The Group
- Wolfgang Amadeus Mozart

*"1001 Ways To Be Romantic. That seems like an **awful lot!** I mean, guys, if the first **thousand** ideas don't work— what are the chances she's going to stick around when you say, 'Okay, just **one more'**?!"*

~ JAY LENO, THE TONIGHT SHOW

Acknowledgments Page Theme Song:
"Thank You for Being a Friend,"
Andrew Gold

Table of Contents

Introduction

This "Author's Annotated Edition" of **1001 Ways To Be Romantic** includes my handwritten comments in the margins.

Many of these are notes I've jotted into my personal copy of the book I carry with me into seminars and interviews.

Enjoy!

~ Gregory Godek

Love may make the world go 'round, but it's **romantic** **love** that makes the ride worthwhile. We *need* love, but we *crave* romance (just like you *need* broccoli, but you *crave* chocolate!). It's romantic love that allows you to say *emphatically* "I'm *in* love with you," instead of merely, "I love you."

This book is about re-igniting passion and deepening intimacy. It is for young and old, singles and marrieds, men and women. It is for *you* if you want to turn your *relationship* into a *love affair*.

Why are many marriages mediocre and boring? Not because they lack *love*, but because they lack *romance*. Love is lukewarm, comfortable— while romance is hot, exciting!

Everyone wants passion and romance in his or her life. But—

✻ Some people are uncertain how to create romance. This book shows you how.

✻ Some people are stuck in cultural stereotypes. This book helps you appreciate your partner as a unique and special individual.

✻ And some people have given up the search for romance out of frustration or cynicism. This book will re-inspire you.

Love in the twenty-first century is about practicing old-fashioned values with a modern twist. It is about honoring the timeless values of honesty, commitment and caring, while expressing them creatively, uniquely and passionately. And this is where romance comes in. Romance, you see, is the expression of love. Romance brings love *alive* in the world. Without romance, love is a sweet but empty concept.

I believe that *expressing love* is our purpose as human beings. Therefore, anything that helps you achieve this purpose is a *good thing*. There are thousands, *millions* of ways of expressing love. These 1001 ideas are just the beginning.

"Greg Godek explains how to get the Woo in wooing."

~ COSMOPOLITAN

Once Upon a Time . . .

. . . two people fell in love. *Just like you.* They did all the classic romantic things. But the passion faded after a few months. Is this *inevitable??*

1a

He gave her a dozen roses *and* a box of chocolates on Valentine's Day.

*The "Classics" of romance are **fine** in the beginning. **Then** what??*

1b

She wrote him long, romantic love letters. He sent her greeting cards.

1c

They talked and cooed on the phone. During work. And late at night.

1d

He took her to see every romantic movie that year.

Infatuation and what I call "Generic Romance" only go so far.

1e

He gave her perfume. She gave him cologne.

1f

They celebrated special occasions with a bottle of champagne.

1g

She served dinner by candlelight. He served breakfast in bed.

. . . They Lived Happily Ever After

Go beyond "Generic Romance." Couples with A+ Relationships* know the secret of creating unique and personal ways to express their love.

*These are the secrets of turning your relationship into a **love affair**!*

2

Give your lover a dozen roses—and do it with a *creative twist*. Give *eleven* red roses and *one* white rose. Attach a note that reads:

> *"In every bunch there's one who stands out—*
> *and you are that one."*

3

Sending a birthday card isn't just a good idea, it's an *obligatory* romantic gesture. But how about doing something *different* this year? On your lover's birthday, send a "thank you" card to his/her mother.

4

Gallantry never *really* goes out of style. So every once in a while kiss her hand with a *flourish*. Note: The *proper* way to kiss a woman's hand is to lower your lips to her hand. You *don't* raise her hand to your lips.

5

Thoughtfulness is merely the beginning! True romantics know how to go "above and beyond the call of duty": Following a bubble bath you've prepared for her, wrap her in a towel that *you've warmed up in the dryer*.

*How would you grade your relationship?

A = Passionate, exciting, loving, fulfilling; not *perfect*—but clearly excellent.

B = Very good, solid, better-than-most, consistent, *improving*.

C = Average, acceptable, status quo, okay— but static, ho-hum, sometimes *boring*.

D = Below average, unhappy, dismal; bad— but not hopeless.

F = Hopeless, depressing, dangerous; tried everything, it didn't work.

Little Things Mean a Lot

6

Giftwrap a wishbone in a jewelry box. Send it to her with a note that says, "I wish you were here."

The relationship "secret" that's not really a secret: Express your love in lots of little ways.

7

Unplug the TV. Put a note on the screen saying, "Turn *me* on instead."

8

Go through revolving doors together.

9

Keep candles in the car. Eat dinner by candlelight the next time you go to McDonald's.

Pick wildflowers from a field or the side of the road.

10

Run your hands under hot water before joining your partner in bed(!)

11

Look—no, *gaze*—into each other's eyes more often.

12

Write him a little love note. Insert it into the book he's reading.

Chapter Theme Song:
"Can't Buy Me Love," The Beatles

Bigger Is Better

13

Go for it in a **BIG** way. Pull out *ALL* the stops. Don't TIPTOE into being more romantic. Be outrageously romantic.

14

GIANT BANNERS are available from Supergram. The banners are printed on white or colored paper, and lamination is optional. The banners are about a foot tall, and tend to run from twelve feet long to thirty feet or more, depending on your message. Call 800-3-BANNER.

15

Make a GIANT greeting card out of a big cardboard box.

Make a gesture that's as big as your heart.

16

Make a custom banner—a BIG banner—to welcome him home from a trip (or just to say "I love you!"). Use construction paper and crayons, or poster board and markers, or old sheets and spray paint.

17

Craig liked doing things in a *big* way. He was a dramatic and loud (though lovable) kind of guy. Mary, on the other hand, was proper and quiet (and just as lovable). Craig sometimes criticized Mary for not being expressive or outrageous enough. Until . . . one day when Craig returned home from a business trip and was greeted by Mary—and two hundred forty-three members of the local high school marching band on their front lawn. (Most people don't consider John Philip Sousa marches to be romantic—but *Craig* does!)

You, too, can probably hire your local high school marching band for a relatively modest donation to its band fund!

Creative Gifts

18

Roses are fine—but a simple daisy can *really* communicate your feelings *if* you give it with flair. Pick a single daisy. Attach a note that says: *"She loves me—she loves me not."* (But don't leave anything to chance: Trim the daisy so there is an *odd* number of petals!)

Get your honey . . .
*Two **small** gifts and one **big** one.*
*Two **red** gifts and three **green** ones.*
*One **funny** gift and two **sweet** ones.*

19

You can create a theme gift-and-gesture by selecting the right love song:

✦ Get the song "I Will Always Love You," by Whitney Houston—
✦ And rent the movie *The Bodyguard*, featuring the song.

➻ Get the song "True Love," by Bing Crosby & Grace Kelly—
➻ And rent the movie *High Society*, featuring the song.

✳ Get the song "When Doves Cry," by Prince—
✳ And rent the movie *Purple Rain*, featuring the song.

20

An "infinite" love note:

I love you,
And you love me;
This is as it ought to be.
Ask me why
And I'll reply—
I love you,
And you love me . . .

Here's how you can create a love note that *never comes to an end*. Structure a short love note or love poem so that it loops back on itself (where the last word leads back to the first word). Then write it on a Möbius strip.*

✦ First, cut a strip of paper about two inches wide and eighteen inches long.
✦ Now, compose your special love note. (See example in the margin.)
✦ Then write it on both sides of the strip of paper.
✦ Then twist one end of the paper strip 180 degrees and tape it to the other end.
✦ You've just created a Möbius strip.

*A Möbius strip is a curious geometric phenomenon through which you can literally turn a common two-sided piece of paper into *a surface with only one side.*

Creative Gestures

21

Fake a power outage at home. (Loosen the fuses or throw the breaker switches.) With no TV to tempt you . . . with no computer to occupy you . . . with no furnace to heat you . . . you pretty much have *no choice* but to get out the candles, huddle around the fireplace and be romantic!

This is why the birth rate always rises nine months after every major power outage. True!

22

Being a liberated gal, the bride wanted use a *hyphenated* last name when they got married. Being a romantic guy, the groom observed that a hyphen is *also* a minus sign. *Hmmm—what to do??* The creative couple now writes their name like this: Mr. & Mrs. J. Smith+Brown.

23

When she's traveling alone, arrange with an airline attendant to have a gift or flower delivered to her after the flight is airborne.

24

Her husband is a handyman. He loves to take things apart and put them back together again. She gave him a fancy VCR for his birthday. Here's the creative twist: She took it apart and gave it to him wrapped in *sixteen* different boxes!

Copy a romantic poem onto fancy parchment paper. Roll it into a scroll, tie it with a red ribbon, and present it to your lover.

25

Play Trivial Pursuit. (In preparation for the game, create some *custom* cards that ask trivia questions about your relationship.)

Romance on a Budget

26a

Write a love letter. Mail it. Cost: 33¢.*

*Postal rates subject to the whims of the U.S. government.

26b

Pick flowers from the side of the road. Cost: Zero.

26c

Watch falling stars together. Cost: Nada.

26d

Walk hand-in-hand together. Cost: Nothing.

Frugal travel tip: When the U.S. dollar is strong compared with foreign currency, travel abroad. When the U.S. dollar is weak, travel within the country.

26e

Memorize her favorite poem or passage from a book—and recite it during lovemaking. Cost: Zilch.

26f

Buy wine and champagne *by the case*. Cost: 20 percent off the per-bottle price.

You can be romantic on a budget without being "cheap."

26g

Go to vacation spots *off-season*. Cost: 20 percent to 50 percent less than usual.

Spare No Expense

27a

The best way to spend the *most* money for the *smallest* gift is to buy *diamonds*.

27b

The best way to spend the *most* money for *food* is to dine at a *five-star restaurant*.

27c

The best way to spend the *most* money for *lingerie* is to buy an outfit from La Perla.

La Perla has three shops, in New York, Miami and Los Angeles. Call 888-307-3752.

27d

The best way to spend the *most* money to *fly* is to travel on the *Concorde*.

27e

The best way to spend the *most* money on *men's clothing* is to have a suit *custom-made*.

27f

The best way to spend the *most* money on *women's clothing* is to buy her *haute couture*.

*Play Monopoly together. Use **real** money!*

27g

The best way to spend the *most* money on a *hotel room* is to reserve the *honeymoon suite*.

The Most Important Things I've Learned in Twenty Years of Teaching Romance

*Life is too short **not** to be romantic.*

28

- ✦ *How* is more important than *why*.
- ✦ Gender stereotyping blinds you to your partner's uniqueness.
- ✦ The speed of love is 1.7 mph.
- ✦ *Everybody* wants an A+ Relationship.
- ✦ Love has no reason. It never needs to be explained or defended.
- ✦ "Good chemistry" has nothing to do with compatibility.
- ✦ You *can't* keep the infatuation—but you *can* keep the passion.
- ✦ The process *must* be respected. (There ain't no shortcuts.)
- ✦ *Everyone* is an amateur when it comes to matters of the heart.
- ✦ The metaphors of love you use create your reality.
- ✦ Romantics are happier than most people.
- ✦ "Communication" is, maybe, 10 percent of an A+ Relationship.
- ✦ Creating a loving long-term relationship is the most difficult, time-consuming and complicated challenge you will face in your entire life. Also the most rewarding.
- ✦ The passion is more important than the happy ending.
- ✦ Life is too short *not* to be romantic.

The Ten Commandments for Loving Couples

29

1. Thou shalt give 100 percent.

2. Thou shalt treat your partner as the unique individual he/she truly is.

3. Thou shalt stay connected through word and deed.

4. Thou shalt accept change and support growth in yourself and your mate.

5. Thou shalt live your love.

6. Thou shalt share: The love and fear, the work and play.

7. Thou shalt listen, listen, listen.

8. Thou shalt honor the subtle wisdom of the heart and listen to the powerful insights of the mind.

9. Thou shalt not be a jerk or a nag.

10. Thou shalt integrate the *purity* of spiritual love with the *passion* of physical love and the *power* of emotional love.

If love is really your top priority, then you never really "sacrifice" for it.

Left-Brained*

*Left-Brained people tend to be logical and practical. They *think* first and *feel* second.

30

For those of you who like to analyze and compute things:

- ❏ Spend 10% more time together.
- ❏ Generate 33% more laughter in your life together.
- ❏ Focus 100% of your attention when listening to him/her.
- ❏ Create a 10% increase in the amount of fun you have together.
- ❏ Reduce your TV watching by 50%.
- ❏ Give up 10% of your hobby time, and give it to your partner.
- ❏ Reduce your complaining by 50%.
- ❏ Reduce your criticizing by 62%.
- ❏ Say "I love you" 300% more often.
- ❏ Spend 10% as much time kissing as you spend watching TV every day.
- ❏ Be 25% more creative in your relationship.
- ❏ Be 10% more thoughtful/considerate.
- ❏ If you're talkative by nature, talk 20% less, and listen 20% more.
- ❏ If you're quiet by nature, open up and talk 20% more.

B.C. © 1978. By permission of Johnny Hart and Creators Syndicate, Inc.

31

Analyze the number of your sexual encounters as a function of the frequency of your romantic gestures. Is there a correlation? (Hmm . . . There just *might* be a lesson here!)

Right-Brained*

32

*Right-Brained people tend to be creative and spontaneous. They *feel* first and *think* second.

Characteristics of true romantics:

❋ Taps into his/her creativity regularly.
❋ Is just a little bit "naughty."
❋ Takes love seriously—
❋ But has a great sense of humor.
❋ Makes his/her intimate love relationship a top priority.
❋ Makes romantic gestures without ulterior motives.
❋ Is flexible.
❋ Celebrates sexuality.
❋ Appreciates his/her partner's uniqueness.
❋ Celebrates both the masculine and the feminine.
❋ Is a pretty good mind-reader.
❋ Sees the world in a slightly offbeat way.
❋ Maintains a deep, spiritual connection with his/her partner.
❋ Is spontaneous.
❋ Defines him/herself as a "lover"—regardless of other roles.
❋ Remembers important dates and anniversaries.
❋ Continuously learns and grows.
❋ Is in touch with his/her feelings.
❋ Pursues new and different experiences.
❋ Gives of himself/herself without expectations.
❋ Does lots of little things.
❋ Gives without being asked.

Who are the better romantics: Right-brainers or left-brainers?

Everyone *thinks* it's the right-brained, creative types by a long shot. But a great many left-brainers are tremendously romantic. It's just that the right-brainers are louder and more spontaneous about it. But those logical types are great planners of surprises and great at noticing little but important things about their partners.

33

One morning, for no particular reason, Susan quietly slipped out of bed, tiptoed to the stereo, selected "Fanfare for the Common Man," (by Aaron Copland), cranked the volume *all the way up*, started the music, and gleefully leaped on a very surprised (but delighted) Michael.

Additional music that gives the same effect:
"The William Tell Overture," Gioacchino Rossini

"The 1812 Overture," Peter Ilych Tchaikovsky

Romance for Dummies

34

Variation on a theme: "Flip-a-Coin" Romance.

Practice "Even-Day/Odd-Day" Romance: On *even* days it's *your* turn to be romantic, and on *odd* days it's your *partner's* turn.

35

No time—or too lazy—to wrap those gifts? Buy fancy bags and pre-decorated boxes for gift-wrapping presents.

36

Ask her best girlfriend—or her mother—for help. Ask her to go shopping with you (secretly!). Tell her you want to spend *one afternoon* shopping for a *year's worth of gifts* for your partner. Establish a budget, let her think about it for a week, then go shopping together.

37

(Shhh! Keep this one under your hat!)

Place a *standing order* with a local florist. Give him your anniversary date, her birth date, and instruct him to send flowers *automatically* on those dates. Also on Valentine's Day, and (if it's appropriate) on Mother's Day, and—just to be safe—have him send a bouquet once a month. Give the florist your charge card number and have him bill you automatically.

This technique is for the forever-forgetful and the terminally unorganized! I know that the true romantics out there will be *aghast* at this suggestion, but hey, sometimes the end justifies the means.

Romance for Smarties

38

Write a love letter in *code*. Give your lover a challenge.

✦ Try a message in Morse Code (see the message to the right).
✦ Here's a simple code, created by shifting all of the letters in the alphabet one place to the right (A becomes B; B becomes C, etc.):

.. / . _ .. ___ ... _ . /
_ . _ _ ___ .. _

Efbs mpwfs:

J mpwf zpv, J bepsf zpv, J offe zpv, J xbou zpv.

Mpwf boe ljttft,
Nf

39

Visit a museum. Visit an art gallery. Walk a formal garden. Attend a symphony. Attend an opera.

40

$$(\ 144 \ \times 3) + (8/ \quad \times \ /2)$$

Attend a lecture. Take a class together at a local college. Expanding your horizons can deepen your relationship.

*Note: Operas aren't as painful as you may **assume** they are. So give one a try!*

What's Your Romantic "Style"? (Men)

41

Which person or character most closely matches your or your lover's style of romance? Identifying the similarities and differences can help you become more aware of your own strengths and weaknesses, and can help you express love in ways that your partner appreciates most.

☞ The *Romeo* Type: Passionate and impetuous

☞ The *Fred Astaire* Type: Sophisticated and elegant

☞ The *Humphrey Bogart* Type: Tough guy with a heart of gold

☞ The *Jimmy Stewart* Type: The boy next door

☞ The *James Bond* Type: The playboy heartbreaker

☞ The *Indiana Jones* Type: Adventurous and charmingly bumbling

☞ The *Rhett Butler* Type: Arrogant but charming

☞ The *Don Quixote* Type: Irrepressible and outrageous

☞ The *Don Juan* Type: Seductive and charming

☞ The *Cyrano de Bergerac* Type: Witty and literary

☞ The *Paul Newman* Type: Rugged and quiet

☞ The *James Dean* Type: The rebel and bad boy

☞ The *Sean Connery* Type: Dashing and experienced

☞ The *Vincent van Gogh* Type: Artistic and moody

☞ The *Lord Byron* Type: Poet and dreamer

☞ The *Frank Sinatra* Type: Tough but suave

☞ The *James T. Kirk* Type: The adventurous seducer

☞ The *Clark Gable* Type: Smooth and smart

You romantic devil, you!

What's Your Romantic "Style"? (Women)

42

Okay ladies, it's *your* turn. What's your romantic style? (Guys: What is your gal's romantic style?)

- The *Scarlett O'Hara* Type: Feisty and dramatic
- The *Meg Ryan* Type: The girl next door, adorable and sweet
- The *Juliet* Type: Passionate and impetuous
- The *Jane Eyre* Type: Romantic and idealistic
- The *Marilyn Monroe* Type: Sultry and seductive
- The *Billie Holiday* Type: Artistic and loyal to a fault
- The *Jane Seymour* Type: Classic and elegant
- The *Elizabeth Barrett Browning* Type: Poetic and artistic
- The *Cher* Type: Exotic and creative
- The *Mae West* Type: Sassy and bold
- The *Ingrid Bergman* Type: Smooth and intriguing
- The *Madonna* Type: Bold and fun
- The *Greta Garbo* Type: Sensual and enigmatic

Is your romantic style subtle or obvious?

Flowers

43

"A flower a day keeps the divorce lawyer away." (Overheard one evening in the Romance Class.)

It's hard to go wrong with flowers!

44

Did you know . . . that different color roses have different meanings?

* Red roses = **LOVE** & **PASSION**
* Pink roses = **A *Romantic* Friendship**
* Yellow roses = Friendship & Respect
* White roses = PURITY & ADORATION

You single folks should pay *special* attention to this. Early in a relationship is often too soon to send *red* roses. If you're not absolutely *certain* that you're both madly, passionately, crazy in love—*don't* give **red** roses! Send pink or yellow.

Fabulous gift idea:

For flower-lovers, nature-lovers and art-lovers alike: Get your partner a beautiful botanical illustration that's personalized with your message or a quote in fabulous calligraphy. Visit www.RosaScript.com.

45

Place a single flower under the windshield wiper of his car.

46

* 1-800-FLOWERS; www.1800flowers.com
* ProFlowers.com
* 1-800-SEND-FTD; www.FTD.com

Chapter Theme Song:

"You Are My Flower," The Carter Family

Chocolate

47

Reliable sources report that chocolate just may *really be* an aphrodisiac. (Great news for chocoholics!) Chocolate contains large amounts of phenylethylamine, a chemical that also is naturally produced by the body when one is experiencing feelings of love.

48

Long-stem chocolate roses! Have a dozen shipped to your sweetie. Call Lila's Chocolates at 415-383-8887.

49

(Inspired by *Willy Wonka and the Chocolate Factory*): Create a custom contest just for your favorite chocoholic. Make a series of *Golden Tickets* to insert in chocolate bar wrappers. Make the tickets redeemable for romantic gifts and gestures. If you use your imagination, this *one* idea could supply the two of you with romantic fun for *years* to come.

50

✳ Ghirardelli Chocolates: 800-877-9338; www.Ghirardelli.com
✳ See's Candies: 800-347-7337; www.Sees.com
✳ Godiva Chocolatier: 800-9-GODIVA; www.Godiva.com
✳ Hershey: 800-437-7439; www.HersheyPA.com
✳ Harry & David: 800-547-3033; www.HarryAndDavid.com
✳ Gevalia: 800-438-2542; www.Gevalia.com

"What's important in life?" When you poll people, you pretty much get these answers—in this order: 1) Love, 2) Sex, 3) Money, 4) Chocolate.

ENGLISH: "Excuse me, where is the nearest chocolate?"

FRENCH: "Excusez-moi, où est le chocolat le plus proche?"

GERMAN: "Entschuldigen Sie bitte, wo ist die nächste Schokolade?"

Jewelry

51

Get her a diamond cut into a heart shape. (It's not the most *brilliant* cut—but it is the most *meaningful*.)

52

✦ Hide a diamond ring in a cake.
✦ Bury a necklace in a pie.
✦ Drape a pearl necklace around her teddy bear's neck.

Note: Talk to your local jeweler before cooking or baking jewelry or hiding gems in your food. Why? Because pearls dissolve in champagne and rubies crack when heated!

53

Here are the twelve birthstones—and their symbolic meanings.

Accompany the jewelry gift with a poem about the symbolic meaning of his or her birthstone:

✳ January: *Garnet*—faith & constancy
✳ February: *Amethyst*—happiness & sincerity
✳ March: *Aquamarine*—courage & hope
✳ April: *Diamond*—innocence & joy
✳ May: *Emerald*—peace & tranquility
✳ June: *Pearl*—purity & wisdom
✳ July: *Ruby*—nobility & passion
✳ August: *Sardonyx*—joy & power
✳ September: *Sapphire*—truth & hope
✳ October: *Opal*—tender love & confidence
✳ November: *Topaz*—fidelity & friendship
✳ December: *Turquoise*—success & understanding

*When it comes to jewelry, bigger is **not** better—**better** is better! In other words, quality is what counts.*

Buying fine jewelry is unlike any other purchase. It's an investment in a gift that should last many lifetimes! Learn more by contacting the Jewelry Information Center at www.JewelryInfo.org.

Songs to accompany your jewelry gifts:

"Love is a Golden Ring," Frankie Laine

"Diamond Girl," Seals & Crofts

"Emerald," Thin Lizzy

"Golden Earrings," Peggy Lee

"Pearl," Sade

"Sapphire," The Clash

"Emerald Eyes," Fleetwood Mac

"String of Pearls," Glenn Miller

"Diamonds are a Girl's Best Friend," Marilyn Monroe

Perfume

54

There probably would be no such thing as perfume if it weren't for the concept of romantic love. Think about it. We'd still have champagne, chocolate, flowers and jewelry. But there would simply be no *reason* for perfume to exist if it weren't for love. So one could say that

Perfume = Romance

Perfume may be the *essence* of romance. Romantic love distilled into a bottle. Interesting, huh?

55

You *could* have a special perfume custom-made for your one-of-a-kind woman! Match the fragrance to her personality: Is she light and breezy, or sophisticated and alluring, or sexy and sensual?

☞ Caswell-Massey, 518 Lexington Avenue, New York City, New York 10017; 212-755-2254.

56

Get the whole "family of products" in the fragrance of her favorite perfume (bath powder, soaps, cremes, candles, etc.)

57

Well of *course* you should get perfume for her that she simply loves. *And* a scent that reflects her personality. And a scent that *you* like!

Send her a message or create a theme gift through the *name* of a perfume:

Romance

Allure

Beautiful

Joy

Destiny

Eternity

Unforgettable

Happy

Red

Impulse

Obsession

Paris

Spellbound

Passion

Pleasures

Tabu

White Diamonds

Champagne

58

Romantic arithmetic: Champagne = Celebration.

59

Buy a case of champagne. Label each of the twelve bottles . . .

1. *His birthday*
2. *Her birthday*
3. *For a midnight snack*
4. *Anniversary (of meeting)*
5. *Anniversary (of marrying)*
6. *For a picnic*
7. *Before making love*
8. *Celebrate a milestone at work*
9. *Christmas/Hanukkah/holiday*
10. *The first day of spring*
11. *The first snowfall*
12. *For making up after a fight*

You do, of course, have two crystal champagne flutes with your initials on them. Don't you?!

60

Buy wine and champagne *by the case*. You'll typically get a 20 percent discount off the per-bottle price. You'll save money, and always have a bottle on hand for those "Spontaneous Celebrations."

61

Always have a bottle of Dom Perignon on hand. (For those extra-special occasions.)

62

Always have several bottles of Korbel on hand. (For those spontaneous little celebrations.)

Chapter Theme Song:
"Champagne Jam," Atlanta Rhythm Section

Lingerie

63

The topic of lingerie is the one place where love, sex and romance all come together. This is why the topic is so enticing, so sexy, so sensitive.

✦ Gals: Guys really, really, really, really, *really* love gals in lingerie.
✦ Guys: Approach this topic *sensitively*.

64

☞ Gals: When in doubt, wear a garter belt and stockings.
☞ Guys: When in doubt, more foreplay.

65

Go through her Victoria's Secret catalog and rate the items one through ten. Write your ratings in the margins.

66

Guys: Spread out on the bed the lingerie outfit you'd like her to wear.

67

I've been asked by several men in the Romance Class to convey this message to the ladies: "Nothing completes a great lingerie outfit like a pair of great high heels."

Special note to gals who have health concerns about high heels: "You don't need to be on your feet for more than a minute or two."

When you're in Los Angeles, California:

Visit the Lingerie Museum, featuring items from Mae West, Zsa Zsa Gabor and Madonna, plus four decades of lingerie history. At Frederick's of Hollywood, 6608 Hollywood Boulevard, in Hollywood. Call 323-466-5151.

It's Not *What* You Do—

Do it with style.

Do it with flair.

Do it with attention to detail.

Do it with a flourish.

68

Don't just walk into the house tonight the way you always do. Pause on the porch; ring the doorbell; and greet her with one red rose and a bottle of champagne.

69

Never give a gift or present without wrapping it. Get extra-nice wrapping paper and fancy bows. If you truly have two left thumbs, get the store to do your gift-wrapping for you.

70

One woman in the Romance Class told us that her husband always manages to incorporate her favorite teddy bear into his many gift presentations.

- He's given her diamond earrings by putting them on the bear's ears.
- He's strung pearls around the bear's neck.
- He's packed the bear inside boxes along with other gifts.
- He's put funny notes in the bear's paw.

71

Not that it really matters, but I was just wondering . . .

- ☞ Why do we have birthday cakes and wedding cakes, but no anniversary cakes or Valentine's cakes?
- ☞ Why do we have Christmas tree ornaments, but no special ornaments with which to celebrate other special occasions?
- ☞ Why is Columbus Day a national holiday, but Valentine's Day *isn't?*
- ☞ Why is it crude to tell jokes that characterize races and religions in stereotyped ways, but it's acceptable to be a "gender bigot" and stereotype men and women?

—But *How* You Do It

72

Want to jazz up the presentation of a special meal? Buy a little hunk of dry ice from a local ice house. Put it in a bowl of water and place it on your serving tray. You'll create wondrous, billowing white clouds!

73

Strings of pearls have been known to appear inside real oyster shells at fancy restaurants.

How about presenting a gift of pearls to the tune of "A String of Pearls," by Glenn Miller?

74

And many diamond rings seem to find their way to the bottom of a glass of champagne.

75

Okay, let's say you've decided to give her the complete collection of The Moody Blues' (her all-time favorite group) albums. Let's now give this gift a creative twist. Instead of simply wrapping the CDs and handing them to her, do this:

Best love songs by The Moody Blues:

"Nights in White Satin"
"Watching and Waiting"
"Want to Be With You"
"So Deep Within You"
"In My World"

* Remove the CDs from their cases.
* Hide the CDs around the house.
* Gift-wrap all the CD cases separately.
* Attach a note to each gift . . .
* Each note gives clues to the location of the CD . . .
* And each note's clues are based on each album's title.
  * *Days of Future Passed* is hidden in a photo album.
  * *To Our Children's Children's Children* is in the kids' toybox.
  * *On the Threshold of a Dream* is hidden in your bedroom.
  * *Long Distance Voyager* is hidden along with airline tickets to Tahiti.

To Do

76

Write "Romantic Reminders" on your "To Do" list at work. (What's the use of being a great success in the business world if you're a miserable failure in your personal life?) Romantic Reminders will remind you that there's another part of your life that's quite important.

77

☞ A do-it-yourself romantic Saturday afternoon: 2 bicycles, 5 hours, 1 bottle of wine.
☞ A do-it-yourself romantic date: 2 movie tickets, 1 Tub-o'-Popcorn, 2 Cokes.
☞ A do-it-yourself romantic picnic: 1 loaf of bread, 1 hunk of cheese, 1 bottle of wine.
☞ A do-it-yourself romantic Sunday afternoon: 1 canoe, 1 lazy day, 2 star-struck lovers.

78

Pay close attention to the subtle signals, the non-verbal clues, the body language and tone of voice that your lover uses.

79

Anticipate your partner.

✳ Is he stressed at work? Would he like a back rub or time alone?
✳ Does she need a dinner out or a movie in?
✳ Does he need extra sleep or a surprise lovemaking session?
✳ Take extra good care of her during the most difficult days of her menstrual cycle.
✳ Does he need a good book to read or a visit to the gym?

*If **some** form of romance is not on your To Do list, you may want to re-evaluate your priorities.*

A great book: *Your Life Is More than Your To Do List,* by Maggie Bedrosian.

I Do

80

Well on its way to becoming a wedding classic, a new tune called "Wedding Song" was the selection Tracey and I chose for our wedding ceremony. This wonderful, touching song is from the album *Illusions and Dreams*, a collection of uplifting and spiritual compositions by singer/composer/guitarist Brit Lay.

✦ *Illusions and Dreams* is available on CD and cassette.
✦ *Heart to Heart* (second album) is available on CD and cassette.

Cassettes are $12, CDs are $15; plus $4 for shipping. Write to: Brit Lay, Box 127, Barnstable, Massachusetts 02630.

81

For those of you who do not want a traditional wedding ceremony . . .

➤ Get married on *skis*—at Heavenly Resort, in Lake Tahoe, California. Call 800-243-2836; or visit www.skiheavenly.com.
➤ Tie the knot on a *beach*—on the tropical island of Fiji. Call 800-932-3454; or visit www.bulafiji.com.
➤ Create a truly *fairy tale wedding*—at Walt Disney World, in Orlando, Florida. Call 407-828-3400; or visit: www.Disney.go.com/disneyworld/morevacations/wed74.html.

Get married *underwater*—at the Amoray Dive Resort, in Key Largo, Florida. Call 800-426-6729; or visit www.amoray.com.

82

Plan ahead—*way* ahead! Get a friend to buy fifty of the top magazines and newspapers that are on the newsstand on your wedding day. (Everything from *The New York Times* to *The New Yorker; Cosmo* and *Playboy; TV Guide* and *Time; Harper's* and *Highlights for Children; Sports Illustrated* and *The National Enquirer*.)

Pack them safely away (in a dark, dry, cool place) and present them to your partner—*on your twenty-fifth wedding anniversary!*

Chapter Theme Song:
"I Do, I Do, I Do, I Do, I Do," Abba

Do's & Don'ts

83

Do be romantic.
Don't wait.

(I mean now—right now!
Put down this book and go
do something romantic!)

■ Don't go out on New Year's Eve—
❏ Do stay home and cozy-up to your lover near the fireplace.

■ Don't buy roses for Valentine's Day—
❏ Do buy flowers that begin with the first letter of her name.

■ Don't go to the beach on crowded weekends—
❏ Do go mid-week.

■ Don't go to popular vacation spots during their busy seasons—
❏ Do go right before or after the busy season.

❏ Do make some sacrifices for each other—
■ But don't turn yourself into a martyr.

■ Don't read the newspaper at the breakfast table—
❏ Do talk with one another over breakfast.

■ Don't give him a birthday present—
❏ Do give him seven gifts, one for each day of his birthday week.

■ Don't leave lovemaking until just before sleeping—
❏ Do schedule more time for foreplay.

■ Don't make love the same way every time—
❏ Do eliminate distractions for two to three hours.

■ Don't rush through lovemaking—
❏ Do slow down! You'll both enjoy yourselves, and each other, more.

■ Don't: Negotiate—as if your relationship were a business deal—
❏ Do: Learn the gentle art of loving compromise.

■ Don't try to change your partner—
❏ Do accept him/her for the special, unique person he/she is.

■ Don't act your age—
❏ Do wacky things; express your quirkiness; be creative.

Don'ts & Do's

84

Don't try to have a "perfect" relationship. There's no such thing. Expecting one will only paralyze you. Once you eliminate the goal of perfection, nothing can hold you back! You'll lose your fear of "doing it right." You'll lose your fear of taking risks. And people who take risks, who live life creatively and spontaneously, live more fun-filled, passionate lives.

85

☞ *Don't* buy gifts at the last minute. (You probably *won't* find a great gift, and you probably *will* pay top dollar.)

☞ *Do* plan ahead. (Less stress for you, more joy for your partner, less effect on your wallet.)

86

Don't relate to your lover as a stereotype. He's an individual, not a statistic. And she's a unique person, not "just like all women." Today's tabloid topics, talk-show trends, and sex surveys have only limited relevance to you and your lover and your relationship. Take it all with a large grain of salt. *You'll never lose by treating your partner as a unique and special person*.

Chapter Theme Songs (and good advice):

"Don't Be Afraid," Aaron Hall

"Don't Be Cruel," Elvis Presley

"Don't Break the Heart that Loves You," Connie Francis

"Don't Cry," Guns N' Roses

"Don't Fight It," Wilson Pickett

"Don't Give Up," Petula Clark

"Don't Let Go," Isaac Hayes

"Don't Let It End," Styx

"Don't Lose the Magic," Shawn Christopher

"Don't Mess Up a Good Thing," Fontella Bass & Bobby McClure

"Don't Say No," Billy Burnette

"Don't Stay Away Too Long," Eddie Fisher

"Don't Stop," Fleetwood Mac

Do

87

Go out of your way for him or her. Being romantic only when it's convenient is like giving flowers on Valentine's Day—it's expected and, frankly, it's no big deal!

✤ *Always* pick him/her up at the airport after a trip—no matter what time the flight arrives.
✤ Offer to stop at the store on the way home from work.
✤ Take care of the kids when it's not "your turn."

88

Decide to fall in love all over again. That's it—just *decide*. You don't need to read books that analyze your relationship. You don't need therapy. You just need to *decide*.

Just think of the great opportunity you have: The less romantic you've been, the more dramatic the change will be! I've had guys in the Romance Class simply *make up their minds* to be more romantic. They've reported that this simple decision led to falling in love with their wives all over again.

89

Accompany each other to doctor appointments. Going along for routine check-ups gives you opportunities for quickie coffee dates. And accompanying him/her when there are difficult problems allows you to provide emotional support.

90

Listen! Listen with your ears, mind and heart. Listen for the meaning behind his actions. Listen for the message behind her words.

Overwhelm him/her!

Honor him/her!

Romance him/her!

Woo him/her!

Date him/her!

Feed him/her!

Stimulate him/her!

Nurture him/her!

Understand him/her!

Support him/her!

Calm him/her!

Surprise him/her!

Delight him/her!

Don't

91

- ✦ Don't gloat when you're right.

- ✦ Don't sulk when you don't get your way.

- ✦ Don't worry—be happy.

- ✦ Don't try to pack too much into the weekend.

- ✦ Don't over-schedule your vacations.

- ✦ Don't make the same mistake twice.

- ✦ Don't undermine your partner's authority with your kids.

- ✦ Don't reveal the ending of a movie!

- ✦ Don't spend your "Prime Time" watching TV.

- ✦ Don't drink and drive—not ever.

- ✦ Don't stop.

- ✦ Don't be a "cover-stealer" in bed.

- ✦ Don't interrupt when he/she's talking.

- ✦ Don't wait—express your love right now.

- ✦ Don't hold grudges.

- ✦ Don't take one another for granted.

- ✦ Don't go a single day without saying, "I love you."

- ✦ Don't let your mind wander during conversations.

- ✦ Don't wait for your partner to read your mind.

- ✦ Don't just sign "Love" on your Valentine's Day card; be eloquent.

- ✦ Don't be so judgmental.

- ✦ Don't wait until the last minute to make Valentine's Day dinner reservations.

- ✦ Don't even *try* to leave the house during a blizzard. Snuggle together for a romantic day off.

"Spoil your husband, but don't spoil your children."

~ LOUISE SEIER GIDDINGS CURREY

Chapter Theme Song:
"Don't Talk Just Kiss," Right Said Fred

You Must Remember This

92

Remember: Romance isn't barter!

You'll lose every time if you use romantic gestures to barter for favors or forgiveness. The following "unspoken agreements" may have had some validity in the past, but they don't cut it anymore: "I'll take you to a movie and dinner if you'll sleep with me." "I'll cook dinner for you if you'll let me nag you." "I'll give you flowers if you'll forgive me for being a jerk."

Romance is the expression of your love for that special person. It's not a bargaining chip. If you use it as one, you cheapen the gesture, devalue your relationship, and up the ante for the next round of bartering.

93

Start saving mementos of your life together. Create a "Memories Box."

☞ Save movie stubs, theater programs and restaurant receipts.
☞ Save sand and seashells from your beach vacations.
☞ Save labels from wine bottles and corks from champagne bottles.
☞ Save restaurant menus and placemats.
☞ Save maps from your road trips.
☞ Save plane tickets, movie tickets, event tickets, theater tickets, etc.

Use these mementos to create a unique gift for a special anniversary. Make a collage, a scroll, a memory box or a scrapbook.

You must remember— **her birthday!** *Or your name is "Mud," bud!*

You must remember— **Valentine's Day!** *C'mon, spring for flowers and chocolates!*

You must remember— *your* **anniversary!** *Why not take a personal holiday?*

A Kiss Is Just a Kiss

94

- ↣ Give her one Hershey's Kiss.
- ↣ Give her *one thousand* Hershey's Kisses.
- ↣ Remove all the little paper strips (that say "Kisses" on them) from a couple hundred Hershey's Kisses. Fill a little jewelry box with them. Wrap 'em up and present them to her.
- ↣ Write a clever certificate explaining that the little paper slips are coupons redeemable for one kiss each.

95

Best movie kisses:

- ✳ *The Way We Were:* When Barbra Streisand and Robert Redford kiss in front of her fireplace.
- ✳ *Life Is Beautiful:* The kiss underneath the banquet table.
- ✳ *Gone with the Wind:* When Rhett steals a major kiss from Scarlett while he's helping her escape as Atlanta burns.

96

Best songs about kissing:

- ➤ "Kiss Me in the Rain," by Barbra Streisand
- ➤ "One More Kiss," from the Broadway musical *Follies*
- ➤ "Kiss," by Prince
- ➤ "Shut Up and Kiss Me," by Mary Chapin Carpenter
- ➤ "Blowing Kisses in the Wind," by Paula Abdul
- ➤ "It's Been a Long, Long Time," by Bing Crosby
- ➤ "Kiss Me Baby," by The Beach Boys
- ➤ "Kiss You All Over," by Exile
- ➤ "Say It with a Kiss," by Billie Holiday
- ➤ "Sealed with a Kiss," by Bobby Vinton
- ➤ "Put That Kiss Back Where You Found It," by Benny Goodman

FYI

33,000,000 Hershey's Kisses are made daily.

FYI

Twenty-nine facial muscles are used when you kiss.

FYI—For love letters and emails:

X's symbolize kisses; O's symbolize hugs.

Use capital X's for smooches; lower case x's for pecks.

Use capital O's for bear hugs; lower case o's for squeezes.

A Sigh Is Just a Sigh

97

Spread rose petals all over the bedroom.

98

*Write a "five-minute love poem."
Set this book down—right now!—
and spend the next five minutes
writing a quick love poem. (Do this
once a day for a week and you'll get
pretty good at it!)*

Do you think you're the only one who writes "mushy," exuberant poetry? Well, think again . . .

> *Miss you, miss you, miss you;*
> *Everything I do*
> *Echoes with the laughter*
> *And the voice of You.*
> *You're on every corner,*
> *Every turn and twist,*
> *Every old familiar spot*
> *Whispers how you're missed.*
>
> *Oh, I miss you, miss you!*
> *God! I miss you, Girl!*
> *There's a strange, sad silence*
> *'Mid the busy whirl,*
> *Just as tho' the ordinary*
> *Daily things I do*
> *Wait with me, expectant*
> *For a word from You.*

> - DAVID CORY, SELECTIONS FROM *Miss You*

99

A well-crafted love letter will bring a sigh to your lover. Love letters also make treasured keepsakes. But many people tell me they feel uncomfortable or silly when attempting to write a real love letter. Some think it's not cool to express their true/passionate/insecure feelings.

Maybe you'd feel more comfortable if you could only see someone *else's* love letters, huh? How about a selection from an unabashed love letter from Napoleon Bonaparte to Josephine De Beauharnais:

A love letter resource: *Love Letters*, edited by Antonia Fraser is a bookful of passionate, emotional, romantic love letters.

> *"I wake filled with thoughts of you. Your portrait and the intoxicating evening which we spent yesterday have left my senses in turmoil. Sweet, incomparable Josephine, what a strange effect you have on my heart!"*

The Fundamental Things Apply

100

Romantics have their priorities straight.

What are your priorities? What I mean is, what are your *true* priorities? In other words, *how do you spend your time?* How you spend your time reflects your true priorities. (Most people *claim* that home and family are most important to them, but their *actions* don't reflect this.)

Living a life full of love is about getting your *actions* into alignment with your *beliefs*.

- ✦ Make an honest appraisal of how you spend your time. Make a chart of how you spend an average week. You'll probably make some interesting discoveries!
- ✦ Say to her, "Let's plan a special outing: A lunch-date, dinner-date, movie—whatever. You choose the time and place, and I'll be there—*regardless of my previous plans*." This shows that she has top priority—over work, friends, hobbies, etc.
- ✦ You sometimes work overtime at work, right? Why not occasionally work "overtime" on your relationship??

"Chains do not hold a marriage together. It is threads, hundreds of tiny threads, which sew people together through the years."

~ SIMONE SIGNORET

101

Romantics know that love is a *process*.

While on the one hand romantics tend to live in the moment, we also expect to be around for a while—so we don't fret too much about today's problems. We know that love, like life, is a *process*. Things change. Things grow. There is a future coming our way, and it's probably going to be pretty good!

- ❖ Adjust your daily schedule *in some small way* to advance the *process* of love in your life.
- ❖ Read a book to increase your understanding of the *process* of love. I suggest *Born For Love*, by Leo Buscaglia.

You might also want to read a book called *Love—The Course They Forgot To Teach You In School*, by some guy named Godek.

As Time Goes By

102

Love is timeless—and to *prove* it, cover up all the clocks in your house for the entire weekend. (Remember that one of the best things about being on vacation is the freedom from schedules and clocks and appointments. You can create a mini-vacation by freeing yourself from the tyranny of the clock for 48 hours.)

103

Get her a wristwatch. Inscribe it with: *I always have time for you.*

104

Inspired by Jim Croce's song "Time in a Bottle."

Get a little bottle. (Maybe an antique bottle or quirky jar.) Fill it with sand. Cork it. Label it: "Extra Time." Give it to your partner.

105

He gave her a simple little music box that plays "As Time Goes By." In the card he wrote: "*As time goes by* I love you more and more."

106

You say you need *more time* in order to be more romantic? So *create* more time! The strategies for how to do so are in a great little book called *How to Put Ten Hours in an Eight Hour Day*, by Kay Johnson.

Chapter Theme Song:
"Time After Time," Carly Simon

(Play It Again, Sam)

107a

Multiple viewings of your lover's favorite movie.

107b

Multiple honeymoons. (Not for newlyweds only!)

107c

Multiple orgasms(!)

108

Renew your wedding vows. You could create a private little ceremony for just the two of you. Or you could restage an entire formal wedding!

109

Revisit the place where you proposed marriage. Take along a bottle of champagne. Toast your good fortune in having found each other.

110

➤ Re-enact your first date.
➤ Relive your first *night* together.

111

When's the last time you sat on his lap and "made-out" like you did in high school??

Familiar gestures—performed with a creative twist—are hallmarks of people with A+ Relationships.

Chapter Theme Songs:
"Let's Get Married," Al Green
"Let's Get Married Again," John Conlee

Love Notes (I)

112

Write *"I love you"* on the bathroom mirror with a piece of soap.

Yes, the writer has to clean the mirror.

113

✳ Write her a love letter or poem on one sheet of paper. Glue it to thin cardboard; cut it up into puzzle-shaped pieces; then mail all the pieces to her.

✳ Or, mail one puzzle piece per day!

114

Write "I love you" on every page of a pack of Post-It Notes. Stick 'em *all over* the house!

115

➡ Write little love notes on the eggs in the refrigerator.

➡ Draw funny faces on the eggs in the refrigerator.

116

Cut-out interesting/suggestive/unusual/funny headlines from the daily newspapers. When you've collected about twenty-five of them, simply dump them in an envelope and mail them to your lover.

Write notes on balloons with markers.

Trace your initials in the dust on the coffee table.

Write funny notes in the margins of her *Cosmopolitan* magazine.

Write sexy notes in the margins of his *Playboy* magazine.

Jot love notes in his appointment calendar.

Write romantic reminders on her To Do list.

117

Write a short note to your lover that's spread out over several postcards. Write a short phrase on each postcard, then mail one at a time. You'll build anticipation for the romantic conclusion on the final postcard. (Maybe deliver that last one *in person*.)

Love Notes (II)

118

Do you remember "passing notes" in school? Do you remember how to fold them up so they tuck into a neat little square? *If not, find a teenager to advise you.*

119

Put notes on various household products:

* Joy dishwashing liquid: "Every day with you is a Joy."
* Cheerios: "Just knowing you love me cheers me up!"
* Old Spice cologne: "You spice up my life!"
* Ritz Crackers: "Let's 'Put On The Ritz' tonight! Let's go dancing!"
* A roll of Lifesavers: "You're a lifesaver!"
* Caress soap: "This is what I'm going to do to you tonight."

120

■ Mail her a pack of matches. Attach a note: "I'm *hot* for you."
■ Mail him a pair of oven mitts: Attach a note: "I'm *hot* for you."
■ Mail her a bottle of Tabasco sauce. Attach a note: "I'm *hot* for you."
■ Mail him a pair of your sexiest panties. The note: "I'm *hot* for you!"

121

Send an old-fashioned telegram. Call Western Union at 800-325-6000; or visit www.WesternUnion.com.

122

Write funny love notes on a roll of toilet paper.

Don't sign your love letters: "You're one-in-a-million." (That would mean that there are six thousand of her in the world.)

Chapter Theme Song:
"Love Letters," Elvis Presley

Freshman Lessons

123

Romance is a *state of mind*. If you have the right mindset, you can make cleaning the bathroom romantic. If you have the *wrong* mindset, you can turn a moonlit stroll on the beach into a miserable experience.

124

Romance is a *state of being*. It's about taking *action* on your feelings. It's a recognition that love in the *abstract* has no real meaning at all! Romance is best defined as "love-in-action." Love is the *feeling*—romance is the *action*. Got it?? Romance often *starts* as a "state of mind," but it must move beyond mere thoughts and intentions, and be communicated to your lover—through words, gifts, presents, gestures, touches, looks—through *action*.

125

Romance is about the *little things*. It's much more about the small gestures—the little ways of making daily life with your lover a bit more special—than it is about extravagant, expensive gestures.

126

There are *two* kinds of romance: 1) **Obligatory**, and 2) **Optional**. *Obligatory* romance is required by law. Look, if you forget to send roses on Valentine's Day, you'd simply better not show up at home! But *optional* romance is really more romantic. It's more genuine. It's making the romantic gesture *when you're not required to*. It's arriving home on a Tuesday after work with a bottle of champagne—just because! It's massages and messages. It's cards and candles and songs and . . .

Freshman Orientation: Start with the basics, be yourself, take it one step at a time.

Chapter Theme Song:
"I've Got a Lot to Learn About Love," Storm

Sophomore Lessons

127

Move beyond what I call "Generic Romance."

Generic Romance is the stuff that our culture has *defined* as "romantic": Chocolate, champagne, dinners, diamonds, movies, roses, lingerie, perfume, flowers, cards and candy. *Yes*, this stuff is romantic—yes, I give roses to my wife Tracey sometimes—but it's only a *start*, it's just skimming the surface.

If you expect your relationship to survive (much less *thrive*) for fifty years or more, you must move waaay beyond Generic Romance.

Are you ready to move beyond "Generic Romance"?

128

Timing is *everything*.

➤ Pulling surprises requires a superb sense of timing.
➤ Belated birthday cards ought to be outlawed.
➤ Chocolate is romantic—*but not if she's on a diet.*
➤ Stick to *small* romantic gestures when he's totally preoccupied with a big work project. (Save the biggies until he can appreciate them.)

129

Flirt with her at a party, as if you both were single.

❐ Freshmen level: Flirt just a little. Wink. Compliment her.
❐ Sophomore level: Act out a complete "pick-up" fantasy, without any of the other guests being aware of what you're doing.
❐ Junior level: Continue the fantasy as you return home!
❐ Senior level: Act out the complete "pick-up" fantasy at the party—and sneak off to an empty room, porch or closet, and make mad, passionate love!

Chapter Theme Song:

"Learning How to Love You," George Harrison

Junior Lessons

130

Turn common, everyday events into "little celebrations"—opportunities to express your love for your partner. We're not talking *passion* here, but *affection*. (*We'll get to passion elsewhere!* . . .) A tiny bit of forethought can turn the ordinary into the special. Eat dinner by candlelight. Tie a ribbon around a cup of bedtime tea. Pop your own popcorn while watching a video at home. Turn his birth*day* into a birthday *month!* Give her a bottle of champagne as a "thank you" for doing the grocery shopping. Leave a greeting card on his car seat when he's about to run errands for you.

"Love is letting go of fear."

~ Gerald Jampolsky

131

Recognize that *one* mode of expression isn't enough.

We all have natural patterns that we follow; behaviors that are easy, natural, habitual; modes of expression that we fall into without even thinking about it. And these modes of expression are not particularly gender-based (even though pop psychology claims otherwise). Do you *talk* about your feelings—or do you *act* on your feelings? Are you quick and spontaneous—or slow and methodical? Do you process information primarily through your head—or through your heart? Do you express yourself directly—or subtly?

There's no "right" and "wrong" here—simply "your" way and your partner's way. So the first lesson is to accept that your partner has a variety of *different* ways of expressing his or her feelings. Honor and respect these differences, and I *promise* that this alone will greatly improve your relationship!

The second lesson is to recognize your *own* modes of communication. Your easiest path to better communication will be through your natural channels. (See the index entry for *The Acorn Principle*.)

Chapter Theme Song:

"Teach Me Tonight," Ella Fitzgerald

Senior Lessons

132

- ➻ **Senior Biology:** When it comes to sex and sexuality, men and women are *different!*

- ➻ **Senior Psychology:** But when it comes to emotions and love, men and women are much more *alike* than we are *different.*

Wow! The things you learn when you read the real psychological literature, instead of relying on pop pyschology!

133

You can be yourself and it works! It's astonishing to me that so many people think that "being romantic" somehow means something *other* than "being yourself."

Men don't *really* expect women to be playmates, and women don't *really* expect men to be Harlequin heroes. What we all *really* want is the spark, the magic, the thrill of love: The experience we all had at the *beginning* of our relationships. This experience can be recreated through romance—that is, through the creative expression of your feelings. You never need to be someone you aren't, but you *do* need to stay in touch with your feelings, and then act on them.

134

Start with any basic romantic concept, then *give it a twist*—build on it, expand on it, exaggerate it, use your creativity, put your personal stamp on it—and you'll create an *endless* supply of new romantic ideas.

Le Boudoir

135

The bedroom is your *private, romantic hideaway*. Don't turn it into an all-purpose room.

* Get rid of that TV!
* No bright lights!
* No exercise equipment.

* Keep flowers on the nightstand.
* Always have candles handy.
* Massage oil is a must.

After she's asleep, quietly place a greeting card in front of her alarm clock. In the morning before she arises, ask her what time it is.

136

Don't simply have breakfast in bed—make it an *elegant feast*. Whip up something special: Blueberry pancakes? Cinnamon toast? Fresh-squeezed orange juice? French-roast coffee?

Serve on your good china and best crystal. Add lots of candles. And flowers, too.

The True Test of Love & Tolerance: Letting her warm her cold feet on you in bed.

137

"Breakfast in bed is 'nice'—but rather *common*, don't you think?" said one couple in the Romance Class. "We think the class would be interested in one of our favorite pastimes: *Dinner* in bed!"

138

Chapter Theme Song:
"Lay Lady Lay," Bob Dylan

➥ Canopy beds: Most Romantic Kind of Bed/Feminine Category
➥ Brass beds: Most Romantic Kind of Bed/Masculine Category

La Cuisine

139

Get to know the owner, manager or *maître d'* at your favorite restaurant. Become a "regular" and you'll get the best tables, best service and best wines, plus inside tips on what's *really* best on the menu tonight.

140

"The Great Search for the Most Romantic Restaurant in Town." Create a list of candidates garnered from restaurant reviews and tips from your friends. Visit a different restaurant each week. Rate them according to your own personal standards.

141

Does your partner have a favorite meal that he/she *always* orders when dining out? If so, write-up a "custom description" of the meal and secretly tape it into his/her menu. ("Pasta Prima Patricia." "Beefy Bob Wellington." "Eggs à la Lisa.")

142

Have lunch or dinner in an *unusual* place. Museums have quirky cafés. Airports have restaurants with great views. All-night diners are cool places to hang out.

143

Get up extra early on a weekday and go *out* for breakfast with your lover. It's a great way to start the day in a totally different way.

Chapter Theme Song:
"Hungry for Love," Patsy Cline

Love Notes (III)

144

Write one love letter on twenty-five different index cards. Hide these all over the house. Finding all of them will be the *first* challenge. Putting them in order will be the *second* challenge.

Write a love letter—but write it in *reversed letters*, so your lover has to hold it up to a mirror to read it!

145

Let comic strips speak for you. Tape them to the refrigerator. Hide them in her purse. Hide them in his briefcase. Pack them in her suitcase.

* Blondie and Dagwood's marriage issues
* Cathy's dating dilemmas
* Charlie Brown's unrequited love
* Rose and Jimbo's ongoing romance
* Brenda Starr's wry observations about love
* Dilbert's disastrous attempts at dating

146

If you're not much of a writer, create an *audio* love letter. Sit down with a tape recorder and just talk to her for ten minutes. Then place the tape in a Walkman, giftwrap it and mail it to her.

147

Add flair to your love notes and envelopes with festive, wacky or personalized rubber stamps. (You can even have a photograph made into a rubber stamp!) Call Ink-A-Dink-A-Do at 800-888-4652; or write to 61 Holton Street, Woburn, Massachusetts 01801; or visit www.inkadinkado.com.

Best Company Name Award to: Ink-A-Dink-A-Do.

Love Notes (IV)
148

Finding special meaning in various items is a romantically useful habit to develop. Here are a few album titles that might inspire you.

Attach an appropriate note to the CD and give it to your lover. Or create a musical "Love Coupon" with a theme that matches the title of the CD.

* *A Night to Remember*, Cyndi Lauper
* *Anticipation*, Carly Simon
* *August*, Eric Clapton
* *Captured Angel*, Dan Fogelberg
* *Desire*, Bob Dylan
* *Fantasy*, Carole King
* *Girls Just Want to Have Fun*, Cyndi Lauper
* *I'm Your Baby Tonight*, Whitney Houston
* *In the Dark*, The Grateful Dead
* *Lawyers in Love*, Jackson Browne
* *One Night of Sin*, Joe Cocker
* *Spend the Night*, The Isley Brothers
* *Still Crazy After All These Years*, Paul Simon
* *True Blue*, Madonna
* *Give and Take*, Eric Tingstad & Nancy Rumbel
* *Romance (Music for Piano)*, on the Narada Label
* *Beauty of Love*, Shardad
* *Euphoria*, Ottmar Liebert & Luna Negra
* *Passion in My Heart*, Nicholas Gunn
* *Let's Talk About Love*, Celine Dion
* *American Beauty*, Grateful Dead
* *Dressed to Kill*, Kiss
* *Heart to Heart*, David Sanborn
* *Let's Live for Today*, The Grass Roots
* *You Got What It Takes*, The Dave Clark Five
* *Dirty Mind*, Prince
* *Love to Love You Baby*, Donna Summer
* *Please Love Me Forever*, Bobby Vinton

*What albums in **your** collection have especially meaningful titles?*

Personal recommendation:

Aaron Skyy's new CD, *Skyy's the Limit*. Includes some great romantic R&B songs like "Love Letter," and "Can't Stop Lovin' You," as well as the hit "The One."

"I Love You"

149

"I love you." The all-purpose, over-used phrase . . . that we never tire of hearing. Say it. Say it often. Say it with *feeling*. Mean it.

150

Upside-down stamps on envelopes mean "I love you."

FYI:

This tradition was started during World War I as soldiers and their gals wrote love letters back and forth, including this "love code."

151

You could learn how to say "I love you" using sign language. These two books will show you how:

❖ *The Joy of Signing*, by Lottie Riekoff
❖ *A Basic Course in American Sign Language*, by Tom Humphries

If you get more ambitious, you could move beyond a simple "I love you" and learn how to have silent and intimate conversations of love with one another across crowded rooms.

152

Call her from work for no other reason than to tell her, "I love you."

Chapter Theme Songs

"I Love You," Climax Blues Band

"I Love You," People

"I Love You," Donna Summer

"I Love You," Vanilla Ice

"I Love You," Otis Leavill

"I Love You," Mary J. Blige

"Ai Shite Imasu"

153

1. English: "I love you"
2. Apache: "Shi ingôlth-a"
3. Arabic: "'Ahebbek"
4. Armenian: "Sírem zk ´ez"
5. Aztec: "Nimitzlaco'tla"
6. Bengali: "Ami tomake bhalo basi"
7. Bulgarian: "Obícom te"
8. Burmese: "Chítte"
9. Cambodian: "Khñoms(r)alañ 'neak"
10. Cantonese: "Kgoh òi nei"
11. Cherokee: "Kykéyu"
12. Cheyenne: "Ne-méhotatsc"
13. Chinese: "Wo ài nei"
14. Czech: "Miluji vás"
15. Danish: "Eg elskar dig"
16. Dutch: "It hous van jou"
17. Egyptian: "Anna bahebek"
18. Eskimo: "Nagligivaget"
19. Finnish: "Mínä rákistan sínua"
20. French: "Je t'aime"
21. Gaelic (Irish): "Mo ghradh thú"
22. German: "Ich liebe dich"
23. Greek: "Sàs agapo"
24. Romany: "Mándi komova toot"
25. Hawaiian: "Aloha wau ia oe"
26. Hebrew: "Aní ohev otakh"
27. Hindi: "Mayn toojh ko pyár karta hun"
28. Hungarian: "Szeretlék"
29. Icelandic: "Eg elska pig"
30. Indonesian: "Saja tjinta padamu"
31. Irish: "Thaim in grabh leat"
32. Italian: "Ti amo"
33. Japanese: "Ai shite imasu"
34. Korean: "Na nun tangshinul sarang hamnida"
35. Kurdish: "Asektem"
36. Latin: "Ego Te amo"
37. Mandarin: "Wo ài ni"
38. Mohawk: "Konoronhkwa"
39. Norwegian: "Jeg elsker deg"
40. Persian: "Aseketem"
41. Polish: "Ja cie kocham"
42. Portugese: "Eu te amo"
43. Russian: "Ya lyablyu tyebya"
44. Samoan: "O te alofa ya te oe"
45. Sanskrit: "Aham twan sneham karomi"
46. Sioux: "Techi ´hila"
47. Somali: "Wankudja'alahai"
48. Spanish: "Te amo"
49. Swahili: "Mimi nakupenda"
50. Swedish: "Jag älskar dig"
51. Taiwanese: "Ngùa ai dì"
52. Thai: "Pom rak khun"
53. Tibetan: "Khyod-la cags-so"
54. Turkish: "Seni severim"
55. Ukranian: "Ya vas kikháyu"
56. Vietnamese: "Anh yêu em"
57. Welsh: "Rwy'n dy garu di"
58. Yiddish: "Ich libe dich"
59. Yugoslavian: "Ja te volim"
60. Zulu: "Ngi ya thandela wena"

Be Creative

154

Create a "Romantic Idea Jar."

✦ Write a hundred romantic ideas on separate slips of paper. Fill a jar with them. Once a week, one of you picks an idea at random and has to implement it within the next week. Take turns being the chooser.

✦ Or, number slips of paper one through 1001. Pick a number, then refer to the corresponding number in this book. (For this activity, you may want to skip the chapter "Spare No Expense"!)

✦ Or, number slips of paper one through 10,000(!)—and use the Romantic Idea Jar to choose items from my book, *10,000 Ways To Say I Love You.*

Everyone has tremendous creative potential inside. You just need to tap into it!

155

Is she a crossword fanatic? Create a *custom* crossword puzzle for her. Make the clues reminiscent of your relationship and life together; include private jokes, funny phrases and names of favorite songs. (And maybe some suggestive stuff! Hmmm?!)

For a *real* surprise: Carefully glue her custom crossword puzzle over the top of the Sunday *New York Times'* crossword puzzle—and wait for her to discover it!

156

Remove the mechanism from a musical card and attach it to the bottom of a dinner plate or to the inside of a heart-shaped box of chocolates.

Be Prepared

157

Be prepared—for *anything!* Create a "Gift Closet." Gather gifts ahead of time; buy things on sale; order quantities of items and get discounts; buy things during end-of-season sales; pick up presents on a whim. Then warehouse them and save them for later!

❖ Never again will you have to rush around at the last minute looking for an anniversary gift.
❖ You'll have more fun giving gifts and presents.
❖ Your partner will appreciate it.
❖ You'll save money!
❖ You'll be prepared to surprise her whenever the inspiration strikes you.

If you live in a *very small* house or apartment, create a "Gift Drawer" or store a "Gift Box" under your bed.

Seems like a paradox, but it's not: "Preparing for spontaneity!"

158

Be prepared for spontaneous romantic escapes! Have "His" and "Hers" overnight bags packed at all times. Keep under the bed or in the car trunk.

159

Be prepared for shopping! Know *all* of your partner's sizes! You should be able to buy *any* item of clothing for him or her, and have it fit 80 percent of the time.

☞ Could you buy her *any* item of lingerie? A coat? A sweater?
☞ Could you buy him a pair of shoes? A pair of gloves? A *hat?*

Be prepared—always have on hand:

A bottle of champagne
A romantic greeting card
A sexy greeting card
Love Stamps
A local/regional "Calendar of Events"
A few candles
Scented bubble bath
A fun little "Trinket Gift"
A little extra cash
A CD of romantic music
A bottle of massage oil

Always, Always, Always

160

Always, always, *always* stay in touch with the special, memorable, unique ways that the two of you have *fun* together.

✱ What's the most fun you've ever had with your clothes on? Well, do it again!

✱ What's the most fun you've ever had with your clothes off? *Well?!*

*When's the last time you really **played** together?*

161

☞ Learn your partner's "hot buttons"—and vow to never hit them.

☞ Learn your partner's pet peeves—and avoid them.

☞ Learn your partner's "blind spots"—and help him/her cope.

☞ Learn your partner's "soft spots"—and indulge them.

☞ Learn what turns your partner off—and avoid those behaviors.

☞ Learn what turns your partner on—and practice, practice, *practice!*

Books to enhance the *fun* in your life:

Simple Fun for Busy People, by Gary Krane.

Deep Play, by Diane Ackerman.

Beyond Love and Work: Why Adults Need to Play, by Lenore Terr.

162

Always remember that there are many—thousands, *millions!*—of ways of expressing love. And remember that your partner has the right to express his/her love in ways that may *not* be what you want or expect. When you *insist* that romance take a *particular* form, this reflects your rigidity or insecurity.

You do, of course, have the right to have *some* of the romance come to you in the form you desire. But don't expect your partner to read your mind! If you want something in your life, you must take responsibility for manifesting it. You might simply talk with your partner about your wants and needs. Some people recognize subtle hints while others need lists and reminders.

If you work *with* you partner's personality instead of *against* it, your relationship will be much happier.

Chapter Theme Songs:

"Always," Sammy Turner (1959)

"Always," Luther Ingram (1973)

"Always," Bon Jovi (1994)

Never, Never, *Never*

163

When you're talking with your lover on the phone, never, never, *never*, interrupt your conversation to answer another call via Call Waiting. Let your answering service pick up that incoming call! A+ Couples know it's important to give one another their undivided, focused attention.

164

* Never, never, *never* wallpaper together.
* Never, never, *never* disrespect her.
* Never, never, *never* embarrass him in public.
* Never, never, *never* give checks as gifts.
* Never, never, *never* nag.
* Never, never, *never* forget your partner's birthday.
* Never, never, *never* throw out something that belongs to him/her.
* Never, never, *never* betray a confidence.
* Never, never, *never* refer to your wife as "My Old Lady."
* Never, never, *never* give her practical gifts.
* Never, never, *never* say, "Yes, dear," just to appease her.
* Never, never, *never* joke about her PMS.
* Never, never, *never* withhold sex to punish him.
* Never, never, *never* give her the "silent treatment."
* Never, never, *never* return his car with an empty gas tank.
* Never, never, *never* say "What's for dinner?" before saying "I love you."

*Never, never, **never** say, "I told you so."*

Gifts, Gifts, Gifts

165

The Forty-Six *Kinds* of Gifts

This list may inspire your thinking, give you a creative kick, or simply serve as a reminder.

1. The Surprise Gift
2. The Trinket Gift
3. The "Just what I always wanted" Gift
4. The Classically Romantic Gift
5. The Perfume Gift
6. The Sexy Gift
7. The "Oh, you shouldn't have!—But I love it!" Gift
8. The Obligatory Gift
9. The Optional Gift
10. The Kooky Gift
11. The Keepsake Gift
12. The "How did you find it?!" Gift
13. The Homemade Gift
14. The Unbelievably Expensive Gift
15. The Gag Gift
16. The Gift that Keeps on Giving
17. The One Gigantic Item Gift
18. Theme Gifts
19. Personalized Gifts
20. The Gift of Travel
21. The Gift of Food
22. The Gift in His/Her Favorite Color
23. The Meaningful Gift
24. The Funny Gift
25. The Practical Gift
26. The Frivolous Gift
27. The First-Class Gift
28. The Custom Romance Certificate Gift
29. The Gift-Within-a-Gift-Within-a-Gift Gift
30. The Beautifully Wrapped Gift
31. Birthday Gifts
32. Anniversary Gifts
33. The Gift of Time
34. The Gift of Cash
35. The Gift Certificate
36. The Gift of Yourself
37. The Cheap Gift
38. The Charming Gift
39. The Gift of Flowers
40. The Gift for No Particular Reason
41. The Family Heirloom Gift
42. The Gift of Art
43. The Decadent Gift
44. The Gift of Chocolate
45. The Gift Cruise
46. The Gift in a Teeny, Tiny Package

Sex, Sex, Sex

166

Here's something that may surprise you: "The *Torah* obligates a man to pleasure his wife so that she reaches sexual climax before [he does]." This practical/sexual/spiritual advice is from the amazing book *Kosher Sex: A Recipe for Passion and Intimacy*, by Rabbi Shmuley Boteach.

167

The Playboy catalog. Call 800-423-9494, or visit www.Playboy.com.

➤ Time yourselves: How *fast* can you make love??

➤ Time yourselves: How *long* can you make sex last??

168

Hang mistletoe over your bed. (Not just for Christmas only!)

✳ Increase the frequency of your lovemaking by 33%.

✳ Increase the time you spend on foreplay by 150%.

✳ Increase the quality of your lovemaking by 21%.

✳ Be 15% less inhibited in your lovemaking.

169

Learn to program your VCR—it could lead to more sex! Tape his/her favorite TV show. *Make love* during that timeslot. (Hint: Choose his favorite *hour-long* show, not his favorite *half-hour* sitcom.)

170

Use *props* to enhance your lovemaking. Here's tonight's assignment: First, buy a derby. (Yes, a *derby*. One of those old-fashioned hats.) Then rent the movie, *The Unbearable Lightness of Being* . You'll learn how to make effective use of the derby.

Chapter Theme Song:
"Sexy, Sexy, Sexy," James Brown

Love Notes (V)

171

Put a tiny little love note *inside* a balloon. Insert the message, blow up the balloon and tie it. Then attach a pin to the string.

172

Be prepared with greeting cards. Go out this weekend and buy $50 worth of greeting cards. Don't ask questions, *just do it!* Head for your nearest card shop and spend a solid hour reading *hundreds* of cards. Get some sentimental cards. Get some sexy cards. Get *several* birthday cards. Get some friendship cards. Get cards with no inscription, so you can exercise your creativity.

♣ Don't forget to file some of these cards at work.
♣ Pre-stamp the envelopes (with *Love Stamps*) to save time later.

173

Some creative twists to your basic love letters, love notes, poetry, verses and romantic quotes:

✳ Write them on nice parchment paper.
✳ Turn them into scrolls, tied with ribbon.
✳ Frame 'em.
✳ Have them rendered in calligraphy.
✳ Have your poem set to music.
✳ Have the new song recorded.
✳ Publish your love letters in a book.
✳ Place a love note in the newspaper classified section.
✳ Create a poster of a love poem.
✳ Write it up on your computer; add flourishes.
✳ Write a letter in *code*.

Cool idea! Have your poem set to music!

See the index listing for "Songsmith."

Love Notes (VI)

174

When traveling, give her a bouquet of roses; one rose for each day that you'll be away. Attach a note that says something like this:

"These three roses represent the three days I'll be away from you. They also symbolize the love, joy and laughter we share together."

175

Another flower-and-note combination for when you're apart from one another: Give her forget-me-nots. The note:

"Forget-me-not while I'm away from you. You're never far from my thoughts as you're always in my heart."

Be creative and have fun with your love notes!

176

Send him *one rose*. The note: "This bud's for you!"

177

Remove all of the thorns from a dozen long-stem red roses before you give them to your lover. The note:

"These roses symbolize my love for you: Perfect, pure and without the thorns of hurt. I'm not perfect, but my love for you is."

178

Give her tulips. ("Tulips"—"Two lips.") *You* write the note!

Pun alert!

Lovesick

179

Send *five* large flower arrangements to her at work, timed to arrive one-per-hour, beginning at one o'clock. Write a five-part love note, with one part accompanying each flower arrangement.

180

During their first date she picked up a penny from the ground and said, "A penny for your thoughts." He shared his thoughts and she paid him. (He saved the penny.) As they continued to date they often gave each other pennies as special little love tokens. One day, two years later, he presented her with two ring boxes. As she opened them he said, "A penny for your thoughts . . . and a diamond for your heart. Will you marry me?"

They named their first daughter Penny. On their tenth anniversary he gave her a rare nineteenth century penny made into a pendant. On their twentieth anniversary they visited the U.S. Mint on vacation. They now collect pennies in giant jars for their two grandchildren.

181

Attend a lousy movie (on *purpose*); sit in the balcony; make out in the dark.

Chapter Theme Song:

"Lovesick Blues," Floyd Cramer

Prescriptions for Love

182

Prescription for Romance #1: Compliment her. Repeat every four to six hours.

183

Prescription for Romance #2: Say "I love you" at least three times today. Repeat dosage every day *for the rest of your life*.

184

Prescription for Romance #3: Hug. Often!

185

Get an empty bottle of prescription pills. Fill it with green M&M's. Create a custom label, something like this:

> PATIENT: (YOUR PET NAME FOR YOUR LOVER.)
> MEDICATION: LIBIDO LIBERATOR—EXTRA STRENGTH!
> SIDE EFFECTS: LOVE SICKNESS & HOT FLASHES.
> DOSAGE: A HANDFUL OR TWO.
> REFILLS: SEE PRESCRIBING PHYSICIAN ONLY!
> PHYSICIAN: DOCTOR OF LOVE, (YOUR NAME).

Additional ideas:

* Create a sexy prescription label for a bottle of massage oil.
* A custom prescription for a bottle of cough syrup filled with liqueur.
* Convince his/her doctor to "prescribe" one of these concoctions to your lover!
* Convince a local pharmacist to dispense one of these creations to your lover!

Write her a prescription for a dozen chocolate chip cookies. Then fill the order.

Chapter Theme Song:
"Vitamin L," B.E. Taylor Group

Help for the Hopeless

186

Freebie Alert!

Get a free one-year subscription to a unique publication from yours truly: *The LoveLetter™—The Newsletter of Romantic Ideas.* It's a $25 value, and it's full of creative, unusual and wonderful ideas, gifts and gestures. Just send your name and address to: LoveLetter Newsletter, P.O. Box 1288, La Jolla, California 92038.

Sign up yourself, your spouse, your boyfriend/girlfriend, your brother, your parents, your friends—anyone who needs help in the Romance Department, or who would appreciate receiving lots of great romantic ideas on a regular basis.

187

Know your anniversaries. *All* of them . . .

Your wedding day

The first time you made love

The day you first met

Your first big blow-out fight

Your first date

The day you moved in together

Your first kiss

The day you bought your home

The day you conceived your first child

The first time you said the words, "I love you"

Are you ready? Take notes now. Here are seventeen creative ways to celebrate Celebrate Valentine's Day:

1. Rent a local hotel's Honeymoon Suite.
2. Take the day off from work on Valentine's Day.
3. One day simply isn't enough! Celebrate for a solid week!
4. Buy ten boxes of kids' valentines, and *flood* your partner with them!
5. Give your partner one card every hour on the hour.
6. Make a batch of heart-shaped cookies.
7. Make a giant Valentine card on the back of a travel poster—
8. And have vacation tickets (to that location) taped to the poster.
9. Plan a solid day's worth of romantic music.
10. Stay at a local bed and breakfast.
11. Send ten Valentine's Day cards.
12. Send a *hundred* Valentine's Day cards!
13. Spend the entire day watching romantic movies.
14. Give your modern gal a piece of antique jewelry.
15. Bake a heart-shaped cake—
16. And decorate it with red frosting and heart-shaped sprinkles.
17. Send a Valentine's Day card each day for a week.

Hope for the Helpless
188

To help you with your romantic planning, here are *The 23 Kinds of Romantic Surprises:*

1. Once-in-a-lifetime surprises
2. Unfolding surprises
3. Bait-and-switch surprises
4. Shocking surprises
5. Mystery-event surprises
6. Total surprises
7. Big surprises
8. Little surprises
9. Expected-but-not-right-now surprises
10. Expensive surprises
11. Surprise tickets
12. Group surprises
13. Surprise vacations
14. Public surprises
15. Private surprises
16. Surprises involving a collaborator
17. Midnight surprises
18. Surprises at work
19. Sexy surprises
20. Funny surprises
21. Meaningful surprises
22. Out-of-character surprises
23. Sweet surprises

> *A Romantic Surprise Coupon*
> Surprise!
> We're escaping together
> to a bed & breakfast this weekend!

Travel Tips

189

I love this one!

Sneak off to the airport the night before she's going to leave for a trip. Take one red rose. Rent one of those small storage lockers in the airline terminal. Put the flower in the locker. Sneak back home. Just before she leaves for the airport, hand her the key to the storage locker.

190

When you're traveling without her: Mail a card or note to her the day *before* you leave town, so she'll get it while you're away.

Visit www.CultureFinder.com to find out what's going on in any city you plan to visit.

191

When you'll be traveling without him, leave him one greeting card for each day you'll be gone.

192

When you'll be traveling for several days without her, leave behind a pile of "I'm Thinking of You" packets.

* Get a large manila envelope for each day you'll be away.
* Label each one with a day of the week, and fill each one with *stuff*. Stuff like: Her favorite candy, poems, little notes, magazines, a photo of you with a funny note, a "Love Coupon" for use when you're back, and an item of lingerie with a note saying, "Be wearing this when I return."

If the two of you love the outdoors, keep your camping equipment in the trunk so you'll be ready for spontaneous overnight outings.

193

When you're going to be away, tape your photo to your pillow.

A Suitcase Full of Romance

194

➤ Pack a card inside his suitcase. Pack a dozen!
➤ Hide little "love notes" everywhere: In his socks and shoes and shirt pockets and pants pockets and suit pockets and briefcase and suitcase and wallet and notebooks and files.
➤ Pack his favorite candies (any kind that won't melt).

195

Give him a custom-made tape in a Walkman just before he goes on a business trip. Tell him not to play it until the plane is airborne.

196

When she's going away by herself, give her a "Trip Survival Kit." (It would be nice to package it in a gift box or fancy bag—but you don't have to. You can make do with a grocery bag or shoebox labeled with a magic marker.) Fill the kit with fun stuff, candy, notes, etc.

197

Get help from hotel concierges! They're great resources, and they'll get nearly *anything* done for you: From normal things like delivering champagne and a note to his room, to the unusual—like filling his room with 100 balloons . . . or hiding a special gift in the bathtub . . . or whatever outrageous thing you can think up!

198

Send a greeting card *to her hotel*, so it's waiting for her when she arrives.

Definition of *spontaneity:*
Deciding this afternoon to fly somewhere—*anywhere*—this evening. Traveling without any luggage at all. Buying what you need along the way.

Plan a surprise trip. Fill her suitcase with helium balloons. Attach to each balloon a note that gives clues about your destination.

Fun & Games

199

Literally make a "game" out of being romantic. Take the spinner from an old board game; cover over the original instructions; divide the circle into twelve quadrants. Write different romantic activities in each quadrant. Take turns giving it a spin every week.

Guys think they should get "points" for being romantic. Well, give it a try!—

Make a "game" out of love, and award him "points." Might be the most fun you've had all year!

200

Go to a carnival, fair or amusement park together. Ride the rides. Play the games. Eat the hot dogs and cotton candy. Win her a stuffed animal. Kiss in the Tunnel of Love.

201

Visit a theater-supply shop together and rent some costumes. (Not just for Halloween, but for adventurous couples . . .)

✦ Guys: Be a cowboy, doctor, policeman, mechanic, astronaut.
✦ Gals: Be a ballerina, policewoman, doctor, cheerleader, elf.

202

Go on a mall-wide "Trinket Gift Hunt." Here's how it works: You each get ten dollars and thirty minutes to shop for each other. The goal is to buy as many different fun/crazy/significant/silly "Trinket Gifts" as possible, for your partner. Meet back in the center of the mall, open your gifts, and be prepared for a hilarious time!

Weird & Wacky

203

Greet him at the door with confetti, noise-makers and party hats.

204

Practice "Telepathy Romance." When you're going to be apart, agree to stop whatever else you're doing and *think about each other and nothing else for one minute*, at a pre-determined time.

205

Practice "Leap Year Romance." When February 29th rolls around, take the day off work and declare it your own personal "Romance Day." Give the gift of time—twenty-four hours worth—to your lover!

206

Have you ever seen $10,000 in one dollar bills strewn about someone's living room? Well, neither have I—but one woman in the Romance Class reported that's what her husband did with a commission check he received one year after a big sale. He handed her a rake and said, "Honey, whatever you can fit into this paper bag is yours to spend!" (Being rather clever herself, she stacked the bills *neatly* and walked away with *all of it!*)

Cats & Dogs

207

Include his/her beloved pet in many of your times together. Pet-lovers can be fanatical, so don't force her to choose between you or Spot, because Spot will probably win!

Get special treats for her dog. Celebrate his cat's birthday. Find hotels that welcome pets.

Eleven percent of cat owners have ended a romantic relationship because of their cat, according to one survey.

208

There's a cat museum in Amsterdam, Holland. Called the Cat Cabinet, it features works of art highlighting the role of the cat in art and society. For more info call the Netherlands Board of Tourism at 312-856-0110, or write to them at 225 North Michigan Avenue, Suite 1854, Chicago, Illinois 60601.

209

Not to be outdone, dog-lovers have a Dog Museum near St. Louis. The museum is devoted to the collection, preservation and exhibition of works of art and literature related to Man's Best Friend. The museum is in the Trot Jarville House, a magnificent Greek Revival building in Queeny Park, 25 miles west of downtown St. Louis. Call 314-821-3647.

FYI:

Cat Fancy Magazine: www.catfancy.com
Cats Magazine: 800-365-4421

FYI:

Dog World Magazine: 917-256-2305 or
    www.dogworldmag.com
Dog Fancy Magazine: www.dogfancy.com

Also:

Aquarium Fish Magazine and
Bird Talk Magazine at www.animalnetwork.com

210

Include his/her beloved pet in some of your romantic gestures.

- Attach a small gift to Fido's collar.
- Attach a little love note to Fluffy's collar.
- Float in the aquarium a bottle with a love note inside it.
- Place a diamond ring in a little treasure chest, sink it in the aquarium, then give clues about the location of the gift.

Satin & Lace

211

Ladies, regarding the sexual side of love, if you remember only *one thing* from this book, remember this: Men *love* lingerie.

Thousands of men in my Romance Classes have confided or complained that having their ladies wear lingerie more often is the one thing they want intensely that their women tend to hold back on.

212

Go lingerie shopping together. Accompany her into the dressing room.

213

Timid about shopping in a lingerie shop? That's what *catalogs* are for!

- ❤ *Victoria's Secret Catalog*—800-888-8200; www.VictoriasSecret.com/
- ❤ *Frederick's of Hollywood Catalog*—800-323-9525
- ❤ *Playboy Catalog*—800-423-9494; www.Playboy.com/
- ❤ *Dream Dresser*—800-963-7326
- ❤ *Three Wishes Lingerie*—www.3WishesLingerie.com/
- ❤ *Barely Nothings*—800-4-BARELY
- ❤ *Maitresse*—800-456-8464
- ❤ *Coquette International*—800-668-5477; www.Coquette.com

Lingerie Coupon

He gets to choose her lingerie outfit.
She gets to choose the sexual fantasy.

Participants must be at least
18 years of age.

Strategies & Examples

214

Use the particulars of your own personal love story to help you create gifts and gestures that are unique and meaningful.

One couple had first met on the subway in Boston.

✳ He once gave her a Boston subway token in a jewelry box, along with this note: "Here's a 'token' of my affection for you."

✳ The following year he had that token made into a pendant by a local jeweler.

✳ She once held a "mobile birthday party" for him on a subway car. All of their friends got on board at different stops along Beacon Street in Boston.

✳ Because they'd met on the "Green Line," green was their "special color," and they used it in many of their gifts to one another.

✳ And, of course, their special song was "(Charlie on the) M.T.A." by The Kingston Trio.

215

"Love is generally confused with dependence; but in point of fact, you can love only in proportion to your capacity for independence."

~ Rollo May

Sometimes one simple concept can provide a *lifetime* of gift-giving opportunities. One guy in my Romance Class told us that he bought his wife a modest diamond necklace for their tenth anniversary: A nice gold chain with one "smallish" diamond on it. For their eleventh anniversary he added another diamond; for Christmas he added *another* diamond; for her birthday he added yet *another* diamond. He's been doing this for twenty-three years now!

During years when money is tight, he simply buys less expensive diamonds. Then, when times are good, he replaces a cheaper diamond with a more expensive one!

He's happy because he saves *tons* of time by not having to really go shopping(!)—and his wife is happy because she really believes that "Diamonds are a girl's best friend!"

Bed & Breakfasts

216

Some favorite bed-and-breakfasts, inns and romantic hideaways recommended by Romance Class participants:

➽ Andrie Rose Inn, Ludlow, Vermont. "The most romantic of a dozen inns we've visited over the years." A variety of rooms and suites in nineteenth century surroundings welcome guests at the base of Okemo Mountain. Call 802-228-4846.

➽ Blue Lake Ranch, outside Durango, Colorado. "So private that there's no sign out front." Choose from the main inn or private cottages near picturesque Blue Lake. Call 970-385-4537.

➽ The Inn on Mount Ada, Avalon, California. "The definition of romance: A Pacific California island that doesn't allow cars!" Six rooms in a stately mansion are elegantly appointed with antiques and working fireplaces. Call 310-510-2030.

➽ The Don Gaspar Compound, Santa Fe, New Mexico. This classic Mission- and Adobe-style home has six private suites that enjoy a secluded garden courtyard. Call 505-986-8664.

➽ The Inn at Long Lake, Naples, Maine. The guest rooms have been restored to their original country warmth with elegant antique furnishings, fluffy comforters and pillows. Call 800-437-0328 or 207-693-6226.

➽ The Terrell House, New Orleans, Louisiana. Circa 1858, this inn is located in the Lower Garden District of New Orleans. The house surrounds you with Southern charm, antique chandeliers, marble fireplaces and elegant parlors. It's located on a street of antique shops and jazz clubs. Call 504-524-9859.

➽ The San Ysidro Ranch, Santa Barbara, California. A favorite of the Hollywood elite: Vivien Leigh and Laurence Olivier got married here; frequented by Jean Harlow, Audrey Hepburn, Fred Astaire. Call 800-368-6788.

Internet resources for B&Bs:
www.InnPlace.com
www.InnCrawler.com
www.BedAndBreakfast.com
www.BBonline.com
www.BedAndBreakfastNetwork.com

Gifts & Presents

217

Understand the difference between a *gift* and a *present*.

✦ A ***present*** is something you're giving the receiver because it's something *you* want him or her to have.
✦ A ***gift*** is something that you're sure the receiver *wants*.

(Don't bother looking up the words "gift" and "present" in the dictionary. Technically, they're synonyms. But then, what does *Webster's* know about romance?)

When a man gives a woman lingerie—guess what?!—nine times out of ten it's a *present*. When he gives her favorite perfume, it's a *gift*. This is not to say that one is better than the other. Gifts and presents are just *different*. Knowing the difference between a gift and a present will help both of you stay "in tune" with each other and avoid unrealistic expectations and possible hard feelings.

Note: Items can sometimes be both gifts and presents at the same time. It depends on the item in combination with the recipient's individual personality.

Gift—Tickets to see his favorite team.
Present—Tickets to the opera.

Gift—Elegant, satin lingerie.
Present—Peek-a-boo panties.

Gift—A new Ping putter.
Present—Clothes you'd like him to wear.

Gift—A book by her favorite author.
Present—A book you'd like her to read.

218

Consciously choose gifts and presents that *symbolize* your love.

Gifts and presents are *things* we give to symbolize our love. It's not about the *stuff*, it's about what the stuff *means*. Frankly, what lovers *really* want is *more of each other!* More time together, more shared experiences, more opportunities to be loving.

The role of gifts and presents is to stand in for you, to represent you, when you're not physically there. So choose them wisely.

What has he *really wanted* for a long time, but held back from buying? Get it for him!

Presents & Gifts

219

Create "theme" gifts and gestures. Combine similar items and ideas to create fun, meaningful gifts.

Give her these three gifts, wrapped separately but ribboned together:

❖ The poetry book *A Friend Forever*, by Susan Polis Schutz
❖ The CD *Forever Friends*, by Justo Almario
❖ The song "That's What Friends Are For," by Dionne Warwick & Friends

220

Another "theme" gift: Give him *all* of Leo Buscaglia's "love" books:

➛ *Love*
➛ *Personhood*
➛ *Living, Loving & Learning*
➛ *Born for Love*
➛ And get some of Leo's wonderful lectures on videotape.

221

➤ "Diamonds are a girl's best friend." Get her one.

➤ "Dogs are a man's best friend." Get him one.

222

And another "theme" gift:

❑ Give her a new pair of walking shoes or hiking boots.
❑ And a copy of the book *Off the Beaten Path—A guide to more than 1,000 scenic and interesting places still uncrowded and inviting.*
❑ And a written invitation to a three-day hiking vacation.

Give a *funny* gift.

Give an *artistic* gift.

Give a *sexy* gift.

Give a *timely* gift.

Give a *meaningful* gift.

Give a *musical* gift.

Give a *tiny* gift.

Give a *seasonal* gift.

Give a *tasty* gift.

Daily & Weekly

223a

A *Daily* Romantic Checklist:

✦ Compliment your partner.
✦ Spend twenty minutes of uninterrupted time together.
✦ Check in with each other during the day.
✦ Perform one small—and *unexpected*—gesture.
✦ Say "I love you" at least three times.
✦ Thank your partner for *something*.
✦ Look for romantic concepts in the newspaper.
✦ Take an extra minute when kissing good-bye.

223b

A *Weekly* Romantic Checklist:

➤ Bring home one *small*, unexpected gift or present.
➤ Share some form of physical intimacy.
➤ Share an *entire* afternoon or evening together.
➤ Share two insights you gained this week.
➤ Write at least one little love note.
➤ Mail *something* to your partner.
➤ Make love!
➤ Plan something *special* for the upcoming weekend.

Seven qualities to focus on:

On Sunday: Be *debonair*.
On Monday: Be *zany*.
On Tuesday: Be *enchanting*.
On Wednesday: Be *sexy*.
On Thursday: Be *funny*.
On Friday: Be *playful*.
On Saturday: Be *romantic*.

Focus on a different sense each day:

Sunday: Sense of *sight*.
Monday: Sense of *hearing*.
Tuesday: Sense of *smell*.
Wednesday: Sense of *touch*.
Thursday: Sense of *taste*.
Friday: Common *sense*.
Saturday: Sense of *humor*.

Monthly & Yearly

223c

A *Monthly* Romantic Checklist
- ❖ Plan one romantic *surprise* for this month.
- ❖ Re-stock your stash of greeting cards.
- ❖ Go out to dinner once or twice.
- ❖ Rent at least two romantic movies.
- ❖ Make love several times!
- ❖ Make plans for a three-day romantic weekend sometime in the next three months.
- ❖ Plan one romantic event with a *seasonal theme*.

223d

A *Yearly* Romantic Checklist
- ❋ Make a New Year's resolution to be a more *creative* romantic.
- ❋ Make plans for your next anniversary.
- ❋ Think of an *unusual* way to celebrate your partner's birthday.
- ❋ Review your plans for your next vacation.
- ❋ Create a special "Romance" category in your household budget.
- ❋ Make plans for Valentine's Day—well in advance!

Rent one romantic comedy every month:

January: All of Me

February: Arthur

March: Frankie and Johnny

April: The Goodbye Girl

May: Groundhog Day

June: The Owl and the Pussycat

July: Tootsie

August: Desk Set

September: Moonstruck

October: Shakespeare in Love

November: Bull Durham

December: French Kiss

Yin & Yang

224a

Romantics are particularly good at balancing opposites.

A lot of problems and misunderstandings—from marital spats to world wars—are caused by people ignoring the fact that everything operates under the principles of Yin and Yang. Everything includes, or works together with, its opposite: Masculine and feminine; love and hate; give and take; funny and serious; life and death.

There is great wisdom and truth in every pair of ideas below—even though each pair represents two *opposite* suggestions! These paradoxes are part of the mystery and magic of life and love.

224b

❖ Celebrate your differences.
❖ Take comfort in your similarities.

224c

✳ Live in the present! *Now* is all there is! Free yourself from the past.
✳ Keep your memories alive. Nostalgia fuels romance.

224d

✳ Read books! They contain wisdom, great ideas and inspiration!
✳ Throw the books away! Listen to your inner voice.

224e

Chapter Theme Song:
"Hello Goodbye," The Beatles

✳ Say what you feel when you feel it. Be *totally honest* with each other.
✳ Choose your words carefully. What you say creates your reality.

Yang & Yin

224f

- Treat her as your *best friend*—You'll build intimacy.
- Treat her as a *stranger*—It will add spice to your life!

224g

- Lighten up! Have more *fun* together. Experience the joy of life!
- Get serious! Successful relationships require work!

224h

- Romance is easy! Just express yourself. Romance is "adult play"!
- Romance is hard! Plan, shop, hide, wrap, write, surprise, deliver, drive, call, remember, woo!

224i

- Actions speak louder than words. *Do* something, don't just *talk*—Talk is cheap!
- Communication is the cornerstone of a good relationship.

*Romantics **thrive** on dynamic tension!*

224j

- Travel inspires romance: Exotic locales, foreign food, new experiences, high adventure!
- Home is where the heart is: A cozy fire, a romantic bedroom, and a hot tub!

224k

- "Shake up" your life! Go to a motivational seminar! Do something outrageous! Go skydiving!
- "Slow down" your life. Meditate. Find your center. Listen. Shhh.

Mozart

225

These twelve pieces, performed on solo piano, are now available on a CD titled *1001 Ways To Be Romantic—The Music*. Available at your local music store or at www.1001WaysToBeRomantic.com.

The dozen most romantic classical compositions of all time?

1. Liszt-Siloti: "Un Sospiro (A Sigh)," Concert Etude in D Flat Major
2. Debussy: "Girl with the Flaxen Hair"
3. Beethoven: "Moonlight Sonata," 1st Movement Op. 27, No. 2
4. Debussy: Arabesque No. 1
5. Mendelssohn: "Venetian Boat Song," Op. 30, No. 6
6. Chopin: Waltz in C Sharp Minor Op. 64, No. 2
7. Beethoven: "Fur Elise"
8. Mendelssohn: "Song Without Words," Op. 62, No. 1
9. Chopin: Nocturne in F Sharp Minor Op. 48, No. 2
10. Brahms: Waltz in A Major, Op. 39, No. 15
11. Brahms: Waltz in E Major, Op. 39, No. 2
12. Saint-Seans: "The Swan" from Carnival of the Animals

226

The *next* twelve most romantic classical compositions of all time?

13. Rachmaninoff: "A Night for Love"
14. Debussy: "Clair de lune"
15. Granados: Spanish Dance No. 2 ("Oriental")
16. Chopin: Rondo in C Major, Op. 73
17. Scriabin: Fantasy in A Minor, OpCustom-made (II) Posthumous
18. Debussy: "Prelude to the Afternoon of a Fawn"
19. Bach: "Jesu, Joy of Man's Desiring"
20. Schubert: Impromptu in G flat
21. Ravel: "Jeux d'eau"
22. Rameau: Gavotte and Six Doubles
23. Schubert-Liszt: "Serenade"
24. Ravel: "Bolero"

Elvis

227

For your Elvis fan . . .

✻ Visit Graceland on your next vacation.
✻ Hold a yearly birthday party on January 8th.
✻ Use Elvis stamps *every time* you mail something to him/her.
✻ Get all *fifty-two* Elvis albums that were certified gold.
✻ Plan your vacations with the help of the book, *The Field Guide to Elvis Shrines*, by Bill Yenne. It's a truly *astounding* resource.

228

Take a favorite 45 RPM record, and paste a new label over the original one: Retitle the song using her name or some personal reference. Or simply rename it "Our Song."

Everybody has a favorite singer, song, group or type of music. Use this knowledge in your romantic gifts and gestures!

229

Get *every recording ever made* by his or her favorite musical group.

230

✻ Musical lovenote: "Play the CD *Music Box*, by Mariah Carey. My message to you is song number nine."

Song #9: "I've Been Thinking About You"

✻ Musical lovenote: "Play the CD *America*, by America. My message to you is song number seven."

Song #7: "I Need You"

✻ Musical lovenote: "Play the CD *Tapestry*, by Carole King. Listen to song number seven."

Song #7: "You've Got a Friend"

✻ Musical lovenote: "Play the CD *Christopher Cross*; my message to you is song number one."

Song #1: "Say You'll be Mine"

✻ Musical lovenote: "Play the CD *A Day at the Races*, by Queen. My message to you is song number two."

Song #2: "You Take My Breath Away"

Lame Excuses (#'s 1-4)

231a

Not true!

Lame Excuse #1: "Real Men aren't romantic."

Sez who?? Somebody on a TV talk show? Some character in a movie? Your buddies? (Experts all, on matters of the heart, no doubt.) Let me tell you something: If Real Men aren't romantic, then Real Men are *lonely*.

231b

Not necessarily!

Lame Excuse #2: "Being romantic is going to cost me a fortune!"

As the Beatles said, "Money can't buy me love." It's true. Money *can* buy you companionship, attention, sex and status—but it *can't* buy you *love* or *happiness*. Being romantic *can* cost you a fortune, but it doesn't *have* to. There is no correlation whatsoever between the size of the sentiment and the size of the price tag.

231c

Give me a break!

Lame Excuse #3: "I don't have time."

Bull! You have 1,440 minutes every day—the same as everybody else. How you use those minutes is up to you. Yes, work is important. Yes, your golf game is important. But do you really need to watch that rerun of *Gilligan's Island* again? The truth is, we all have time for what's *truly important* to us.

231d

Uh-Huh!

Lame Excuse #4: "I forgot."

That's okay. *Just don't do it again.* You're allowed to forget *occasionally*, but not consistently. If forgetting is a *habit*, you're sending a clear signal that he or she just is not that important to you.

Lame Excuses (#'s 5-8)

231e

Lame Excuse #5: "I'll be romantic *later*—after I get my career in order."

The busy executive excuse.

"Later" usually comes in about *forty years*—much too late for most partners to wait. And I know this next comment is a cliché, but it's so, so true: No one, on his death bed, ever wished that he'd spent more time at work.

231f

Lame Excuse #6: "I shouldn't have to *prove* my love by being romantic."

The belligerent excuse.

Romance isn't about *proving* anything. It's about *expressing* something.

231g

Lame Excuse #7: "Maybe *next* week."

The procrastinator's excuse.

* Question 1: How many weeks have you been saying this??
* Question 2: (Sorry to be morbid—*but* . . .) How would you feel if your lover passed away without you having expressed your true love for him/her?

231h

Lame Excuse #8: "What will the *guys* think?"

The pseudo-macho excuse.

First, why should you *care* what the guys think? Second, who says that you need to *tell* the guys how romantic you are? Third, even though many guys won't admit it, most of them would *love* to know the relationship secrets of romantic guys!

Lame Excuses (#'s 9-12)

231i

One of the most common excuses.

Lame Excuse #9: "Oh, heck, she *knows* I love her."

She knows that you loved her *at one time*—but she may not be so sure about *right now*. Love must be *expressed* in order stay alive. Otherwise it simply withers away.

231j

*A really **feeble** excuse!*

Lame Excuse #10: "It's simply not *me* to be romantic."

What you *probably* mean is that you're not "typically" romantic, or that you're not very *openly* demonstrative. This is fine, as long as you do express your love in *some* way, in a way that works for you *and* that your partner recognizes.

231k

A lazy excuse.

Lame Excuse #11: "I'm just not creative."

Untrue. *Everyone* is creative. It's simply a matter of *where* you apply your creativity. Most people use their creativity all day at work, then come home and shut it off.

231l

Grasping at straws!

Lame Excuse #12: "I'm simply not eloquent."

Great news, Shakespeare! You don't *have* to be eloquent in order to be romantic! A simple "I love you" usually does the trick. And besides, I'll *bet* that she knows you well enough to suspect that your talents lie in areas other than poetry.

Lame Excuses (#'s 13-14)

231m

Lame Excuse #13: "I'm just too *tired* to be romantic."

Oh, my! Poor baby! Let's help. No, not by propping up your feet so you can watch TV more comfortably—but by *really* helping you. First, we'll take you to the doctor, to make sure you're not anemic. Then we'll start you on an exercise program. Then we'll improve your diet. Then we'll get you started on a yoga program. Then we'll make sure you stop working overtime, and get home to your loving partner at a reasonable hour.

ZZZZZZZzzzzzzzzzzzzzzz . . .

231n

Lame Excuse #14: "It's been so long since I've been romantic that if I brought home a dozen roses her first reaction would be to ask me what I've been up to."

I'd say she has a *right* to be skeptical, don't you? She really wants to be reassured that this romantic gesture isn't just something you've done because you read it in a book(!) She needs to know that the gesture is genuine—and that it's not a one-time occurance. You're just going to have to prove yourself over time. (Believe me, it's worth it!)

Get over it!

Bonus *Lame Excuse!*

"I'm afraid she'd be so shocked if I were to be romantic that she'd have a heart attack and die."

For Men Only

232

Women **love** how a man looks in a tuxedo. I think it's genetic.

Wear a tuxedo home from work.

233

A shopping trip for men (store-specific). Buy one item from each store. Giftwrap in separate boxes.

* A bath shop
* A lingerie boutique
* A card shop
* A liquor store
* A flower shop
* A quality jewelry store

234

Another shopping trip for men (product-specific): Pick-up all these items in coordinated fragrances:

* Body lotion
* Hand lotion
* Foaming bath gel
* Dusting powder
* Potpourri
* Shampoo
* Conditioner
* Perfumed soap
* Fragrance candles
* Oils

235

This one is worth **10 zillion** points in the Relationship Accounting Department!

Secret Romantic Idea for Guys Only. Videotape the Super Bowl—and take your wife out to dinner during the game!

Think about it: You only have to do this *once*. She'll be *thrilled*. She'll be telling all her friends how wonderful you are. (More bonus points for you!) And you *will* get to see the game—just three hours later than everyone else. And heck, the game is usually a letdown anyway.

For Women Only

236

Send him a letter sealed with a kiss. (Use your reddest lipstick.)

237

Send him a *perfumed* love letter.

A heartfelt appreciation for the positive, powerful, endearing and enduring qualities of men: *What There is to Love About a Man*, by Rachel Snyder.

238

Send flowers to him at work.

239

Don't position yourself against his passions. Please don't force him to choose between you and his golf/football/basketball/cars/fishing! There's room for football *and* females in most guys' lives. If you're in love with a fanatic, you have to remind him why he *used to be* fanatical about you, too—and why it's worth his while to be a fan once more!

The rules have changed for the new millennium: It's now appropriate and acceptable for women to give flowers to men.

240

Read the book *Iron John*, by Robert Bly. It offers a fresh and insightful look at masculinity. Learn that the "Wild Man" inside him need not turn him into an insensitive macho guy; see the partnership that the book offers between the masculine and the feminine. (If your guy hasn't already read this book, give it to him when you're finished with it.)

Chapter Theme Song:
"Stand By Your Man," Tammy Wynette

For Singles Only

241a

Think Like a Married Person: Strategy #1
Build intimacy

Dating as a "lifestyle" is okay for a few years, but most singles long for a serious, monogamous, intimate relationship. Ask yourself what your *real* goals in dating are. (Making the scene? Looking good? Scoring?) If, instead, intimacy is your goal, you'll share more of yourself sooner, you'll communicate honestly, and you'll listen to one another more attentively.

*Think like a **married** person!*

241b

Think Like a Married Person: Strategy #2
Think long-term

The single brain is consumed with *short-term* goals. (This Saturday night. What will I wear? Will he kiss me tonight? Will she sleep with me on the second date?) *Chill out*, singles! A *long-term* mindset will relieve a lot of your stress, help you be more "yourself," and give you a better perspective on things.

241c

Think Like a Married Person: Strategy #3
Communicate!

Have you ever noticed that single people often do a lot of *talking* without really *communicating*? The singles scene is characterized by a lot of posturing, boasting and clever bantering. Those who get beyond these superficial things most quickly tend to end up in the best relationships.

Chapter Theme Song:

"Girl That I Marry," from the musical *Annie Get Your Gun*

For Marrieds Only

242a

Think Like a Single Person: Strategy #1
Flirt!

When's the last time you actually *flirted* with your own spouse? Try it the next time you're out in public together. You'll give your partner a pleasant jolt—and *you'll* have fun, too. Think back to all those little things you used to do while you were courting one another—and try them out again.

242b

Think Like a Single Person: Strategy #2
Pursue instant gratification

The typical mindset of a married person is *long-term*. The *positive* side of this is that *long-term* can mean security, commitment and comfort. The *negative* side is that it can also mean boredom, laziness and complacency. One way to combat this negative side is to adopt the mindset of a single person: It's a mindset of *instant gratification*. Horny?—Make love *now*. Thinking of her?—Call her *now*. Appreciate him?—Hug him *now*. Walking through a mall?—Pick up a little love-gift *now*.

242c

Think Like a Single Person: Strategy #3
Seduction

When's the last time you *seduced* your spouse? How often do you bother to set the mood, play the music, dress the part, say the right words, do the little things? Think back to your seduction techniques from when you were single. (C'mon—don't play innocent with us here!)

*Think like a **single** person!*

Chapter Theme Song:
"Husbands & Wives," Neil Diamond

A Month of Romance: Week 1

243—Sunday

Buy a guidebook for the city or region in which you live. Visit someplace you've never been before.

244—Monday

Clip your partner's horoscope from the newspaper. Attach a note describing how you're going to make certain that the astrological prediction comes true. Give it to your partner as you part ways for work.

245—Tuesday

After you say good-bye, turn back one more time and blow her a kiss.

246—Wednesday

Buy a lottery ticket. Give it to her with a little note attached:
"I hit the jackpot when I married you!"

Alternative notes:
"Take a chance on me!"
"You're one-in-a-million!"

247—Thursday

Thursday is "Gift Day"! *(Why? Because I said so, that's why!)* Bring home a bottle of scented massage oil. Use it!

248—Friday

Page through your photo albums together. Relive the memories.

Chapter Theme Songs:

"Come Sunday," Johnny Mathis
"Beautiful Sunday," Daniel Boone
"Loving You Sunday Morning," Scorpions
"Easy," The Commodores
"On Sunday," 'Til Tuesday
"Sunday Kind of Love," Ella Fitzgerald
"Sunday Morning Sunshine," Harry Chapin

249—Saturday

Touch more. Hold hands. Rub her neck. Massage his feet. Hug! Cuddle!

A Month of Romance: Week 2

250—Sunday

Go for a walk. (No headphones allowed.) Hold hands.

251—Monday

Get up with the sun. Enjoy the morning for a change, instead of rushing through your shower, grabbing your coffee and dashing out the door.

252—Tuesday

Get up with the sun. Make love. Go to work.

253—Wednesday

Take a class together. Sign up for a dance class. Or a cooking class. Or a wine-tasting class. Or a massage class.

254—Thursday

Thursday is Gift Day! Bring home a bouquet of flowers. Write a poetic note about their symbolic significance.

255—Friday

Have "your song" playing on the stereo when your partner returns home from work.

256—Saturday

Visit a museum giftshop and get a poster print by her favorite artist. Have it framed for her. They may also have greeting cards, note cards, journals or blank books featuring the artwork of her favorite artist.

Chapter Theme Songs:

"Come Monday," Jimmy Buffett
"Another Monday," John Renbourn
"Born on a Monday," Michael Quatro
"Goodbye Monday Blues," Si Kahn
"Monday Monday," Mamas & The Papas
"Manic Monday," Bangles
"Monday Love," Tara Kemp
"Monday Morning in Paradise," Tom Paxton

"Tuesday Afternoon," The Moody Blues
"Ruby Tuesday," Cat Stevens
"Tuesday's Gone," Hank Williams, Jr.
"Tuesday Next," Stan Getz
"Sweet Tuesday Morning," Badfinger

A Month of Romance: Week 3

257—Sunday

Remove the lightbulbs from the lamps in your bedroom. Replace them with candles. You take it from there.

258—Monday

Head to your local music store. Get the *Heartstrings* CD by Earl Klugh.

259—Tuesday

Start the day in a special way. Read out loud an inspirational passage from a favorite book.

260—Wednesday

End the day in a special way. Give him/her a massage.

261—Thursday

Yes—today is Gift Day! Buy him a wild tie. Buy her a stuffed animal.

262—Friday

Share a bubble bath.

263—Saturday

Make love tonight—*without using your hands*.

Chapter Theme Songs:

"Wednesday," Detroit Emeralds
"Wednesday Car," Johnny Cash
"Wednesday Morning, 3 AM,"
Simon & Garfunkel

"Misty Thursday," Duke Jordan
"Thursday," Count Basie
"Thursday Afternoon," Brian Eno

A Month of Romance: Week 4

264—Sunday

Spend *all day* in bed. Read the Sunday funnies aloud to her. Make love. Enjoy breakfast in bed. Take a nap. Watch old movies on TV. Make love again. Have Domino's Pizza deliver dinner. Make love again.

265—Monday

Call in sick to work. Repeat yesterday.

266—Tuesday

Send loving thoughts to your lover via mental telepathy.

267—Wednesday

Pack a picnic lunch. Meet him at work. Close his office door. *Bon appétit!*

268—Thursday

Another Gift Day. Today's gift won't cost you a *dime*. Write a list titled "Ten Reasons I Love You." Present it to him/her over dinner.

269—Friday

Today's assignment is to find one romantic idea/concept/gift in the newspaper. Act on it within the next two weeks.

270—Saturday

Make a couple of *incredible* banana splits. Make sure to use your partner's favorite ice cream flavors.

Chapter Theme Songs:

"Friday," Joe Jackson
"Friday I'm in Love," Cure
"Friday's Angels," Generation X
"Never on Friday," Willie Smith
"Quiet Friday," Stan Kenton Orchestra

"Saturday," Carpenters
"Come Saturday Morning," Sandpipers
"Saturday Afternoon," Jefferson Airplane
"Saturday Evening," Ronnie Laws
"Saturday in the Park," Chicago

The Golden Rules of Romance

271a

Time and effort expended are more appreciated than money spent.

Gifts are great, but they can't make up for lost time. Maintaining a loving, romantic connection with your lover means lingering over dinner, spending lazy Sunday afternoons together, walking and talking, etc.

271b

Planning doesn't destroy spontaneity—it creates opportunity.

Plan a special gesture for your next anniversary. Plan a surprise birthday party. Plan your work life with time built in for romance.

*Romance is often—but not **always**—a spontaneous thing. Sometimes it's the **planning** that makes the romance come alive!*

271c

The *receiver* defines what's romantic.

✷ If you give her flowers, and she hates flowers, it ain't romantic.
✷ If you've spent all day cooking a gourmet meal, and he'd rather call Domino's for a pizza . . . guess what?
✷ If you've spent a fortune on an outfit for her, and she says it isn't her style, you have no right to be resentful. (This is why you must listen to her and learn her likes and dislikes.)

271d

Romantics give their relationship the top priority in their lives.

Everything else flows *from* the relationship, *through* the relationship, and *because of* the primary love relationship, if your life is operating in a successfully dynamic manner. This does not mean that one becomes a martyr on behalf of the other. Martyrs hurt themselves, and thus harm the relationship. Healthy relationships always support and nurture each member of the couple.

Rules Were Made to be Broken

272

- Rule: *Don't* give cash as a gift.
- Breaking the Rule: Unless it's done *creatively*.

  * Tape one hundred one-dollar bills together, creating a long banner out of them, and string them throughout the house.

  * If his favorite color is green, tie a stack of one-dollar bills with a green ribbon.

  * Attach a one-hundred-dollar bill to a Victoria's Secret catalog, along with a note saying, "You choose."

  * Wrap a one-hundred-dollar bill around the stem of a flower.

273

- Rule: *Don't* give gift certificates.
- Breaking the Rule: Gift certificates generally don't work because they're too generic. So if you can make them specific, personalized, and "just right" for your partner, go for it!

  * For gals: A generous gift certificate for her all-time favorite boutique, catalog or service.
  * For guys: A gift certificate from Sears or The Sharper Image or Radio Shack.
  * Exception #3, for both: *Custom-made* gift certificates that express your affection in a special, creative, unique and/or touching way.

Romantics like to break the rules, be unconventional, express themselves and be spontaneous.

Chapter Theme Song:
"Breaking All the Rules," Peter Frampton

Be My Valentine!

274

For future reference: Buy an *extra* bag of Valentine Conversation Heart candies and save them for use *six months later*.

275

While sharing stories from their childhoods, Pete told Deb that, because he grew up poor, he was unpopular in grammar school. Every Valentine's Day when the children would decorate their shoeboxes so they could deliver Valentines to each other, Pete's box always remained empty. Deb thought this was the saddest thing she'd ever heard.

For the next Valentine's Day she decorated a shoebox and *filled* it with Valentines. And Deb promised him that he would *never* go without a Valentine again.

276

Gals: Stumped about what to get him for Valentine's Day? Try this idea this year: Forget the *gift!* Just greet him at the front door wearing a big red ribbon—*and nothing else.*

Kiss Me, You Fool!

277

Of course you know how to kiss, but perhaps a refresher course might add a little spark to your lives. Pick up a copy of a fun little book called *The Art of Kissing*, by William Cane. In it are instructions for (among other things) . . .

- ❤ The Candy Kiss
- ❤ The Music Kiss
- ❤ The Perfume Kiss
- ❤ The Sliding Kiss
- ❤ The Surprise Kiss
- ❤ The French Kiss
- ❤ The Counter Kiss
- ❤ The Vacuum Kiss
- ❤ The Japanese Kiss

278

"Butterfly Kisses": You're butterfly kissing when your face is very close to your lover's cheek, and you blink your eye rapidly, softly grazing your eyelashes against her skin.

279

Rent the classic movie *Singin' in the Rain*. Then . . .

- ✦ Take a walk the next time it rains—
- ✦ And sing and dance in the rain together!
- ✦ Buy her an umbrella in her favorite color.
- ✦ Buy a golf umbrella—so you can walk comfortably together.
- ✦ Buy a tiny travel umbrella—so you have to huddle together!
- ✦ Get him a new overcoat; stuff the pockets with your lingerie.
- ✦ Vacation in Seattle.

1) Steal a kiss.
2) Give it back.

"Kiss: A contraction of the mouth due to an enlargement of the heart."

~ ANONYMOUS

Trivia: The rock group Kiss has not recorded *any* romantic songs.

The Mathematics of Romance

280

Great relationships aren't 50/50. They're 100/100.

Having a "fifty-fifty" relationship *sounds* like a good goal—but it's *not*. An *equitable* relationship is not the same thing as a *loving* relationship. Fifty-fifty *really* means "I'll meet you half way." In other words, "I'll work only this hard, I'll give only this much, then it's your turn to meet me halfway." Love is about giving 100%, not merely 50%.

Nobody can give 100% of himself 100% of the time—it's impossible. But you *can* aim for it, and when you (inevitably) fall short, it'll still be okay. Even if you each fall short by as much as 50%, you'll still be in fine shape; it'll still add up to something close to 100%. The problem is when you're both trying to limit your giving to "your fair share"—usually defined as 50%. If you do that, you'll *definitely* fall short of 100%.

Give 100% to your relationship. But don't fall into the trap of trying to "give 150%." It sounds impressive, but it's impossible to give more than you have. It will just frustrate you and make you feel guilty.

Here's the mathematical formula for romance:

$r = a\,(1\text{-}cosA)$

Actually, this is the formula for a "cardioid"— a somewhat *heart-shaped curve*. More precisely, for you romantic mathematicians , a cardioid is "the path of a point on a circle that rolls externally, without slipping, on another equal circle." (Who *says* nerds can't be romantic?!)

281

5 minutes devoted to romance = 1 day of harmony

Think of all the times that your failure to do some *little thing*—like calling to tell her you'll be home late from work, or mailing her birthday card on time—has caused a full day of unhappiness. Consistent attention to your lover will keep your relationship balanced and happy. It doesn't take much! Little gestures go a long way.

Best Mathematical Love Poem of All Time:

See the story titled, "Trurl's Electronic Bard," in *The Cyberiad* by Stanislaw Lem.

282

+ Celebrate your *1,000th* day together. (That's about 2 years, 8 months and 26 days—depending on when the leap years fall.)

+ Celebrate your *10,000th* day together! (That's about 27 years, 4 months and 23 days.)

The Calculus of Love

283

Be prepared for romantic weekend get-aways. Get a road map of your state. Now draw a circle on the map. Make your house the center of the circle, and measure a radius of 120 miles. You've just identified a 45,238-square-mile region that lies within a mere two-hour drive of where you live. Unless you live in *Antarctica,** there must be *many* romantic, exciting, new and different things to within a 45,238-square-mile area!

Once you've got your circle inscribed on your map, it's time to do a little research:

- ➨ Locate every bed & breakfast in your circle.
- ➨ Find every park and walking path.
- ➨ Locate every art gallery, museum and theater.
- ➨ Find every mall and store of interest to you and your partner.
- ➨ Make a list of twenty restaurants that look interesting.

284

Figure out how many *days* you've been together (don't forget to add in leap years). In ten years you'll have spent 3,652 days together! Reflect on the highlights of your time together. How have you changed? What have you accomplished together?

- ✳ Write a short letter sharing your feelings about your time together.
- ✳ Create a timeline, noting highlights of your relationship.

285

Use *numbers* to create *theme* gifts and gestures. Use your partner's *age* or the number of *years* you've been together or his/her lucky number. Send that number of greeting cards. Spend that amount of money on a gift. Get that *number* of gifts. Spend that many days on vacation. Spend that many minutes giving him/her a massage. Buy a piece of jewelry with that number of gemstones in it.

*Romantic things to do in Antarctica:

Go tobogganing.
Host a formal party. Invite penguins.
Stay in bed all night. (Nights last *six months!*)

Couplehood

286

15 Ways to Really Be a *Couple* in Public:

1. Always make your "entrance" arm-in-arm.
2. Wear outfits that match in a subtle way.
3. Compliment her in front of her friends.
4. Hold her chair for her at the table.
5. Whisper your pet name to her.
6. PDA.*
7. Brush against him in a sexually suggestive way.
8. Wear matching baseball caps.
9. Open doors for her with an extra little flourish.
10. Hold hands.
11. Give him a seductive smile.
12. Order for her when dining out.
13. Wink at him from across the room.
14. Blow her a kiss.
15. Buy her one rose from a street vendor.

* PDA—Public Displays of Affection.

Very funny (and insightful) books, both by Paul Reiser:

Couplehood

Babyhood

Q: How do you know when you're a "couple"?
A: When you say, "Hi, it's *me*," on the phone—and he/she *knows* it's you.

Q: How do you know when it's *really* love?
A: When it doesn't feel like you're *pretending* or *hoping* it's love.

287

Switch roles with your lover for a day, a weekend or a week. Trade responsibilities, chores and daily routines; trade sides of the bed, trade as many aspects of your lives as you possibly can. You'll gain new insights into your partner. You'll get to know him or her better. Guaranteed. And this knowledge will make you both more patient and understanding with each other. It will also help you make romantic gestures that are more personal, intimate, appropriate and appreciated.

Parenthood

288

Guys: Hang this sign on your wall at work:

"The best thing a father can do for his children is to love their mother."

"WHY DO YA WANT TO BE ROMANTIC? YOU'RE **ALREADY** MARRIED!"

289

Create a neighborhood "Child-Sharing Program." Arrange entire weekends when one family on the block plays host to "The World's Biggest Slumber Party," while the rest of you get romantic.

Erotica

290

"Christen" every room in your house or apartment by making love in it. (Don't forget to include the stairways, hallways and closets.)

291

For women: Fulfill a fantasy—Greet him at the door wearing the lingerie outfit that you *know* makes his eyes bulge out of his head!

The goal of this fantasy is to get your guy to react the way Roger Rabbit does when he sees Jessica!

292

For men: Fulfill a fantasy—Become her vision of Prince Charming, whether it involves dressing in a tuxedo or in a sexy muscle shirt and hard hat! Indulge her.

293

When he's traveling on business, give him a sexy wake-up call at 6 a.m.

294

Kiss every square inch of her body . . . S-L-O-W-L-Y.

295

Why not mail a lingerie gift to her—*at work*.

Picture this: She opens her mail about 11 a.m.; she gets your package. After she recovers and regains her composure, she's totally distracted for the rest of the day. Sounds good to me!

Chapter Theme Song:
"Erotica," Madonna

Exotica

296

One of the most exotic places in the world you could *possibly* visit is Nepal—the tiny Asian country where Mount Everest resides. If your partner loves adventure, just imagine trekking through the Himalayas, discovering the Nepalese culture, shopping in the open-air markets, exploring Katmandu. The expert on trekking in Nepal (and in trekking vacations to other countries, as well) is Steve Conlon, founder of Above the Clouds Trekking. (Isn't that a *fabulous* name for a company?!) Call 800-233-4499 or write to P.O. Box 398, Worcester, Massachusetts 01602; or visit www.gorp.com/abvclds.htm.

297

If you'd rather ride than walk, consider a trip on the Trans-Siberian Railroad in a vintage private train! You'll travel in original antique carriages that were once part of the fabled Orient Express. Call TCS Expeditions at 800-727-7477, or write to 2025 First Avenue, Suite 450, Seattle, Washington 98121; or visit www.TCS-Expeditions.com.

298

Equitour organizes horseback vacations as far afield as India and Australia. Trips through the American Wild West are also available. The trips are wonderfully diverse: On the Wyoming trip you camp out in tents, while on the Vermont trip you stay in quaint country inns. Call Equitour at 800-545-0019.

Everyone has a different idea of what constitutes an "exotic" experience or location. For some folks, exotic means roughing it in Africa. For others it means lounging in Tahiti. For some, New York City is exotic. Others prefer Paris.

Creating an A+ Relationship

299

The A+ Relationship is a powerful concept that reveals unique insights into loving relationships. It is a technique, a tool that can help you accomplish two things. First, it helps you *understand* your loving relationship on a deep level that is impossible to achieve in any other way. And second, it helps you *take action* on your love in ways that fulfill you and your partner as individuals and nurture the two of you as a couple.

My twenty years of teaching Relationship Seminars, my research, and my discussions with *thousands* of couples has convinced me that the A+ Relationship concept can help *any* couple improve their relationship.

How do you *achieve* an A+ Relationship? You commit yourself to excellence, you work hard (and *play* hard!), and you work on your relationship skills together. In other words, to the best of your ability, you *live your love*. Great relationships are acts of conscious creation, and the two of you are artists working to create one life out of two. While falling in love *does* "just happen," *staying* in love *never* happens by itself.

You—and every couple—have the power to establish your own "rules" and expectations for your relationship. This is one of the great benefits of the social changes we've been experiencing since the 1960s. This kind of empowerment is a major factor in why the twenty-first century marks a new epoch in the evolution of human relationships: We're free to break away from the rigid, stereotyped thinking that characterized relationships in the 1950s. You have the opportunity to create a "custom-fit" relationship that incorporates the best of the timeless values (commitment, faith, honesty, etc.) with the best of the modern values (equality, flexibility, creativity, etc.). You can create your *own* set of standards and establish your own goals for your relationship.

The A+ Relationship concept focuses on *behavior*, not on *personality*. It's not about making value judgments of people, it's about making honest evaluations of people's behavior. It helps you look directly at how you're doing right now, and then helps you achieve your future relationship goals. What more could you ask for?!

A+ Relationship (a • plus • ri la' shen ship), n.
1. The best intimate relationship you can possibly create. 2. A loving monogamous relationship that is excellent, superior, awesome, exciting, passionate, growing, fulfilling, fascinating and romantic. 3. An act of creation involving two individuals—two artists whose lifework is creating love through the medium of their relationship.
4. A relationship that, while not perfect, ranks in the ninety-fifth percentile.

Chapter Theme Song:
"Straight A's in Love," Johnny Cash

The Relationship Report Card

300

Master these skills for an A+ Relationship

Take the "Relationship Report Card": Grade yourself and your partner
(A+ through F, like in school):

	GRADE YOURSELF	GRADE PARTNER		GRADE YOURSELF	GRADE PARTNER
AFFECTION	____	____	HONESTY	____	____
ARGUING SKILLS	____	____	HOUSEHOLD MGMNT.	____	____
ATTITUDE	____	____	LISTENING SKILLS	____	____
COMMITMENT	____	____	LOVEMAKING	____	____
COMMUNICATION	____	____	PATIENCE	____	____
CONSIDERATE	____	____	PLAYFULNESS	____	____
COUPLE THINKING	____	____	ROMANCE	____	____
CREATIVITY	____	____	SELF-AWARENESS	____	____
EMPATHY	____	____	SELF-ESTEEM	____	____
FLEXIBILITY	____	____	SENSE OF HUMOR	____	____
FRIENDSHIP	____	____	SENSITIVITY	____	____
GENEROSITY	____	____	SPONTANEITY	____	____
GIFT-GIVING SKILLS	____	____	TOLERANCE	____	____

Don't be deceived by the seeming simplicity of this exercise!

It opens communication, uncovers profound insights and provides a practical tool for change and improvement.

Instructions:

✦ You grade yourself and your partner.
✦ Get your partner to grade him/herself and you.
✦ Compare and discuss your grades; you'll gain great insight into your relationship.
✦ Celebrate everything from a B- to an A+.
✦ Work to improve your Cs and Ds.

How would you grade your relationship?

A = Passionate, exciting, loving, fulfilling; not *perfect*—but clearly excellent.

B = Very good, solid, better-than-most, consistent, *improving*.

C = Average, acceptable, status quo, okay— but static, ho-hum, sometimes *boring*.

D = Below average, unhappy, dismal; bad— but not hopeless.

F = Hopeless, depressing, dangerous; tried everything, it didn't work.

Common Sense

301

Common sense says, "Do what you do best," and, "Use your talents." Sounds good, but the problem is that *simple* advice is rarely *easy* to apply.

In a great book, *The Acorn Principle*, Jim Cathcart explains in detail how you can "nurture your nature." He provides exercises and examples that will help you discover, explore and grow the seeds of your greatest potential. *The Acorn Principle* is one of those rare books that will help you improve your work life *and* your love life.

You fell in love. You decided to spend your lives together. Isn't it simply common sense to make the most of it??

302

Dot your i's and cross your t's. In other words, pay attention to details.

- Don't buy just *any* flowers—get her *favorites*.
- Make a point of *always* wrapping his gifts in his favorite color.
- Don't buy her *gold* jewelry when she prefers *silver*.

303

Remember that relationships are not self-regulating! They're delicate creations that require attention, adjustment and regular oiling.

304

"Walk a mile in his shoes," then rethink your romantic gestures.

- After an especially tough week, he'd probably prefer a massage to going out dancing.
- Don't bring her flowers when what she *really* needs is two hours of peace and quiet.
- Does she need a quiet respite—or an exciting change of pace? Plan accordingly.

*Un*Common Sense

305

The "Golden Rule" doesn't always work: *"Do unto others as you would have them do unto you,"* would lead sports fans to get Super Bowl tickets for their wives; clothes-lovers to buy their partners outfits; workaholics to buy their partners briefcases; and handymen to buy their gals tools!

Try the "Platinum Rule" instead: *"Do unto others as they want to be done unto,"* is a philosophy that gives you deeper insights into your partner. The Platinum Rule helps you see the world through your lover's eyes; it enhances your intuition; it improves your gift-giving skills!

For further insights into this way of thinking, I highly recommend the book *The Platinum Rule*, by Tony Alessandra.

Romantics are good at thinking in uncommon ways.

306

Contrary to popular belief, you should *not* use romance to apologize after a fight! If you do, you'll taint *all* your romantic gestures for a long time to come. (After a fight, a simple, sincere apology is best. Resume romantic gestures *after* you've both cooled down, or after a week—whichever is later.)

It's the Thought That Counts

307

Couples with A+ Relationships understand that they need to balance these two concepts in their lives: 1) Actions speak louder than words, and 2) It's the thought that counts.

These concepts are two sides of the same coin. Sometimes the action, the gesture, the gift says it all. And other times it's the thought, the meaning, the intention, the words that say it all.

308

➤ Guys, let's stop: Stereotyping women, assuming we know what they think, feeling threatened by feminism, ignoring our feelings, acting macho and superior . . .

➤ And start: Being real, getting in touch, reviving gallantry, giving of ourselves, making our relationships a top priority, listening more.

309

➤ Gals, let's stop: Male-bashing, assuming that *all* men are romantic boneheads, feeling superior about your relationship skills (which, admittedly, very often *are* superior), putting down the fledgling men's movement, being a martyr . . .

➤ And start: Giving him the benefit of the doubt, appreciating his quirks, putting yourselves in his shoes, sending him flowers.

310

Chapter Theme Song:

"Thinking of You," Loggins & Messina

If you're like me, you probably can't afford to buy an original Renoir for your partner. You might be happy with a poster print, but that may not seem classy enough. Well now you can get replicas of famous paintings on canvas. Many classic masterpieces are available from The Masters' Collection. Call 800-2-CANVAS; or visit www. MastersCollection.com.

Actions Speak Louder Than Words

311

Cuddle up in front of a roaring fire. (No TV. No kids. No phone.)

312

Carve her initials and yours in a tree.

313

Leave a trail of your clothes, leading from the front door to your bedroom.

314

Fill a basin with hot water. Take off his shoes and socks for him. Sit him down in his favorite chair. Wash his feet. Let them soak for ten minutes. Dry off his feet. Resume life as before.

315

Sara loved Christmas, especially those classic, snowy New England Christmases in Boston. One December was unseasonably warm. And as Christmas approached, Sara was downhearted—and doubly so when her husband Jim announced that he had to work on Christmas Eve.

Jim, a contractor, secretly drove his dumptruck three hours north into Maine, loaded it with man-made snow from a ski resort, then drove home, spread the snow on the front lawn, and presented a delighted Sara with a White Christmas.

G.G.
+
T.B.

S.W.A.K.

316

Use postage stamps that reflect your partner's hobby or interests. There are, for example, stamps picturing:

Patsy Cline & Hank Williams & Bob Wills

Dogs & cats & fish & birds

Spacecraft & astronouts & planets & stars

All fifty states

Lions & tigers & bears (Oh, my!)

Flowers & flowers & flowers & *more* flowers

State birds & state flowers & state flags

Historical themes & places & people

The Olympics

Inventions & contraptions

Gone with the Wind, The Wizard of Oz

Trains, planes & automobiles

Peace themes & ecology themes

Presidents, presidents, presidents!

Elvis & Marilyn Monroe & James Dean

Glenn Miller & Count Basie

Cancer awareness

Fruits & rocks & shells

American history, decade by decade

Christmas & holiday themes

Bugs Bunny!

Dinosaurs & comic strips

Frank Lloyd Wright & the Wright Brothers

And, of course, *Love*

FYI, you can get postage stamps for almost *any* interest or passion your partner may have. The U.S. Postal Service has issued stamps over the years that illustrate *thousands and thousands* of topics. This book is a great resource: *The Postal Service Guide to U.S. Stamps.* Call 800-782-6724 and ask for the Philatelic catalog.

317

Did you know that the United States federal government actively promotes love and romance? Well, sort of. They *do* issue Love Stamps through the U.S. Post Office. Use the latest Love Stamps for all of your love letters, cards and gifts sent via mail.

318

Mail a greeting card to him or her *at work*. A sure way to brighten your lover's work day.

319

* Get a framed print of "The Kiss," by Gustav Klimt.
* Get a reproduction of the sculpture "The Kiss" by Auguste Rodin.

➺ A romantic ritual: Pause and kiss at your front door.
➺ Ask him to pick a number between one and fifty. Reward him with that number of kisses.

G.M.F.L.

320

G.M.F.L. ("Geese Mate For Life.") This phrase reflects that eternal love is symbolized by two geese.

- ➤ Some people sign their love letters with G.M.F.L.
- ➤ Some couples have G.M.F.L. engraved on the inside of their wedding bands.
- ➤ Some folks have gotten the 14K gold G.M.F.L. pin from Cross Jewelers. Call 800-433-2988.

321

Jill gave Howard a birthday card with this inscription:

For your birthday I'm giving you a week of E.S.P.N.*

Love, Jill

*E.S.P.N. stands for "Exciting Sex Practiced Nightly."

322

For true romantics . . .

- ✦ CEO means "Chief Erotic Officer."
- ✦ RN means "Really Naughty" or "Romantic Nut."
- ✦ CPA means "Cupid's Personal Agent."
- ✦ MD means "My Darling."
- ✦ CFO means something really, really dirty.
- ✦ ASAP means "As Sexy As Possible."

"A man is already halfway in love with any woman who listens to him."

~ BRENDAN FRANCIS

Can't Buy Me Love

323a

The best way to spend the *most* money on a *car* is to buy a *Lamborghini Diablo.* (The *second* best way is to buy a *Ferrari F50.*)

323b

The best way to spend the *most* money for a *show* is to get *front row center seats* for whatever is the current hottest show on Broadway.

323c

The best way to spend the *most* money for *stereo equipment* is to get one of Bang & Olufson's amazing, high tech, beautifully designed systems.

324

You *could* update his *entire* album collection! Convert his aging LP collection of beloved Beatles albums, Moody Blues tunes, and Rolling Stones records to compact discs. Converting a lifetime collection of five-hundred-some albums would cost about $6,500.

325

Consider buying a fine vintage wine from the year of your lover's birth— or the year of your anniversary. The Antique Wine Company of Great Britain Ltd., has a huge wine cellar of aged fine wines, dating back to 1893. The value of each gift depends on the year. Prices start at $450. Call 800-827-7153; or visit www.AntiqueWine.co.uk.

Give your partner a proof set of coins from the year you were married.

Chapter Theme Song:

"I Found a Million Dollar Baby," Nat King Cole

I Want to Hold Your Hand

326

✦ Simple question: When is the last time the two of you simply went for a *walk* together?

✦ Complex answer: Now let's be *specific* here: Part of the definition of "a walk" is that you must hold hands. Also, neither of you can be wearing a Walkman during the so-called "walk." Your *speed* is important, too. Running and jogging are obviously *not* romantic. The proper speed is a saunter.

The speed of love is 1.7 mph—the speed of a casual saunter.

327

Does your partner like *speed* and *thrills?* Plan your vacations around the top five roller coasters in the U.S., according to *Park World* magazine:

☞ Superman the Escape, at Six Flags Magic Mountain, in Valencia, California: Accelerates from zero to 100 mph in seven seconds.

☞ Georgia Cyclone, at Six Flags Over Georgia, in Atlanta, Georgia: Based on the famous Coney Island Cyclone.

☞ Magnum XL-200, at Cedar Point, in Sandusky, Ohio: During portions of the ride you actually float off your seat!

☞ Thunderbolt, at Kennywood, in West Mifflin, Pennsylvania: Begins with a terrifying drop into a ravine.

☞ Beast, at Kings Island, Ohio: The world's longest wooden roller coaster.

328

Definition:
Interdigitation: Holding hands.

As a couple, dedicate yourselves to *learning something new every day*.

It might be a new word, it might be a fact from the newspaper, it might be something new about each other. And on a regular basis, take a class together. Learn to paint, learn to play piano, learn to speak French, learn new massage techniques.

Help!

329

Give your partner choices: Classic or avant-garde? Conservative or outrageous? Public or private? Here or there? Loud or quiet? McDonald's or Burger King? Big or small? Light or dark? Fast or slow? Today or tomorrow? Active or lazy? One or many? Gold or silver? Red or blue? Day or night? Expensive or inexpensive? Now or later? Right or left? Modern or antique? Serious or funny?

330

A basic romantic concept: "The Gift-of-the-Month Clubs." Here are some creative twists: Create your own . . .

* Beer-of-the-Month Club
* Romantic-Restaurant-of-the-Month Club
* New-Ice-Cream-Flavor-of-the-Month Club
* Lingerie-Outfit-of-the-Month Club
* New-Sexual-Position-of-the-Month Club
* Stuffed-Animal-of-the-Month Club

Knowing your lover's interests and preferences will help you create your own, unique Gift-of-the-Month Clubs.

All You Need Is Love

331

You've heard it said that "There are no guarantees in life." Well, that's true. You can't get a *guarantee*—but you just may be able to get a *warranty*. One fellow in my Romance Class told us that he surprised his new bride at the conclusion of their wedding ceremony by presenting her with a written "Lifetime Relationship Warranty."

"Many waters cannot quench love, neither can floods drown it."

~ SONG OF SOLOMON 8:7

332

It's winter, it's ten degrees below zero, and the wind chill factor makes it feel like *forty* below. At a time like this, love isn't about preparing a cup of tea—it's about going outside to warm up her car for her!

333

✦ Once a week for a year: Jot down two reasons why you love him/her.
✦ Once a week for a year: Jot down one great thing he/she did.
✦ Once a week for a year: Jot down one inspirational thought.

At the end of the year: Print all this out on a big scroll and present it to your lover.

334

Number One Tip for Being Romantic in the Twenty-first Century: *Remove yourself from the electronic and media grid* on a regular basis—over a weekend, during vacations, and on random days.

In order to slow down and connect one-on-one with your lover, it helps immensely if you occasionally disconnect from the Internet and Email, from TV and radio, from newspapers and magazines, from cable and videos, from mobile phones and pagers, from computers and gizmos, from ATMs and credit cards, and from the media in all its forms.

Chapter Theme Song:
"Endless Love," Diana Ross & Lionel Richie

At Home

335

Carry her over the threshold of your house or apartment.

Not for newlyweds only!

336

Your home should be a *romantic hideaway.* You should be ready at a moment's notice to transform your house or apartment into a love nest through the creative use of candles, music, flowers, wine and food.

337

Make a path of lighted candles leading from the front door to your bedroom. Be waiting for your lover, and let your own flame burn bright!

When dining at home, enhance the mood with soft candlelight.

338

Don't wait until Saturday night to go out dancing. Dance by yourselves at home in your living room. Move the furniture and roll up the rug!

339

When most people decorate or redesign their homes, they plan and sketch, read home-improvement magazines, hire interior designers, spend big bucks, consider color, space, texture and style. But how many of them consider "romance" as a design element or a goal of the entire project? Consider designing a home with "romance" as its primary guiding principle.

Jot a little love note on a sheet of paper, fold it into a paper airplane, and sail it across the living room to your partner.

At Work

340

Find out where he's having lunch today. Then have flowers delivered there. (Or deliver them yourself!)

341

Instruct your secretary that *all* calls from your wife are to be put through—regardless of what you're doing, or with whom you're meeting. (*Prove* to your wife that she's the top priority in your life.)

342

Copy your face (or other body parts) on the Xerox machine. Mail it to him with a funny or suggestive note.

Call from work simply to say "I love you!" (There's rarely an acceptable reason to go eight straight hours without touching base.)

343

Pack a pillow and a blanket in a picnic basket and surprise your partner by appearing in the office at noon. Tell the secretary to hold all calls. Lock the office door. Turn off the intercom. Close the blinds. Make love on the desk.

344

Same as above, but pack a *real* lunch. (Not as much fun, but more nutritious.)

345

Mail him a Rolodex card with your name and number on it. Write on it: "Your instant resource for love. Call when lonely."

Sweet Stuff

346

Fill a Victoria's Secret box full of green m&m's. Fill an m&m's bag with new lingerie. Present both of them to her in bed.

And if you want to be scandalously romantic, you can get "adult" pastries and chocolate body parts!

347

◆ Smooth the top of an Oreo cookie, then scratch a heart and your initials into the surface.
◆ Remove the white frosting from the top of a Hostess Cupcake, then write your *own* message using red frosting.

348

Give your partner his or her favorite kind of Girl Scout cookie.

Cheese Toret Royales, Australian Dessert Apricots, Chocolate-Filled Peppermint Sticks! From the Norm Thompson catalog: 800-547-1160; or visit www.NormThompson.com.

349

Think up fun/clever/suggestive notes to attach to these candies: Good 'n Plenty, Mounds, Snickers, Almond Joy, Fire Balls, Double Bubble, Life Savers or Hershey's Kisses.

✳ "Where would I be without you, gal? You really *are* a **Life Saver**."
✳ "Wow! You certainly were a **Fire Ball** last night!"
✳ "Here are a few **Kisses** to hold you over until we're together again."

350

Fill the cookie jar with love notes. Fill the mailbox with cookies.

Chapter Theme Song:
"Sweets for My Sweet," The Drifters

Kid Stuff

351

Rediscover and nurture the "child" inside of you. It's the key to your creativity, spontaneity, sense of wonder and joy.

352

When's the last time you watched cloud formations? Take your lover for a walk in a field. Find an unobstructed view. Flop down on a hilltop. What do you see in the clouds? What do you imagine?

*What **else** might you be able to do together in a field??*

353

✦ Surprise her with a little "Trinket Gift" hidden inside a McDonald's Big Mac container.
✦ Surprise him by hiding a favorite stuffed animal inside his gym bag.

354

Seventy-eight percent of all women love stuffed animals.

355

Most men love gadgets, electronic stuff or tools . . . "boys' toys." Men never really grow up—our toys simply get more expensive.

356

Get a favorite toy or item from his childhood: A toy, book, report card or picture from the wall. (Call his parents; they'll *love* to be a part of this idea.) Wrap it up and include a touching note.

Funny Stuff

357

Make copies of some favorite comic strips, then rewrite the captions to make them refer to you and your partner! With the application of a little White-Out and a little creativity, you can have lots of fun turning Blondie and Dagwood into the two of you. Or, picture her as Cathy or Sylvia, or him as Snoopy or Doonesbury.

358

Basic: Tape relevant comics to the refrigerator or the bathroom mirror.

There are two kinds of people in the world: People Who Don't Consider the Day Complete Unless They've Read the Comics, and People Who Don't Know Snoopy from Ziggy. If your partner is a Comics Person, ask who his/her favorite characters are, then incorporate them into some of your romantic gifts and gestures.

359

Give him a book of collected comics. What's his favorite? "The Far Side," "Calvin and Hobbes," "Peanuts," "Cathy," "Funky Winkerbean," "For Better or For Worse," "Blondie," "Andy Capp," "Pogo"?

360

Beyond "basic":
➤ Tape a comic to the rearview mirror in his car.
➤ Insert comics in dinner napkins.
➤ Stick them in cereal boxes.
➤ Attach them to the underside of the toilet seat.

361

Funny stuff? You want *funny stuff?!* Why didn't you *say* so? If you want *funny stuff,* you've got to check out The Lighter Side catalog. They've got piles of silly, funny, curious and odd things. Call 'em at 800-232-0963, or write to Post Office Box 25600, Bradenton, Florida 34206.

Cool Stuff

362

- Wouldn't it be cool to take a Japanese flower-arranging course?
- Wouldn't it be wild to rent a classic roadster for an afternoon?
- Wouldn't it be fun to stay in bed together all day on Sunday?

363

Place a full-page ad in your local hometown newspaper to announce your anniversary, or celebrate his birthday, or simply to celebrate your love!

364

Present him with a "favor" (a gift bestowed as a token of goodwill; as a maiden's kerchief given to a knight)—something he'll carry around with him as a reminder of you.

- Classic: A kerchief or scarf
- Meaningful: A short verse printed on a tiny slip of paper
- Intimate: Panties
- Silly: A little toy
- Personal: A lock of your hair

How would your partner define "cool"?

Get a kit of Magnetic Poetry, and write little poems to each other on the refrigerator door.

365

If your partner is into puzzles—jigsaw puzzles—then you've got to get in touch with Stave Puzzles and Bits & Pieces. They create the most wonderful, fun, beautiful and challenging jigsaw puzzles in the world.

These companies will also create custom puzzles that you can use for all kinds of personal occasions. People have used them to spell out marriage proposals, to send personalized birthday greetings, and to help celebrate anniversaries.

- Stave Puzzles: 802-295-5200; www. Stave.com
- Bits & Pieces: 1-800-JIGSAWS; www.BitsAndPieces.com.

Dirty Stuff

366

Plant and care for a garden together. Crawling around in the dirt together has a funny way of bringing a couple closer.

367

They shared a love of gardening. But while his flower garden was a wild riot, her vegetable garden was organized and labeled. One day she did a double-take as she noticed the seed-packet sign on her row of carrots had been changed to read "karats." While her husband barely suppressed a smile, she dug carefully until she found a sealed box containing a three-karat diamond ring!

368

If the two of you enjoy hiking together, try *barefoot* hiking! The Dirty Sole Society can help you find the best trails. Check them out at www.barefooters.org/hikers/.

369

He was an avid gardener. One year, as a surprise for his wife, he planted his flowers in a pattern that spelled out "I LOVE YOU." The message appears only when the flowers are in bloom, and can only be read from their second-story bedroom window.

He changes the message every year. He has great fun, and his wife is thrilled every spring.

Sex!

370

Here's how one couple turned foreplay into a "game," using five dice. First they erased the dots using White-Out. Then they re-labeled all the dice in this manner:

* On a pink ("Hers") die: They wrote a different body part on each of the six sides.
* On a blue ("His") die: They wrote a different body part on each of the six sides.
* On the third die: They wrote a *verb* on each side: "Rub," "Lick," "Kiss," "Massage," etc.
* On the fourth die: They wrote an *adverb* on each side: "Softly," "Quickly," "Slowly," etc.
* On the fifth die: They wrote *time-related* words: "Five minutes," "Half an hour," "As fast as you can," etc.

371

Do you always make love at *night?* How about a little *afternoon delight?!*

372

Go in search of her G Spot. You may not find it, but you'll have a great time looking! (Pick up a copy of *The G Spot*, by Alice Kahn Ladas.)

Funniest relationship book ever written: **Is Sex Necessary?** *by James Thurber & E.B. White.*

Chapter Theme Song:
"Sex," Berlin

Surprise!

373

Surprise her by giving *her* a gift on *your* birthday.

*This is one **heck** of a great surprise!*

374

The Time-Delay Tactic. Learn what she likes/wants. Get it for her, but hold on to it for a few weeks—or months. (This gives her time to forget about it, or think that *you've* forgotten.) Surprise her with it when she least expects it.

375

*Don't worry, lying in the service of romance is **not** a sin. Lovers receive special dispensation.*

The Little White Lie. Setting up surprises sometimes involves a subtle touch, a smooth manner or *outright lying*.

376

Surprise him by performing one of his chores for him. (And I don't mean a little thirty-second chore like taking out the garbage! I mean something *time-consuming*, like cutting the lawn or washing his car.)

377

Surprise her by performing one of her chores for her. (And I don't mean something *easy* like carrying the groceries in from the car! I mean something that requires some time and effort. Something like cooking all the meals over a weekend, or cleaning the entire house.)

Note: Because I'm addressing *millions* of people here, I've chosen chores that a majority of people assign along classic gender lines. You certainly have the freedom to choose who does what in *your* household!

Celebrate!

378

Balloons! Balloon bouquets. Helium-filled balloons. Heart-shaped red balloons. Mickey Mouse/Snoopy/Garfield balloons. Silvery, shiny Mylar balloons. Giant-sized balloons. Balloons with your names on them. Balloons with personalized messages on them.

379

New Year's Eve in Times Square! It's a little crowded, but it's tons o' fun!

380

Celebrate the birthday of your partner's favorite cartoon or comic strip character. Buy a birthday cake. Get a book of collected comic strips. Get a T-shirt picturing this character.

* Bugs Bunny's birthday: July 27th
* Garfield's birthday: June 19th
* Mickey Mouse's birthday: November 18th
* Snoopy's birthday: October 2nd

381

Create a "Count-Down Calendar" to mark the time remaining until a birthday, wedding, anniversary, vacation or "Mystery Day."

382

Celebrate your partner's favorite movie star's birthday. Go out to dinner. Toast the chosen star. Recite the star's famous lines; maybe have these lines rendered in calligraphy or printed on a scroll. Make a gift of a book about this star.

Celebrate the 4th of July . . . with fireworks—in bed.

Celebrate Thanksgiving . . . by vowing to stop being a turkey.

Celebrate Halloween . . . by dressing as sexy fantasy characters.

Celebrate Valentine's Day . . . at the most elegant B&B within one hundred miles.

Celebrate your anniversary . . . with a bottle of Dom Perignon.

Celebrate her birthday . . . aboard a cruise ship in the Mediterranean.

Celebrate his birthday . . . at the Indianapolis 500.

Celebrate next Tuesday . . . by playing hooky from work together.

Chapter Theme Song:
"Celebrate," Kool & the Gang

Outrageous!

383

"The Grand Gesture." The once-in-a-lifetime event.

Wouldn't it be a shame to look back on your life and not be able to say that you did one *incredible, unbelievable, outrageous and wonderful thing* for and with your lover?

❑ One bold husband in the Romance Class went out and *replaced his wife's entire wardrobe* instead of going on vacation one year! "It cost me $7,500, but it was worth it!" he exclaimed.

❑ One woman, whose husband is a partner in a prestigious law firm, arranged a *surprise three-week vacation tour of Europe's vineyards* for her husband. He nearly had a heart attack when he realized that his flight to Chicago was really a flight to *Paris*, that his wife was on board the flight, and that all his work was being taken care of by another partner. His wife reports that he *did* finally calm down and had the time of his life.

384

Gals: Greet him at the front door wearing your wedding gown.

385

Do the impossible for your lover:

✦ Get Super Bowl tickets.
✦ Find that out-of-print book for her.
✦ Meet her at the airport—when she knows you're busy elsewhere.
✦ Get tickets to the World Series.
✦ Get tickets to the NBA or Stanley Cup finals.
✦ Cook a meal.
✦ Get tickets to a *sold-out* Broadway show.

Outrageous!

The surprise three-week vacation.

The new red Porsche.

The dancing lessons.

*The **ten** dozen red roses.*

Passionate!

386

Romantics are passionate (#1).

I'm not talking about *sexual* passion here, but about a passion for *life*. (Don't worry, we'll get to sexual passion in just a moment!) Romantics don't allow any aspect of their lives to slide into boredom.

✳ What is your *partner* passionate about? What are *you* passionate about? What passions do you share?
✳ List three specific ways that you could enhance your partner's enjoyment of his/her passion.
✳ Within the next week, figure out a way to give your partner five hours of uninterrupted time to pursue and enjoy his/her passion.

387

Romantics are passionate (#2).

Yes, as a matter of fact, romantics *do* tend to be more sexually passionate than the average mortal. (Just another of the many side-benefits of the romantic lifestyle!)

Being romantic means *expressing* love. And that expression is often a *physical* expression. The real magic of romance lies in the fact that it includes/weaves together/reflects all facets of love: Physical, spiritual and emotional.

"A kiss can be a comma, a question mark, or an exclamation point."

~ Mistinguett

388

Gals, if you want to stimulate a little bedroom passion, try wearing one of his dress shirts to bed. A surprising number of men *and* women find this to ba a great turn-on!

Games People Play

389

"The First Date Game." A role-playing game. Pretend that you're going out on your first date together. Re-enact your fondest memories of that first date. (Where did you go? What did you do? What did you eat? What did you talk about?)

390

Many couples play a curious little game that goes by various names: "Where's the Bunny?" or "Hide and Go Seek" are two favorites.

The rules are simple: You pick a small inanimate object (like a little stuffed animal, a wind-up toy, seashell, piece of plastic fruit, etc.). You take turns giving it to each other in creative, funny ways. Some couples keep the object in constant rotation. Others will wait *months* before giving it back, and go to *incredible* lengths to surprise their partners.

World-class players have reportedly:

➻ Had the object sealed inside a Coke can.
➻ Sent the object via Federal Express.
➻ Had an airline attendant deliver it while in flight.
➻ Had the object appear in a corporate board room.
➻ Had it delivered by a parachutist.
➻ Had the object frozen in an ice cube.
➻ Placed the object in a store display window.

*People with A+ Relationships don't take themselves too seriously. But they **do** take their partners seriously.*

Declare today "Couple's Day." Do *everything* as a couple. Don't leave one another's sight— even for a moment!—from the time you wake up until the time you go to sleep tonight.

Games Lovers Play

391

"All-Day Foreplay." Plan in the morning to make love tonight. Call each other all day long with "reminders," ideas and suggestive suggestions. By the time evening rolls around you'll both feel like you've engaged in foreplay all day long!

392

A surprising number of couples in my Romance Classes play various "Car Games." Here are some of them:

- Kissing at every stop light.
- Kissing whenever you spot a red Corvette.
- Making love at highway rest areas.
- And variations of *"How Far Will You Go?"*

Book recommendation: *The Couples' Guide to Erotic Games*, by Gerald Schoenewolf.

393

"The Affair Game." (Recommended especially for those married ten-plus years.) Another role-playing game. Pretend that you're not married to him/her, but you're having an affair with your spouse. How would you act? Where would you go? What would you do? What would you talk about? How and where and when would you make love?

394

Here's a sexy game: "Connect the Freckles"!

"An Enchanting Evening." A fun and revealing board game. Check your local toy store or call 800-776-7662; or write to Time for Two, 116 New Montgomery, Suite 500, San Francisco, California 94105; or visit www.TimeForTwo.com.

Off the Wall

395

* Tie a piece of string to the inside doorknob of your front door. String it throughout the house, tracing a path that leads to the bathtub, which you've prepared especially for him.
* Variation on a theme: Tie one end of the string to the doorknob, string it through the house—then tie the other end of the string to *yourself.* Wait patiently in the bedroom.

396

Write her a check for a million kisses.

397

Test drive a Porsche together.

398

Hide a (very) small gift somewhere on your body.

Then say to your lover, "I've got a gift for you, and it's hidden on me somewhere! Find it and it's yours!" Use your imagination—and be sure to leave enough time to participate in any "extracurricular activities" that may result from the search!

399

Some custom T-shirts that Romance Class participants have created:

* *It's the real thing. Love.*
* *Just do it. Love.*
* *W.W.R.D.? (What Would Romeo Do?)*
* *Got romance?*

Chapter Theme Song:

"Still Crazy After All These Years," Paul Simon

On the Wall

400

Several "off the wall"—or rather, "*on* the wall"—ideas from Romance Class participants:

✦ The Mosaic Room: A bulletin board for tacking up mementos overflowed onto the wall and eventually took over the entire den!

✦ The Photo Gallery: Many couples have special walls full of funny, sentimental, meaningful and romantic photos.

✦ The Memory Wall: Some couples frame everything from ticket stubs and menus to dried flowers and greeting cards.

✦ The Wine Wall: Two wine enthusiasts have wallpapered their dining room with wine labels from their favorite bottles.

✦ The Travelogue Room: Two travel bugs have wallpapered two rooms (soon to be three) with maps of all the places they've visited.

401

Make a collage for her. The theme: Her favorite fairy tale. Clip illustrations from several different books. Intersperse photos of the two of you! Combine classic verses from the story with phrases from your own lives.

402

Hire an artist to create a poster illustrating her favorite fairy tale or children's story—and have *her* pictured as the heroine!

One creative guy wrote a "proposal poem" with which to ask his girlfriend to marry him. He had the poem written in calligraphy and beautifully framed. He then went to the owner of a romantic little restaurant and arranged to have his poem hung on the wall next to a cozy booth. He then took his gal out to dinner and waited for her to notice the "unique" artwork on the wall!

The Myths of Romance (I)

403

Beware the power of metaphors!

Myth: "The Battle of the Sexes."

What a *foolish* concept! Yes, it makes cute headlines in women's maga-zines, and exciting segments on TV talk shows, and funny scenes on sitcoms. However, *there ain't no such thing as a battle of the sexes.* There certainly are some psychological and physical differences *("Vive la différence!"),* but there's nothing worth terming a "battle."

Here's the problem with this kind of thinking: It leads to stereotyping: You end up treating your partner like "all men" or "all women," and ignore the fact that he or she is really a unique individual. This stereotyping blocks *real* communication, it short circuits *true* intimacy, and it becomes a barrier to true love.

404

True or False?—
"Nice guys finish last."

Myth: "Nice guys finish last."

Think about it: If you believe that "Nice guys finish last," I suppose that means that "Jerks and bullies finish first." Perhaps this *is* true in the business world and maybe in the world of sports, but it is *definitely* not true in the realm of intimate human relationships.

Note: "Nice" doesn't mean "wimpy" or "feminine." Nice means *courte-ous, mature, gentlemanly, thoughtful, loving.*

405

Myth: "Romance will save my relationship."

It's not quite that simple. If the romance is an expression of the love you feel, then it *will* save your relationship. But if the romance is just a *show,* just something you do to pacify your partner, then it *won't.*

The Myths of Romance (II)

406

Myth: "Romance will cover up my faults."

Sorry. A jerk who gives flowers is *still* a jerk. Romantic gestures may disguise your faults in the short-run—but your true personality will always reveal itself. Having realistic expectations about romance will enhance your relationship and help your love grow.

407

Myth: "Give her an inch and she'll take a mile."

This is a myth promulgated in men's locker rooms and in high school bull sessions. The key word here is "bull."

If you "give an inch" on a consistent basis, you'll satisfy nearly *any* woman. It's when you're stingy with those romantic gestures that a woman builds up so much resentment that she demands "a mile" from you. And rightfully so.

408

Myth: "I can change him."

No you can't. People can be *influenced*, they can be *adjusted*, they can be *manipulated*—but they can't be *changed* or "fixed."

What you *can* do is help your partner learn better skills for expressing his or her feelings. If the feelings of love are in there somewhere, then *you* can help him to be more romantic.

True or False?—

"Give her an inch and she'll take a mile."

Men Are From Mars

409

Be aware that *men and women tend to have different styles of communicating*. Deborah Tannen, author of *You Just Don't Understand*, says that a man engages the world as "an individual in a hierarchical world social order in which he [is] either one-up or one-down." A woman, on the other hand, approaches the world as "an individual in the world of connections. In this world, conversations are negotiations for closeness in which people try to seek and give confirmation and support, and to reach consensus."

Without falling into the trap of simplistic stereotypes, Tannen explores the communication styles of men and women, and helps build bridges.

410

Ladies: Do you really think that *he* thinks the way *you* think?
Gentlemen: Do you really think that *she* thinks the way *you* think?
Everyone: *Think again!*

* He gives her lingerie:
  - *What he means*: "You'd look great in this."
  - *How she takes it*: "He wants me to look like a slut!"

* She wants to go out for dinner and a movie:
  - *What she means*: "I want to go out for dinner and a movie."
  - *How he takes it*: "I'm going to go broke!"

* He gives her one red rose:
  - *What he means*: "This symbolizes my love for you."
  - *How she takes it*: "He's too cheap to buy a dozen."

* She gives him this book:
  - *What she means*: "This will improve our relationship."
  - *How he takes it*: "She's trying to turn me into someone else."

Chapter Theme Song:

"Why Can't a Woman be More Like a Man?" from *My Fair Lady*

What to do? Talk more. Assume less. Listen more. Open your heart. Check your assumptions. And keep trying.

Women Are From Venus

411

When *women* use the word "romance," they're usually referring to *love*. When *men* use the word "romance," they're often referring to *sex*. (So be careful! The word "romance" can be slippery.)

412

Sales figures show that women tend to prefer pink and white and pastel colors for lingerie, while men perfer to see women in black and red.

✳ Women: Ask yourself if you're dressing to please him or yourself.

✳ Men: Ask yourself if the goal of your lingerie gift is to please her or please yourself.

413

❖ Women: Stop nagging. Even if you're right. (*Especially* if you're right!) Hundreds of women in the Romance Class have told me that nagging and complaining are the quickest ways to drive a man into a resentful—and far from romantic—silence.

❖ Men: Stop judging. Stop correcting. Stop lecturing. She doesn't need it and doesn't want it. You're not her father or teacher—you're her *lover*.

414

✦ For women: Place a red rose on the lawnmower along with a note: "I appreciate the work you do. And I'll demonstrate just *how much* I appreciate you when you're done with the lawn—so hurry!"

✦ For men: Float a flower in the kitchen sink along with a note: "Have I told you lately how much I appreciate you? Well I do. I'm warming-up a bottle of massage oil just for you. So hurry!"

Men and women tend to be "thermally incompatible." It is a biological fact that at "room temperature," most women are chilly and most men are warm.

Chapter Theme Song:
"Venus," Frankie Avalon

Men Are (Not) From Mars*

*Mars, mythologically, was the god of *war*, not the god of *masculinity*.

415

Love is not gender-specific. Therefore, *romance* is not gender-specific. Nearly every idea in this book applies to *both* men and women, even though I sometimes say "her" and other times "his." Don't forget that deep down, we all want the same things in life. Men and women have different *styles*—not different *needs*.

416

Note: Things have changed since the 1950s—men like flowers, too. My last survey indicates that 74 percent of American men would feel comfortable receiving flowers and would appreciate the gesture.

Proof that men are from Earth:

1
A man wrote *Romeo and Juliet*.

2
A man wrote *The Bridges of Madison County*.

3
Fred Astaire was a man.

4
There is an organization called the Order of the Manly Men. They hold a good-natured Manly Man Festival in Roslyn, Washington complete with a Manliest Vehicle Contest and Manliest Tool Belt Competition. Founder R.M. "Bob" Crane is the self-proclaimed "manliest florist in the United States," according to *The Wall Street Journal*.

417

The next time you're tempted to fall into using simple gender stereotypes, think about *The Odd Couple*. Felix and Oscar are both "regular guys"—but they're as different as night and day! Their differences arise from their individual *personalities*, not from their *gender*.

The same applies to you and your partner. Not all women are emotional, intuitive and communicative. Not all men are logical, aggressive and practical. While generalizations are generally true, it's *also* true that it's the quirks and idiosyncracies—the qualities that make people unique—that we fall in love with.

A very useful exercise is to talk together about *how* and *why* you first fell in love with each other. The challenge is to answer very, very specifically. You'll notice that the qualities most people identify are rarely gender-specific ("His eyes." "Her sense of humor." "The way he smells." "His solid values." "We both *love* the same books.")

People with A+ Relationships tend to stay in touch with these qualities in themselves and support those qualities in their partners.

Women Are (Not) From Venus*

418

Robin shares this story: "The most romantic gift my husband ever gave me was a pair of needle-nose pliers.

"You see, my family draws names for Christmas gifts, and my wish list always includes tools—I just like to *fix* things—but nobody ever gives me any! The year I didn't get the needle-nose pliers I requested, I happened to mention to my husband, Mark, that it bothered me that my family didn't take me seriously.

"When December arrived and we were short on cash, Mark and I decided not to give each other any gifts. Celebrating Christmas with Mark's family, I found a tiny wrapped gift from my husband under the tree. His family simply didn't understand why a pair of pliers would bring tears of happiness to my eyes!"

419

Be aware of the differences in men's and women's styles of communicating, *but don't over-emphasize them*. If you focus on the gap, you'll overlook the bridges!

➤ Bridge #1: The fact that underneath all our differences in style, men and women all want the same things: To be loved, cared for, respected and appreciated; to have a place of safety and security where we can be ourselves, grow, experiment and mature.

➤ Bridge #2: Romance itself. Romance is a bridge between the sexes, as it is the expression of love. Romance is a language that uses words, gestures and tokens to communicate the subtle, multifaceted and complicated feelings of love.

*Venus, mythologically, was the goddess of love, not the goddess of femininity.

"Men are from Earth. Women are from Earth. Deal with it."

~ GEORGE CARLIN

Tuning In

420

"Tune in" to romantic ideas on TV, ads, billboards, in store windows, newspapers, magazines, articles, bookstores, card shops and catalogs.

"Tune in" to romantic opportunities. They're all around you. *Listen* for them. *Watch* for them. Raise your awareness of how you actually "screen out" ideas, resources, tips and opportunities that you could use to enhance your relationship. For example, observe how you read newspapers and magazines. First, notice the kinds of items that automatically catch your eye. Then go back, slow down, and notice what you've skimmed over. Train yourself to notice potentially romantic items. You can eventually pass this task on to your subconscious mind—and the process can become rather automatic.

421

Lots of romantic ideas will appear if you focus on your partner's "orientation." An orientation isn't really a "hobby"—it's more an intense interest or generalized passion. It's something that tends to occupy his or her mind, time and interest. (Someone who is really *into* his Irish heritage isn't exactly practicing a *hobby*, but his "Irishness" is a great focus for you when thinking up romantic ideas for him.) Here are a variety of orientations expressed by Romance Class participants:

➼ Cats	➼ Shopping	➼ WW II
➼ Dogs	➼ Specific sports	➼ Ethnic heritage
➼ Comics	➼ Specific actors	➼ Puzzles
➼ Hometown	➼ Clothes	➼ Golf
➼ College	➼ Music, classical	➼ Science fiction
➼ Comics	➼ Music, specific type	➼ Do-it-yourself
➼ Lingerie	➼ Music, specific artist	➼ Food!

Do you know what *your* lover's orientation is? Does he/she know *yours?*

Get your southpaw sweetie a subscription to Lefthander Magazine: Box 8249, Topeka, Kansas 66608.

Fine Tuning

422

Everyone has a sense of humor (even accountants!) But the question is, what *kind* of sense of humor? What tickles his/her funny bone? Robin Williams? Rosie O'Donnell? David Letterman? Jay Leno? Paula Poundstone? Monty Python? Abbott and Costello? The Three Stooges? Intellectual humor? Slapstick? Visual humor? Puns? Standup comedy? Funny movies? Saturday Night Live? Romantic comedies?

Take your partner's specific sense of humor into account when you plan dates, buy gifts, and choose movies.

The reason that practical jokes are more often cruel than funny is that they're based on the *joker's* sense of humor, and not on the sense of humor of the *victim*. Be *really careful* when pulling practical jokes on your partner!

423

+ You know that her favorite color is *blue*. But do you know what *shade* of blue? *Sky* blue? *Navy* blue? *Teal* blue? *Turquoise* blue? *Powder* blue? Blue-*green*?

+ You know that his favorite TV show is *Star Trek*. But do you know if he prefers the original series, *The Next Generation, Deep Space Nine* or *Voyager?* Also, do you know his favorite *episode?* His favorite *character?*

+ You know that she *loves* chocolate. But does she prefer *dark* chocolate or *milk* chocolate? Does she have a favorite candy bar? Does she have one (or two) favorite brands?

+ Coke or Pepsi? Diet or classic? Decaf or regular?

+ McDonald's or Burger King or Wendy's or KFC?

Ordinary is what *everyone* does—like renting a movie for Friday night.

Fine tune your romantic gesture: Let's say your partner is a Barbra Streisand fan. Here's the line-up for your "Weekend-Long Barbra Streisand Film Festival":

Funny Girl
Funny Lady
The Way We Were
The Owl and the Pussycat
Yentl
What's Up Doc?
Prince of Tides
A Star is Born

424

❏ Do you know your partner well enough to make a *perfect* cup of coffee for him/her? How much cream and sugar?

❏ Do you know your partner well enough to order coffee for him/her at Starbucks? Regular coffee? Decaf? Café mocha? Café latte? Espresso? Double espresso? Cappuccino? Light roast? Dark roast?

Starstruck!

425

A great idea for **dreamy** romantics.

If you'd like to spend a romantic summer night making wishes on falling stars, mark the second week in August on your calendar. The earth passes through the Perseides Meteor Belt around August 12th every year, which usually results in *spectacular* shows for two to three nights. (You may want to plan an evening of stargazing for the 12th, without telling her about the Perseides. She'll be amazed when about a hundred stars per hour streak across the sky!)

426

A great idea for **science fiction** fans!

Also great for coming through on your promise to give her "the moon and the stars."

Speaking of falling stars—those that make it all the way to earth are called meteorites. You can buy small meteorites at some rock and gem shops. Have a custom piece of jewelry created to showcase your falling star.

427

If it's the stars of *Broadway* who interest your partner, why not get him a poster from his favorite show? Today's and yesterday's Broadway hits are represented at the Triton Gallery, 323 West 45th Street, New York City, New York 10036. Call them at 212-765-2472 or 800-626-6674.

428

Chapter Theme Song:

"Starry Eyed," Gary Stites

If your interest in the ☆ stars is more mystical, call Eric Linter, one of the best ☆ astrologers in the U.S. While well-versed in the basics of birth charts and astrological ☆ predictions, Eric has a dual focus on "spiritually oriented" astrology readings and on "couple ☆ dynamics." He prepares individual ☆ charts, couple's charts and special-purpose readings. Many couples ask him for advice on specific dates and times for when to get ☆ engaged or married. Call Eric at 617-524-5275. ☆

Lovestruck!

429

22 Creative Ways to Celebrate Valentine's Day:

1. Devote yourself 100 percent to each other on Valentine's Day.
2. Rent a local hotel's Honeymoon Suite.
3. Take the day off from work on Valentine's Day.
4. One day simply isn't enough! Celebrate for a solid week!
5. Buy several boxes of kids' valentines, and flood your partner with them!
6. Give your partner one card every hour on the hour.
7. Make a batch of heart-shaped cookies.
8. Make a giant Valentine card on the back of a travel poster—
9. And have vacation travel tickets (to that location) taped to the poster.
10. Plan a solid day's worth of romantic music.
11. Stay at a local bed & breakfast.
12. Send ten Valentine's Day cards.
13. Send a hundred Valentine's Day cards!
14. Spend the entire day watching romantic movies.
15. Give your modern gal a piece of antique jewelry.
16. Bake a heart-shaped cake—
17. And decorate it with red frosting and heart-shaped sprinkles.
18. Spend every Valentine's Day together—no matter what.
19. Send a Valentine's Day card each day for a week.
20. Send a Valentine's Day card each day for a month.
21. Find the best "Lovers' Package" at a local hotel.
22. Spend the entire day in bed together.

"One does not fall 'in' or 'out' of love. One grows in love."

~ LEO BUSCAGLIA

Chapter Theme Song:
"Saving My Heart," Yes

I'm in the Mood for Love

430

Create special "signals" to let your lover know you're in the mood for love. Herewith, some ideas from creative Romance Class participants:

* Have "your song" playing when he returns home from work.
* Play anything by Billie Holiday on the stereo.
* For men: Casually say, "I think I'll shave tonight . . ."
* One couple has "His" and "Hers" Japanese kimonos. The interested party changes into his or her robe . . . and if the other is interested too, he or she changes, also.
* One couple has a special pillow that says "TONIGHT" on one side, and "NOT TONIGHT" on the other side.

431

Some couples have created signals or gestures for use in *public*, all of which mean "Let's blow this joint, rush home, and make love together!"

☞ Holding hands and giving three quick squeezes.
☞ A code word, such as using the word *red* several times in a row.
☞ A code phrase, such as, "Is it *hot* in here, or it just me?"
☞ Hum "your song" in her ear.
☞ Scratch your left ear with your right hand.

432

Create a bouquet of "Long Stem Panties" for her. Buy a dozen red, pink and white panties; buy some plastic roses; remove the plastic buds and replace them with the rolled-up panties.

Chapter Theme Song:

"I'm in the Mood for Love," Little Jack Little

I'm in the Mood for Chocolate

433

A lifelong passion for chocolate inspired one couple in the Romance Class to embark on a round-the-world search for the Ultimate Chocolate. They actually arrange their vacations so they can visit all of the major chocolate manufacturers in various countries! Now *that's* fanatical!

- ✦ Visit the Nestlé chocolate factory in Broc, Switzerland. Call (41) 296-5151; or visit www.nestle.com.
- ✦ "The Swiss Plan" is an organization that arranges package tours to several Swiss chocolate factories. Call them at 800-777-9480; or visit www.SwissPlan.com.
- ✦ Or stay closer to home . . . Visit Chocolate World at the Hershey Chocolate factory in Hershey, Pennsylvania. Call 717-534-4900; or visit www.Hersheys.com/chocworld.

434

People hold wine-tasting parties, right? So why not hold a *chocolate-tasting party*? Invite your best friends, ask them to bring samples of their favorite chocolates, and create a formal methodology for judging the qualities of the finest chocolate. Conduct blind taste comparisons; rank each chocolate for its aroma, texture, sweetness, depth, initial taste, aftertaste, combination of ingredients, etc.

435

- ✳ *Chocolate: The Consuming Passion*, by Sandra Boynton
- ✳ *All Things Chocolate: The Ultimate Resource to the World's Favorite Food*, by Carole Bloom
- ✳ *All Things Chocolate*, by Armand Eisen
- ✳ *The Book of Chocolate*, by Natalie Bailleux
- ✳ *Chocolate Kisses*, by Margaret Brownley

Best Chocolate-Related Book Title (non-fiction):

Death by Chocolate: The Last Word on a Consuming Passion, by Marcel Desaulniers

Best Chocolate-Related Book Title (fiction):

Bittersweet Journey: A Modestly Erotic Novel of Love, Longing, and Chocolate, by Enid Futterman

The Gospel According to Godek

436

Romantic gestures have no ulterior motive. Their only purpose is to express love and appreciation; to show that you've been thinking of your partner; to bring love alive in the world.

This is a goal to *strive for*, but one that we rarely achieve perfectly. That's okay. Don't worry about it. Love isn't about *perfection*, it's about *love*. And romance isn't about perfection either; it, too, is simply about love.

437

When it comes to *love*—the emotional side of relationships—men and women are much more *alike* than we are *different*.

When it comes to *sex*—now *here's* where most of the differences kick in!

You see, humans are a complex mixture of physical and psychological attributes. The more you move down the physical/sexual end of the scale, the more pronounced the *differences* between men and women are. The more you move up the psychological/emotional end of the scale, the more *similar* men and women are.

*Love is **simple** but it's not **easy**.*

438

☞ Romance is an art, not a science.
☞ Love is a cooperative sport, not a competitive sport.
☞ Romance is not a business. There's no bottom line.
☞ Love is not a battle. "War" metaphors are harmful to your health.

The Gospel According to Godek (Revisited)

439

↦ You can lose yourself in love without losing your individuality.

↦ You can compromise without compromising *yourself*.

↦ You can change without losing your uniqueness.

↦ You can grow without growing apart.

↦ You can give without losing *anything*.

↦ You can open up without being judged.

↦ You can disagree without arguing.

↦ You can feel without losing control.

↦ You *can* keep the passion alive in a long-term relationship.

↦ You can be mature without losing the child inside of you.

↦ You can only be *truly known* in an intimate, long-term relationship.

*You can be **insanely** romantic and still be yourself.*

✳ You cannot be known unless you open your heart.

✳ You cannot love without being vulnerable.

✳ You cannot be intimate without taking a risk.

✳ You cannot share feelings in a non-supportive environment.

✳ You cannot enter a relationship demanding a guarantee.

✳ You cannot be interdependent unless you're first independent.

✳ You cannot be controlling and spontaneous at the same time.

✳ You cannot live without making mistakes.

✳ You cannot realize your dreams if you don't have well-defined goals.

✳ You cannot grow unless you learn from your mistakes.

✳ You cannot forgive another until you've forgiven yourself *first*.

✳ You cannot heal a broken heart until you risk it again.

■ You have the power to choose how your feelings affect you.

▲ You have the ability to alter your reality with your beliefs.

● You have all the talents and capabilities to fulfill your Purpose.

Getting Down To Business

440

Mark *all* significant dates in your appointment book or business calendar. Note: You and your partner may not consider the same occasions to be "significant." Make sure you *think like your partner* when you mark these dates.

And here's the key to staying on top of things so these dates don't "sneak-up" on you: Write reminders to yourself in your calendar *two weeks in advance* of each date to remind yourself to send a card, buy a gift, or make reservations.

- ❏ His/her birthday
- ❏ Your anniversary
- ❏ Valentine's Day
- ❏ First day of each season
- ❏ A "mystery date"
- ❏ Dinner dates
- ❏ Major vacations
- ❏ Three-day weekends
- ❏ Kids' birthdays
- ❏ Pseudo-holidays that he/she likes
- ❏ Favorite rock star's birthday
- ❏ Favorite movie star's birthday

441

Another way to ensure that you get those greeting cards, notes and gifts out on time is to get a three-ring binder with twelve pocket dividers. Label them with the months, and insert relevant items into each pocket. Attach a "Master List" of significant dates to the inside cover. This way, you'll be prepared well in advance of every event that comes along.

→ Insert greeting cards, notes, poems, articles, reminders to yourself, ads, catalog pages, etc.
→ Make sure *every* pocket has stuff in it—especially for those months that include no "official" anniversaries or holidays. Make up your own holidays and reasons for celebrating!

442

Delegate more at work. Come home at a reasonable hour!

443

Place a flower in his briefcase. Maybe a dozen. Just because.

Funny Business

444

Write wacky notes, memos and things, based on your profession:

- ❖ Teacher: Write a report card.
- ❖ Lawyer: Write out a motion.
- ❖ Trucker: Make a packing slip.
- ❖ Executive: Write a business plan.
- ❖ Doctor: Write a prescription.
- ❖ Secretary: Write a memo.
- ❖ Salesman: Place an order.
- ❖ Policeman: Write a ticket.
- ❖ Anyone: Write a resumé.
- ❖ *Your* profession: (_____)

445

Call your lover on the phone. Make up a lovesong *on the spot* and sing it to her! Make up a tune, make up the words— and just keep singing! (You'll generate laughter as well as appreciation!)

*I **know** this sounds kind of goofy, but it's really lots of fun!*

446

Don't let your serious business executive fool you: Most of them love to "play" at their desks. Executive "desk toys" make great gifts. Note: There are several categories of desk toys. Which kind does your partner like?

- ✦ Wind-up toys
- ✦ Cartoon characters
- ✦ Nostalgic items
- ✦ Prestige items
- ✦ Toy cars and trucks
- ✦ Electronic gizmos
- ✦ Sports memorabilia
- ✦ Puzzles
- ✦ Hobby-related items
- ✦ Things that move or swivel
- ✦ Things to fiddle with

Resources (I)

447a

- ✦ The Celebration Fantastic (weddings & other): 800-527-6566
- ✦ Croke's Comedy Catalog (ha!): 888-222-9304
- ✦ Figi's Gift Catalog (you name it!) 715-384-6101
- ✦ For Counsel (for lawyers!): 800-637-0098
- ✦ Golf House (duffers' gifts): 800-336-4446
- ✦ Into the Wind (kites 'n stuff): 800-541-0314
- ✦ Levinger (reader's tools): 800-544-0880
- ✦ Littleton Coin Company (¢): 800-258-4645
- ✦ Museum of Fine Arts, Boston (artsy): 800-225-5592
- ✦ Nature Company (cool & natural): 800-227-1114
- ✦ Neiman Marcus (clothing & related): 800-825-8000
- ✦ Norm Thompson (all kinds of stuff): 800-547-1160
- ✦ The Paragon (miscellany): 800-343-3095
- ✦ The San Francisco Music Box Company: 800-227-2190
- ✦ Seasons (fun stuff): 800-776-9677

Get this book before you buy a diamond: *How to Buy a Diamond: Insider Secrets for Getting Your Money's Worth*, by Fred Cuellar.

And before you buy *any* jewelry, become an educated buyer. Visit www.JewelryInfo.org.

Resources (II)

447b

* The Sharper Image (techie & cool stuff): 800-344-4444

* Signals (great gifts): 800-669-9696

* The Smithsonian (curious items): 800-322-0344

* Stave Puzzles (jigsaw puzzles): 802-295-5200

* Sundance (Western & rustic): 800-422-2770

* Vermont Teddy Bear Co. (hand-made!): 800-829-2327

* Victorian Papers (elegant papers): 800-800-6647

* Williams-Sonoma (cooking tools): 800-541-2233

* The Wood Workers' Store (practical tools): 800-279-4441

* Worldwide Games (games & puzzles): 800-888-0987

* White Flower Farm (great flowering plants): 800-411-6159

* Calyx & Corolla (exotic flowers): 800-800-7788

* Smith & Hawken (gardening stuff): 800-776-3336

* Harry & David (gourmet food): 800-345-5655

Sundance was founded by Robert Redford, one of the best romantic stars of all time.

White Flower Farm unconditionally guarantees all of its plants: They'll replace *anything* that dies!

Resources (III)

448

Bridal magazines are great resources for finding romantic vacation destinations. (If you think that honeymoons are just for newlyweds, you're missing some great romantic opportunities!) Pick-up a copy of *Bride's, Modern Bride, Bridal Review, Bridal Trends, Bride & Groom, Brides Today* or *Bridal Guide.*

For the scientifically minded, shop for gifts at:

The American Museum of Natural History, New York City: 212-769-5100

The Smithsonian Institution, Washington, D.C. 202-357-2700

449

Resources around town: Call 'em, ask 'em questions. Send for their catalogs and brochures.

- Adult education programs
- Convention & Visitors Bureaus
- Dance studios
- Music studios
- Cooking schools
- Local amateur theaters
- Professional theaters
- Museums
- Nightclubs
- Golf courses
- Tennis clubs
- City Hall
- Recreation Department
- The Parks Department
- Bookstores
- Concert halls
- The YMCA and YWCA
- Comedy clubs

Catalogs are great resources. Not only for specific gifts, but also for ideas and concepts you can implement on your own.

450

She *loves* flowers. He planted a flower garden "to keep the bloom on our love." The challenge, of course, is that most flowers only bloom for a few weeks of the year. Following fifteen years of many different combinations of flowers, he finally found the perfect resource, *Birthflowers of the Landscape*, by Linton Wright McKnight. This book lists *thousands* of flowers and when they bloom.

Resources (IV)

451

For researching music for your music lover: *Rolling Stone* magazine's web site is a great resource with lots of song clips, videos, profiles of 85,000 artists, and more. Visit www.rollingstone.com.

452

Looking for a movie for your lover, or movies by a particular director or actor, or movie reviews, or background info on a particular flick? Visit the Internet Movie Database at www. imdb.com.

453

A great resource for old magazines (great for birthday or anniversary gifts!) is the Avenue Victor Hugo Bookstore, in Boston, Massachusetts. Call 617-266-7746; or visit www.AvenueVictorHugoBooks.com.

*Do you know a couple with an A+ Relationship? They can be a **great** romantic resource for you.*

454

If you'd be interested in "a connoisseur's worldwide guide to peaceful and unspoiled places," then you should subscribe to *Andrew Harper's Hideaway Report*, a monthly newsletter devoted to upscale travel. For more info, visit www.HideawayReport.com. The *Report's* recent list of Hideaways of the Year included:

❖ Woodlands Resort, in Summerville, South Carolina: A restored Georgian mansion near Charleston. Call 800-774-9999.
❖ Blantyre, in Lenox, Massachusetts: A Tudor structure with turrets and gargoyles. Call 413-637-3556.
❖ Timberhill Ranch, in Cazadero, California: Elegance amid 6,000 acres of beautiful wilderness. Call 707-847-3258.
❖ Rancho de San Juan, in Espanola, New Mexico: In the foothills of the Black Mesa. Call 800-726-7121.

Slightly Outrageous

455

Visit a karaoke bar and surprise your lover by getting up and singing "your song" to him/her.

456

Overdo something. Don't hold back. Go for it! Give it everything you've got. Be creative. Be wild. Be expressive.

- ❐ Does he love m&m's? Fill a one-gallon glass jar with them for him.
- ❐ Make love every day for a week. (For a month!?)
- ❐ Take your lover on a *surprise* two-week vacation to Paris.
- ❐ Call her from work, *every-hour-on-the-hour,* just to say "I love you."
- ❐ Send a birthday message via *skywriting!*

457

Go skinny-dipping: In the ocean, in a pond, in a lake, in a river, in a creek, in your pool, in the neighbor's pool!

458

Fill an entire packet of Post-It Notes with romantic sentiments:

- ✳ Write twenty-five *sexy* notes.
- ✳ Write sixteen *romantic* ideas.
- ✳ Write thirty-one *silly* notes.
- ✳ Write seven *romantic* song lyrics.
- ✳ Write twelve *suggestive* suggestions.
- ✳ Write nine *intriguing* questions.

Now stick the whole pack of romantic Post-It Notes throughout the house. Or stick up three new notes per day for several weeks!

Be outrageous!

Do something unexpected.

Overdo something.

Quite Outrageous

459

Gals: Hire a limousine to pick up your husband at the airport upon his return from a business trip. Send the driver into the terminal to locate and help your husband. Be waiting in the back seat of the limo . . . dressed in your finest lingerie, sipping champagne, and listening to a recording of *Heartstrings*, by Earl Klugh.

460

How about a balloon adventure—over *Switzerland?* (Or France. Or Italy. Or Austria.) Call Bombard Balloon Adventures at 800-862-8537, or write to 333 Pershing Way, West Palm Beach, Florida 33401.

And once you get hooked on ballooning, you'll want to know about "In the Air: The Ultimate Catalog for Balloon Enthusiasts"! Call 800-583-8038; or visit www.InTheAir-online.com

461

Kidnap her! Blindfold her. Drive her around town until she's thoroughly lost. Then reveal your destination: Her favorite restaurant, or maybe a romantic inn.

462

You want more time for love in your life? Shoot your TV.

TV is a black hole that sucks time into it. Have you ever noticed how you're drawn toward a television set when it's on—*even when you're not particularly interested in what's on?* The average American watches about four hours of TV per day.

"Outrageous" is giving her ten pounds of Hershey's Kisses.

"*Quite* outrageous" is filling the bathtub with Hershey's Kisses.

"Outrageous" is getting Super Bowl tickets for your sports fan.

"*Quite* outrageous" is getting seats on the fifty-yard line.

"Outrageous" is a balloon bouquet delivered to his office.

"*Quite* outrageous" is a hot-air balloon vacation over Switzerland.

Slightly Naughty

463

Musical accompaniment: "Back Seat of My Car," by Paul McCartney.

Fill the back seat of your car with pillows. Go for a little drive in the country. Use your imagination.

464

Talk Dirty to Me: An Intimate Philosophy of Sex, by Sallie Tisdale, is a thought-provoking book on a subject that embarrasses many people. Tisdale observes that our society is publicly lascivious yet Puritanical at heart. "We're vicariously living out, in a public way, sexual permissiveness—because we don't have one-to-one, intimate, mature conversations about sex." A little "talking dirty" might just be a good thing.

"*Slightly* naughty" is a garter belt and stockings.

"*Quite* naughty" is a *black* garter belt, matching black bra and panties, black *seamed* stockings and *three-inch* spike heels.

465

* How about staging a personal Lingerie Fashion Show for him?
* Or how about creating a Lingerie Fashion Show *videotape* for him?!

"*Slightly* naughty" is the movie *Henry and June.*

"*Quite* naughty" is the movie *Nine-1/2 Weeks.*

466

Gals: Buy some specially selected items of *cheap* lingerie—so he can literally *rip* them off your body!

"*Slightly* naughty" is sharing your sexual fantasies with each other.

"*Quite* naughty" is role playing and acting out your sexual fantasies together.

467

Buy these items of clothing in matching colors: A necktie and silk boxer shorts for *him*, and a bra and panty outfit for *her*. Make a relationship rule that whenever one of you wears your items, your partner must wear his/her matching items. Guaranteed to keep your partner envisioning you all day long!

Quite Naughty

468

Join the Mile High Club.

Fly the friendly skies!

469

Make love in other unusual places, too: Cars, trains, beaches, pools, boats, ponds/lakes/oceans, store dressing rooms, libraries, elevators, bathtubs, fire escapes, porches, rooftops, tree houses, boardrooms, saunas, airplanes, kitchen tables and hot tubs.

470

♣ One couple in the Romance Class confided that they have a tradition of making love at every wedding reception they attend!

♣ Another couple keeps a U.S. map in their den with pins marking the many places where they've made love!

471

☞ Gals: Perform a personal striptease for him. You might be spontaneous about it or you might choreograph and practice your routine. Note: Some stripteases emphasise the *strip* part, while others emphasize the *tease* part. You choose!

If you want a little inspiration—and some choreography—for performing a personal striptease for your lover: Check out the movie *Nine-1/2 Weeks*, and fast-forward to 1:18:20 into the film. Take notes, practice, and you're sure to get a rise out of your guy.

☞ Guys: Does the word "Chippendale" mean anything to you? And for additional inspiration, watch the movie *The Full Monty*. Grab your black bow tie, grab your top hat, drop your inhibitions and drop your pants!

Best songs to accompany a striptease:

"The Stripper," the classic song, by David Rose and his Orchestra

"You Can Leave Your Hat On," by Joe Cocker

Shopping for Dummies

472

When window-shopping together, pay close attention to items that she *really likes*. Sneak back later and get them for her. (Store them in your "Gift Closet" for use at your discretion.)

473

Get help!

Get professional help. No, no, I don't mean a *psychiatrist*—I mean hire a *personal shopper*. He or she can help you run those errands and pick up those gifts that you always seem to forget about. Set a budget, provide your personal shopper with some key information about your partner, then set him or her loose in the mall!

474

Around your town are all the stores you'll need to inspire and satisfy your romantic urges. Try browsing in each of these types of shops with nothing specifically in mind . . . and see what romantic possibilities jump out at you:

* Bookstores
* Used bookstores
* Card shops
* Stationery stores
* Toy stores
* Lingerie shops
* Second-hand shops
* School supply stores
* Nostalgia shops
* Sporting goods shops
* Music stores
* Paper stores
* Dress boutiques
* Hotel gift shops
* Video stores

475

Get to know the owner and manager of her favorite clothing boutique. Ask them to inform you of new arrivals that they feel your lover will love. (This is an easy way to get surprise gifts that are guaranteed to please her.)

Advanced Shopping Strategies

476

While out shopping with her: If she's trying on an outfit she *adores* (or that *you* find sexy)—pay for it quickly while she's still in the dressing room. (A good reason to carry *cash* on these little outings.) Return to the dressing room with a pair of scissors, cut off the price tags, and announce that she can wear the outfit out of the store. Watch her jaw drop. Then watch her leap into your arms.

477

Go shopping with no specific task, and no specific goal in mind. *Let the gift find you.*

Introducing the practice of "Zen shopping."

478

Always be in a "gift-buying mode." I don't mean that you should be shopping *all the time*—but that you should be prepared to buy a great gift whenever you happen upon one. If you have this mindset, you'll usually have birthday and anniversary gifts already purchased long before you need them.

479

Sign up for a Bridal Gift Registry and then go "fantasy shopping." Do this even if—*especially* if— you're already married! Here's what you do: Before going into the department store remove your wedding rings and prepare to pretend you're single. Filling out the registry form together will be fun and will probably reveal some surprises about each other. Then browse throughout the store and discuss items that you *wish* you could get as gifts. In other words, pretend that money is no object. Do you want that expensive crystal vase? *Put it on your list!*

This tip will give your partner ideas for future gifts for you!

Note: If you hold a formal rededication wedding ceremony, you just might *really* get some of these dream gifts!

Words of Love/Shakespeare's
480

Use these elegant words on a homemade Valentine card this year:

Doubt thou the stars are fire;
Doubt that the sun doth move
Doubt truth to be a liar
But never doubt I love.

~ HAMLET

World-Class romantic date: Go see the play Romeo and Juliet.

And it wouldn't hurt to rent one of the many film versions of Romeo and Juliet.

Write this sonnet on a scroll. Add your own note, something like, "I can't write this poetically, but I *can* love you this passionately."

Shall I compare thee to a summer's day?
Thou art more lovely and more temperate:
Rough winds do shake the darling buds of May,
And summer's lease hath all too short a date:
Sometime too hot the eye of heaven shines,
And often is his gold complexion dimm'd;
And every fair from fair sometime declines,
By chance, or nature's changing course untrimm'd;
But thy eternal summer shall not fade,
Nor lose possession of that fair thou ow'st,
Nor shall death brag thou wander'st in his shade,
When in eternal lines to time thou grow'st;
> *So long as men can breathe, or eyes can see,*
> *So long lives this, and this gives life to thee.*

~ SONNET 18

Or how about some "verbal foreplay"?

Graze on my lips; and if these hills be dry,
Stray lower, where the pleasant fountains lie.

~ VENUS AND ADONIS

Use these words to accompany a jewelry gift:

Win her with gifts, if she respects not words,
Dumb jewels often in their silent kind
More than quick words do move a woman's mind.

~ TWO GENTLEMEN OF VERONA

Words of Love/Poetic

481a

How do I love thee? Let me count the ways.
I love thee to the depth and breadth and height
My soul can reach, when feeling out of sight
For the ends of Being and ideal Grace
I love thee to the level of everyday's
Most quiet need, by sun and candle-light.
I love thee freely, as men strive for Right;
I love thee purely, as they turn from Praise.
I love thee with the passion put to use
In my old griefs, and with my childhood's faith.
I love thee with a love I seemed to lose
With my lost saints,—I love thee with the breath,
Smiles, tears, of all my life!—and, if God choose,
I shall but love thee better after death.

~ ELIZABETH BARRETT BROWNING

To see how the power of *eloquent words* can affect the course of romance, see the movie *Roxanne*, starring Steve Martin.

481b

She walks in Beauty, like the night
          Of cloudless climes and starry skies;
And all that's best of dark and bright
          Meet in her aspect and her eyes:
Thus mellow'd to that tender light
          Which heaven to gaudy day denies.

~ LORD BYRON, FIRST STANZA OF *She Walks In Beauty*

A great marriage is a love poem with two authors.

481c

Memorize her favorite poem, or the lyrics to her favorite love song. Recite it at private times, or while making love.

Love one another
But make not a bond of love.
Let it rather be a moving sea
Between the shores of your souls.

~ KAHLIL GIBRAN

Words of Love/ *Your* Words

482

You can use these ideas for scrolls or cards or frameable items for many romantic occasions.

Write your *own* words of love. Here are some ideas to get you started:

✦ List "Ten Reasons I Fell in Love With You."
✦ List "Ten Reasons I *Still* Love You."
✦ List "Ten Ways You Turn Me On."
✦ List "Ten Reasons You Should Stick With Me."
✦ List "Ten Reasons You Should Marry Me."

483

Keep a journal. Every day or so, write down your thoughts about your partner, about your relationship, about your lives together. Some days you'll just jot a quick "I love you"—other days you may be inspired to write page after page. Do this for an entire year. Then present it to her on your anniversary or her birthday.

484

Write your *own* version of Elizabeth Barrett Browning's famous poem *"How do I love thee, let me count the ways . . ."*

485

Place an ad in the Personals column of your local newspaper. Let your lover know why he or she is so special. Write it in "code," possibly using your private pet name for her. This is a great opportunity to exercise your creativity and express your feelings in just a few clever words.

✳ When the ad appears, circle it and leave it on the kitchen table when you leave for work.
✳ Or call him at work on the day the ad appears, and tell him there's a secret message for him on a certain page of the morning newspaper.

Words of Love/From the Ancients

486

* *"To be able to say how much you love is to love but little."*
  ~ PETRARCH

* *"One word frees us all of the weight and pain of life. That word is Love."*
  ~ SOPHOCLES

* *"Take away leisure and Cupid's bow is broken."*
  ~ OVID

* *"The anger of lovers renews the strength of love."*
  ~ PUBLILIUS SYRUS

* *"No act of kindness, no matter how small, is ever wasted."*
  ~ AESOP

* *"The happiness of your life depends on the quality of your thoughts."*
  ~ MARCUS ANTONIUS

* *"To be loved, be lovable."*
  ~ OVID

* *"The more a man knows, the more he forgives."*
  ~ CONFUCIUS

* *"Union gives strength."*
  ~ AESOP

* *"When male and female combine, all things achieve harmony."*
  ~ TAO TE CHING

* *"From their eyelids as they glanced dripped love."*
  ~ HESIOD

* *"He is not a lover who does not love forever."*
  ~ EURIPIDES

* *"My love for you is mixed throughout my body."*
  ~ ANCIENT EGYPTIAN LOVE SONG

"Love is a grave mental disease."

~ PLATO

"The madness of love is the greatest of heaven's blessings."

~ PLATO

Memorize This List
487a

You should know these things about your lover!

Exploring these topics will help you get to know your partner's likes and dislikes a little bit better. Discussing these things will bring you closer together. And knowing these things will also help you express your love more effectively and buy more appropriate gifts.

Chapter Theme Song:

"These Are a Few of My Favorite Things," from the musical *The Sound of Music*

1. Favorite color
2. Lucky number
3. Favorite flower
4. Favorite author
5. Favorite book (fiction)
6. Favorite book (non-fiction)
7. Favorite fairy tale
8. Favorite children's book
9. Favorite Bible passage
10. Favorite saying
11. Favorite proverb
12. Favorite poem
13. Favorite poet
14. Favorite song
15. Favorite singer
16. Favorite musical band
17. Favorite kind of music
18. Favorite dance tune
19. Favorite romantic song
20. Favorite slow dance tune
21. Favorite rock 'n roll song
22. Favorite ballad
23. Favorite country song
24. Favorite Gospel song
25. Favorite jazz number
26. Favorite R&B tune
27. Favorite songwriter
28. Favorite magazine
29. Favorite meal
30. Favorite food
31. Favorite vegetable
32. Favorite fruit
33. Favorite cookie
34. Favorite ice cream
35. Favorite kind of chocolate
36. Favorite snack food
37. Favorite restaurant (expensive)
38. Favorite restaurant (frugal)
39. Favorite fast food joint
40. Favorite TV show (current)
41. Favorite TV show (old)
42. Favorite comedian
43. Favorite actor (living)
44. Favorite actor (of any era)
45. Favorite actress (living)
46. Favorite actress (of any era)
47. Favorite movie of all time
48. Favorite adventure movie
49. Favorite erotic movie
50. Favorite romantic comedy
51. Favorite comedy film
52. Favorite action movie
53. Favorite Broadway play
54. Favorite musical
55. Favorite show tune
56. Favorite breed of dog
57. Favorite breed of cat
58. Favorite animal
59. Favorite comic strip
60. Favorite comic character
61. Favorite TV cartoon
62. Favorite TV cartoon character
63. Favorite artist
64. Favorite style of artwork
65. Favorite painting
66. Favorite sculpture
67. Favorite hero/heroine
68. Role model (actual person)
69. Role model (fictional)
70. Favorite athlete
71. Favorite sport (to watch)
72. Favorite sport (to play)

Memorize This List, Too
487b

73. Favorite Olympic sport
74. Favorite sports teams
75. Favorite board game
76. Favorite foreplay activity
    (to receive)
77. Favorite foreplay activity
    (to perform)
78. Favorite lovemaking position
79. Favorite sexy outfit
    (for partner)
80. Favorite sexy outfit (for self)
81. Favorite erotic fantasy
82. Favorite time of day to
    make love
83. Favorite place on body to
    be touched erotically
84. Favorite music to make love to
85. Favorite season
86. Favorite time of day
87. Favorite holiday
88. Favorite hobby
89. Favorite type of jewelry
90. Preferred jewelry metal
    (silver, gold or platinum?)
91. Preferred style of clothing
    (for self)
92. Preferred style of clothing
    (for partner)
93. Favorite designer
94. Favorite erotic clothing
    (for self)
95. Favorite erotic clothing
    (for partner)
96. Dream vacation spot
97. Favorite vacation activity
98. Favorite city

99. Favorite foreign country
100. Favorite wine
101. Favorite champagne
102. Favorite beer
103. Favorite soft drink
104. Favorite way to spend a
     lazy afternoon
105. Favorite room in your
     home
106. Favorite perfume
107. Favorite cologne
108. Favorite brand of
     make-up
109. Favorite aroma
110. Favorite fictional
     character
111. Favorite historical
     personality
112. Best gift ever received
113. Favorite way to relax
114. Favorite way to get
     energized
115. Favorite store
116. Favorite side of the bed
117. Favorite TV sitcom
118. Favorite TV drama
119. Favorite joke
120. Favorite classical
     composer
121. Favorite symphony
122. Favorite opera
123. Favorite album/CD
124. Favorite car
     (make & year)
125. Favorite color for a car

Also—

126. Favorite gemstone
127. Favorite day of the week
128. Favorite month of the year

Togetherness

488

Invite her to accompany you on your next business trip. (All work and no play makes hubby a bore.)

489

Read the Sunday newspaper in bed together. Read the Sunday comics aloud (use appropriate voices).

490

Explore together: Auctions, flea markets, second-hand stores, garage sales and rummage sales. They're great places to find "Trinket Gifts," little surprises and gag gifts.

491

Cook a meal *together*.

492

Go into a bookstore together. Buy each other two books:

☞ One that you know your *partner* will like.
☞ And one that *you* want your partner to read.

493

Sit down together on the first day of every month and review your calendars. Make your romantic plans *first*, and *then* fit your other meetings, appointments and commitments into your schedule. Couples who have an A+ Relationship keep their love life a number one priority.

---

*Familiarity does **not** "breed contempt"—it's boredom and lack of creativity that breed contempt.*

Dependence isn't healthy in a love relationship. It leads to co-depencency.

Independence doesn't work well, either. What's the point of being a *couple* if your main goal is to be *independent?*

Interdependence is the goal that people in A+ Relationships aim for.

Chapter Theme Song:

"Friends & Lovers," Bread

Twogetherness

494

Some Things that Come in "Twos"

- ✦ Bicycles built-for-two
- ✦ Double sleeping bags
- ✦ Two-seater sports cars
- ✦ A Chinese pu-pu platter for two
- ✦ Mozart's Sonata in D Major for Two Pianos, K. 448
- ✦ Two-person kayaks
- ✦ Two-for-the-price-of-one specials at stores
- ✦ Two-for-the-price-of-one specials at restaurants
- ✦ Duets: "Endless Love," by Luther Vandross & Mariah Carey
- ✦ Loveseats

495

Many couples have "His" and "Hers" matching towels. With a little creative romantic thinking, here's what you can come up with:

- ✳ "His" and "Hers" matching silk pajamas
- ✳ "His" and "Hers" bottles of red and white wine
- ✳ "His" and "Hers" matching motorcycles
- ✳ "His" and "Hers" matching T-shirts
- ✳ "His" and "Hers" overnight bags (have packed at all times)
- ✳ "His" and "Hers" matching coffee mugs
- ✳ "His" and "Hers" jack-o-lanterns at Halloween
- ✳ "His" and "Hers" rocking chairs
- ✳ "His" and "Hers" bicycles
- ✳ "His" and "Hers" mobile telephones
- ✳ "His" and "Hers" Porsches (millionaires need love, too)
- ✳ "His" and "Hers" VW Bugs (love for the rest of us)
- ✳ "His" and "Hers" tennis rackets
- ✳ "His" and "Hers" matching heart-shaped tattoos!
- ✳ "His" and "Hers" Christmas tree ornaments
- ✳ "His" and "Hers" matching beach towels

Some *more* things that come in "twos":

Stravinsky's Concerto for Two Pianos

Singing songs in two-part harmony

Doubles solitaire

Wedding rings

Double beds

See-saws

Double-scoop ice cream cones

Two-person hot tubs

Chapter Theme Song:

"Tea for Two," Nino Tempo & April Stevens

Two

496

There are two kinds of people in the world:
Detail People and *Overview People*.

Detail People focus on the little things; they notice details. Overview People focus on the big picture; they see general trends. Neither is right or wrong, these are simply character tendencies.

It will be much easier for you to pull romantic surprises if you're a Detail Person and your partner is an Overview Person. Detail People are good at covering their trail, paying attention to the little things, and acting "normal." The overview partner won't even notice any little slips. If *you're* the Overview Person, you'll need to be extra careful when planning surprises. Those detail-oriented partners will notice every unusual phone call, every little change in your schedule, and that mischievous look on your face!

There are two kinds of people in the world: High Maintenance People—and Low Maintenance People. (For further insights into this concept see the movie *When Harry Met Sally*.)

497

There are two kinds of people in the world:
Object People and *Experience People*.

Object People see love symbolized in gifts, in *things:* Roses, jewelry, socket wrench sets. Experience People see love expressed in time spent together, in *experiences:* Dinner, movies, bowling. Neither is better than the other, they're just personal preferences. And, interestingly, neither preference is related to gender.

Why do you need to know this? Because if your partner is an Object Person, and you take her to the best restaurant in town and drop $200 on an elegant *experience*, she'll still be expecting a *gift* at the end of the evening! She's not being selfish, she's simply being herself.

There are two kinds of people in the world: People Who Will Spend Hours to Find that Three Cents Needed to Balance the Checkbook—and People Who Will Round Off to the Nearest Hundred Dollars Just to be Done With It.

Tip: Don't argue about it. Neither of you will *ever* change the other!

Object People love items that have special *meaning*. Experience People love activities that create special *memories*.

Two (II)

498

There are two kinds of people in the world:
Left-Brained People and *Right-Brained People*.

Left-Brained People tend to be logical and analytical. Right-Brained People tend to be emotional and intuitive. The current cultural stereotype is that men are logical and women are emotional. This is often—but not nearly always—true. Studies show that this generalization is true for about 60 percent of people. The important lesson for lovers is to treat your partner as an *individual*, not as a stereotype.

499

There are two kinds of people in the world:
People Who Sleep With the Windows *Open*, and People Who Sleep With the Windows *Closed*.

The serious point here is this: It's not about being *right* or *wrong*. It's about working things through, compromising, appreciating each other's quirks, and laughing a lot. (An on the practical side, an electric blanket with *dual controls* just might be a relationship-saving gift!)

500

There are two kinds of people in the world:
Morning People and *Night People*.

Morning People leap out of bed at daybreak and are raring to go, then they close up shop by 8 p.m. Night People are just getting warmed up by sundown, do their best work after midnight, then sleep until noon.

Don't take Morning People on late night dates—they'll doze off. Brisk morning walks and elegant breakfasts are more their style.

Don't serve Night People breakfast in bed. They shine at dinner parties. They love late-night movies and midnight lovemaking.

There are two kinds of people in the world: People With One Left Foot and One Right Foot, and People With Two Left Feet. Note: The dancers and the non-dancers *always* marry each other. Nobody knows why.

There are two kinds of people in the world: Dog People and Cat People. Don't trifle with either kind!

The 99 Best Love Songs of the Twentieth Century (#'s 1-25)

500a

*What are **your** Top Ten love songs?*

1. "You Are So Beautiful (To Me)," Joe Cocker
2. "As Time Goes By," from *Casablanca*
3. "Something," The Beatles
4. "The Rose," Bette Midler
5. "Endless Love," Diana Ross & Lionel Richie
6. "Still," Commodores
7. "Colour My World," Chicago
8. "Lady," Kenny Rogers
9. "Unchained Melody," The Righteous Brothers
10. "Come Rain or Come Shine," Ray Charles

11. "Crazy for You," Madonna
12. "Just the Way You Are," Billy Joel
13. "The One I Love," Frank Sinatra
14. "Love Me Tender," Elvis Presley
15. "Through the Years," Kenny Rogers
16. "Tonight, I Celebrate My Love," Peabo Bryson & Roberta Flack
17. "Unforgettable," Nat King Cole
18. "I Will Always Love You," Whitney Houston
19. "Wind Beneath My Wings," Bette Midler
20. "The First Time Ever I Saw Your Face," Roberta Flack

FYI: Frank Sinatra said that the best love song ever written was "Something," by The Beatles.

21. "(I've Had) The Time of My Life," Bill Medley & Jennifer Warnes
22. "My Eyes Adored You," Frankie Valli
23. "With You I'm Born Again," Billy Preston & Syreeta
24. "I Won't Last a Day Without You," Paul Williams
25. "I Honestly Love You," Olivia Newton John

The 99 Best Love Songs of the Twentieth Century (#'s 26-50)

500b

26. "Up Where We Belong," Joe Cocker & Jennifer Warnes
27. "Baby Come to Me," Patti Austin & James Ingram
28. "We've Got Tonight," Kenny Rogers & Sheena Easton
29. "Let's Talk About Love," Celine Dion
30. "Ain't No Sunshine," Bill Withers

31. "Ain't No Mountain High Enough," Diana Ross & The Supremes
32. "Goin' Out of My Head/Can't Take My Eyes Off You," The Lettermen
33. "If I Fell," The Beatles
34. "One Hundred Ways," Quincy Jones & James Ingram
35. "Somewhere My Love," Frank Sinatra
36. "The Dance," Garth Brooks
37. "Truly," Lionel Richie
38. "Three Times a Lady," The Commodores
39. "Unchained Melody," Rodney McDowell
40. "Can't Help Falling in Love," Elvis Presley

41. "All My Loving," The Beatles
42. "Only Wanna Be With You," Hootie & the Blowfish
43. "You and I," Eddie Rabbitt & Crystal Gayle
44. "Devoted To You," Everly Brothers
45. "Love Will Find Its Way to You," Reba McEntire
46. "So Far Away," Carole King
47. "When a Man Loves a Woman," Percy Sledge
48. "Islands in the Stream," Kenny Rogers & Dolly Parton
49. "Melody of Love," Billy Vaughn
50. "Embraceable You" from the musical *Crazy for You*

What are *your* favorite love songs of all time?
Vote at www.1001WaysToBeRomantic.com.

The 99 Best Love Songs of the Twentieth Century (#'s 51-75)

500c

Is "your song" on this list?

51. "Babe," Styx
52. "Beauty and the Beast," Celine Dion & Peabo Bryson
53. "Evergreen," (Theme from *A Star Is Born*), Barbra Streisand
54. "The Right Thing To Do," Carly Simon
55. "I Want You, I Need You, I Love You," Elvis Presley
56. "Always On My Mind," Willie Nelson
57. "I'll Be There for You," Bon Jovi
58. "Just the Way You Are," Billy Joel
59. "Leather and Lace," Stevie Nicks & Don Henley
60. "Longer," Dan Fogelberg

61. "Missing You Now," Michael Bolton
62. "My Girl," Temptations
63. "Nights In White Satin," The Moody Blues
64. "Oh, Pretty Woman," Roy Orbison
65. "Straight from the Heart," Bryan Adams
66. "Suddenly," Olivia Newton-John & Cliff Richard
67. "The Anniversary Song," Richard Tucker
68. "The Wedding Song," Peter, Paul & Mary
69. "Time In A Bottle," Jim Croce
70. "To Be Loved By You," Wynonna

71. "Touch Me in the Morning," Diana Ross & The Supremes
72. "You Are The Sunshine of My Life," Stevie Wonder
73. "You Make Me So Very Happy," Blood, Sweat & Tears
74. "You're a Special Part of Me," Marvin Gaye & Diana Ross
75. "You're the First, the Last, My Everything," Barry White

The 99 Best Love Songs of the Twentieth Century (#'s 76-99)

500d

76. "(Everything I Do) I Do It For You," Bryan Adams
77. "Coming Around Again," Carly Simon
78. "An Everlasting Love," Andy Gibb
79. "Flame in Your Eyes," Alabama
80. "Head Over Heels," Tears for Fears

81. "Hopelessly Devoted to You," Olivia Newton-John
82. "How Sweet It Is (To Be Loved By You)," James Taylor
83. "I Go Crazy," Paul Davis
84. "I Just Want to be Your Everything," Andy Gibb
85. "We've Only Just Begun," The Carpenters
86. "When I Fall in Love," Celine Dion & Clive Griffin
87. "You Send Me," Sam Cooke
88. "In Your Eyes," Peter Gabriel
89. "A Whole New World," Peabo Bryson & Regina Belle
90. "Reunited," Peaches & Herb

91. "Say You'll Be Mine," Christopher Cross
92. "I Need Your Love Tonight," Elvis Presley
93. "Sexual Healing," Marvin Gaye
94. "Everlasting Love," Howard Jones
95. "(They Long To Be) Close To You," The Carpenters
96. "Magic," Olivia Newton-John
97. "This Heart of Mine," Judy Garland
98. "Til There Was You," from *The Music Man*
99. "Love Is a Many-Splendored Thing," Four Aces

What love song do you think deserves to be number *one hundred?!* Let me know via www.1001WaysToBeRomantic.com.

Songs to Help Express Your Feelings

500e

Friendship & Appreciation
- ✳ "Bridge Over Troubled Water," Simon and Garfunkel
- ✳ "Stand By Me," Ben E. King
- ✳ "Thank You for Being a Friend," Andrew Gold
- ✳ "That's What Friends Are For," Dionne & Friends
- ✳ "You've Got a Friend," James Taylor

Falling in Love
- ↔ "Could It Be I'm Falling in Love?" The Spinners
- ↔ "Could It Be Magic," Barry Manilow
- ↔ "Fallin' In Love," Hamilton, Joe Frank & Reymolds
- ↔ "If I Fell," The Beatles
- ↔ "Knocks Me Off My Feet," Stevie Wonder

New Love
- ❖ "We've Only Just Begun," The Carpenters
- ❖ "(I've Been) Searchin' So Long," Chicago
- ❖ "Puppy Love," Paul Anka
- ❖ "The First Time Ever I Saw Your Face," Roberta Flack
- ❖ "All My Loving," The Beatles

Love & Joy
- ✳ "How Sweet It Is (To Be Loved By You)," James Taylor
- ✳ "It Had to Be You," Harry Connick, Jr.
- ✳ "Let's Hang On," The Four Seasons
- ✳ "Love Me Do," The Beatles
- ✳ "The Way You Do the Things You Do," Temptations
- ✳ "What a Wonderful World," Louis Armstrong

Gentle & Sweet
- ❖ "All Right," Christopher Cross
- ❖ "Hearing Your Voice," The Moody Blues
- ❖ "My Love," Paul McCartney & Wings
- ❖ "Strange Magic," Electric Light Orchestra
- ❖ "Summer Soft," Stevie Wonder
- ❖ "(They Long To Be) Close To You," The Carpenters

Songs to Help Express Your Feelings

500f

Love & Tenderness

➤ "Always On My Mind," Willie Nelson
➤ "First Time Ever I Saw Your Face," Roberta Flack
➤ "I Honestly Love You," Olivia Newton John
➤ "In My World," The Moody Blue
➤ "Through the Years," Kenny Rogers
➤ "Longer," Dan Fogelberg
➤ "Evergreen," (From *A Star Is Born*), Barbra Streisand
➤ "Still," Commodores

Intense Love & Infatuation

✳ "Can't Take My Eyes Off You," Frankie Valli
✳ "Do the Walls Come Down," Carly Simon
✳ "Every Breath You Take," The Police
✳ "Head Over Heels," Tears for Fears
✳ "I Am Waiting," Yes
✳ "I Fall to Pieces," Patsy Cline
✳ "I Will Always Love You," Whitney Houston
✳ "Nights In White Satin," Moody Blues
✳ "When a Man Loves a Woman," Percy Sledge
✳ "(Your Love Has Lifted Me) Higher and Higher," Rita Coolidge

Loneliness & Missing You

"So Far Away," Carole King
"I Miss You," Klymaxx
"I Miss You Like Crazy," Natalie Cole
"Missing You Now," Michael Bolton
"Missing You," Jim Reeves
"Wishing You Were Here," Chicago
"You've Lost That Lovin' Feeling," Daryl Hall & John Oates

Songs to Help Express Your Feelings

500g

Longing & Yearning

* "Against All Odds (Take a Look at Me Now)," Phil Collins
* "Ain't No Sunshine," Bill Withers
* "Baby Come to Me," Patti Austin & James Ingram
* "Closer to Believing," Emerson Lake & Palmer
* "How Can I Tell You," Cat Stevens
* "I Need You," America
* "If Ever You're in My Arms Again" Peabo Bryson
* "If I Can't Have You," Yvonne Elliman
* "Need Her Love," Electric Light Orchestra
* "Until the Night," Billy Joel
* "Watching and Waiting," The Moody Blues
* "When I Need You," Leo Sayer
* "You Take My Breath Away," Queen

Forgive Me/Don't Leave Me!

➤ "Baby Come Back," Player
➤ "Don't Give Up on Us," David Soul
➤ "Hard to Say I'm Sorry," Chicago
➤ "If You Leave Me Now," Chicago
➤ "One More Night," Phil Collins
➤ "Sorry Seems to be the Hardest Word," Elton John

Fun & Whimsical

➤ "Can't You Hear My Heartbeat," Herman's Hermits
➤ "Crazy Little Thing Called Love," Queen
➤ "Groovy Kind of Love," Phil Collins
➤ "Hello Goodbye," The Beatles
➤ "I Think I Love You," The Partridge Family
➤ "If I Had a Million Dollars," Barenaked Ladies
➤ "I'm Gonna Be (500 Miles)," Proclaimers
➤ "Let's Call the Whole Thing Off" (1937)
➤ "Nobody Does It Better," Carly Simon
➤ "Silly Love Songs," Paul McCartney and Wings
➤ "When I'm Sixty-Four," The Beatles

Songs to Help Express Your Feelings

500h

Devotion & Commitment

- "Ain't No Mountain High Enough," Diana Ross
- "An Everlasting Love," Andy Gibb
- "As Long as He Needs Me," Shirley Bassey
- ✦ "Hopelessly Devoted to You," Olivia Newton-John
- "I Just Want to be Your Everything," Andy Gibb
- "I'll Cover You," from the Broadway musical Rent
- "I'll Never Leave You," Harry Nilsson
- "Love of My Life," Abba
- ✦ "The Right Thing To Do," Carly Simon
- ✦ "Say You'll Be Mine," Christopher Cross
- ✦ "You're My Everything," The Temptations

Adoration

- ✱ "Cherish," The Association
- ✱ "Heaven Must Be Missing an Angel," Tavares
- ✱ "I Just Want to be Your Everything," Andy Gibb
- ✱ "My Eyes Adored You," Frankie Valli
- ✱ "My Love," Paul McCartney & Wings
- ✱ "Wind Beneath My Wings," Bette Midler

Anniversaries & Celebrations

- ✤ "Always and Forever," Heatwave
- ✤ "The Anniversary Song," Richard Tucker
- ✤ "Celebration," Kool & The Gang
- ✤ "Forever and Ever, Amen," Randy Travis
- ✤ "More Today Than Yesterday," Spiral Staircase
- ✤ "Our Love Is Here to Stay," Harry Connick, Jr.

Poignant

- ✳ "Do You Love Me?" from Fiddler on the Roof
- ✳ "One More Night," Phil Collins
- ✳ "Truly," Lionel Richie
- ✳ "Without You," from the Broadway musical Rent

Songs to Help Express Your Feelings

500i

Suggestive

- ✦ "In the Mood," Glenn Miller
- ✦ "Lay Lady Lay" Bob Dylan
- ✦ "Light My Candle," from the Broadway musical *Rent*
- ✦ "Makin' Whoopee!" (1928)
- ✦ "Physical," Olivia Newton-John
- ✦ "So Deep Within You," The Moody Blues
- ✦ "We've Got Tonight," Kenny Rogers & Sheena Easton

Desire & Sexual Attraction

- ❤ "Afternoon Delight," Starland Vocal Band
- ❤ "Feel Like Makin' Love," Bad Company
- ❤ "I Want Your Sex," George Michael
- ❤ "Kiss You All Over," Exile
- ❤ "Let's Spend the Night Together," Rolling Stones
- ❤ "Natural Woman," Aretha Franklin
- ❤ "Sexual Healing," Marvin Gaye
- ❤ "Slave to Love," Bryan Ferry
- ❤ "The Sweetest Taboo," Sade

Hot Passion

- ✳ "All I Wanna Do Is Make Love To You," Heart
- ✳ "Deeper and Deeper," Madonna
- ✳ "Do You Wanna Make Love," Peter McCann
- ✳ "Hot Stuff," Donna Summer
- ✳ "I Do What I Do" (*Nine-1/2 Weeks* theme), John Taylor
- ✳ "I'm Your Baby Tonight," Whitney Houston
- ✳ "Kiss You All Over, "Exile
- ✳ "Light My Fire," The Doors
- ✳ "Make Me Lose Control," Eric Carmen
- ✳ "Touch Me (I Want Your Body)," Samantha Sang

Songs to Help Express Your Feelings

500j

Country Love Songs

- "Blue," LeAnn Rimes
- "Diamonds and Dirt," Rodney Crowell
- "Dream On, Texas Ladies," John Michael Montgomery
- "Everything I Love," Alan Jackson
- "Flame in Your Eyes," Alabama
- "He Stopped Loving Her Today," George Jones
- "Hello Darlin'," Conway Twitty
- "I'll Always Love You," Dolly Parton
- "It's Your Love," Tim McGraw & Faith Hill
- "Look at Us," Vince Gill
- "Love Me Like You Used To," Tanya Tucker
- "Love Will Find Its Way to You," Reba McEntire
- "Stand By Your Man," Tammy Wynette
- "Take the Ribbon From Your Hair," Tammy Smith
- "The Dance," Garth Brooks
- "This Night Won't Last Forever," Sawyer Brown
- "To Be Loved By You," Wynonna
- "Unchained Melody," Rodney McDowell
- "You Win My Love," Shania Twain

Love Songs that Put Women on a Pedestal

- "Island of Life," Jon Anderson & Kitaro
- "Lady," Kenny Rogers
- "Oh, Pretty Woman," Roy Orbison
- "She's a Lady," Tom Jones
- "Three Times a Lady," The Commodores
- "When A Man Loves A Woman," Percy Sledge

Best Love Song *Duets*

500k

- ❤ "A Whole New World," Peabo Bryson & Regina Belle
- ❤ "Ain't No Mountain High Enough," Marvin Gaye & Tammi Terrell
- ❤ "Ain't Nothing Like the Real Thing," Marvin Gaye & Tammi Terrell
- ❤ "All My Life," Linda Ronstadt & Aaron Neville
- ❤ "Baby (You've Got What it Takes)," Dinah Washington & Brook Benton
- ❤ "Beauty and the Beast," Celine Dion & Peabo Bryson
- ❤ "Can't We Try," Dan Hill & Vonda Sheppard
- ❤ "The Closer I Get to You," Roberta Flack & Donny Hathaway
- ❤ "Friends and Lovers," Gloria Loring & Carl Anderson
- ❤ "I Can't Help It," Andy Gibb & Olivia Newton-John
- ❤ "I Finally Found Someone," Bryan Adams and Barbra Streisand
- ❤ "I Got You Babe," Sonny & Cher
- ❤ "I Just Can't Stop Loving You," Michael Jackson & Siedah Garrett
- ❤ "I Knew You Were Waiting (For Me)," Aretha Franklin & George Michael
- ❤ "I Like Your Kind of Love," Andy Williams & Peggy Powers
- ❤ "Islands in the Stream," Kenny Rogers & Dolly Parton
- ❤ "Leather and Lace," Stevie Nicks & Don Henley
- ❤ "Let It Be Me," Jerry Butler & Betty Everett
- ❤ "Mockingbird," Carly Simon & James Taylor
- ❤ "The Next Time I Fall," Peter Cetera & Amy Grant
- ❤ "One Man Woman/One Woman Man," Paul Anka & Odia Coates
- ❤ "Put a Little Love in Your Heart," Annie Lennox & Al Green
- ❤ "Set the Night to Music," Roberta Flack & Maxi Priest
- ❤ "Somewhere Out There," Linda Ronstadt & James Ingram
- ❤ "Then Came You," Dionne Warwick & the Spinners
- ❤ "Tonight, I Celebrate My Love," Peabo Bryson & Roberta Flack
- ❤ "True Love," Elton John & Kiki Dee
- ❤ "What Kind of Fool," Barbra Streisand & Barry Gibb
- ❤ "Where is the Love," Roberta Flack & Donny Hathaway
- ❤ "You're a Special Part of Me," Diana Ross & Marvin Gaye
- ❤ "You're All I Need to Get By," Marvin Gaye & Tammi Terrell

*And a few **more** romantic duets:*

"With You I'm Born Again,"
Billy Preston & Syreeta

"You and I,"
Eddie Rabbitt & Crystal Gayle

"Close Your Eyes,"
Peaches & Herb

"Somethin' Stupid,"
Nancy Sinatra & Frank Sinatra

"Suddenly,"
Olivia Newton-John & Cliff Richard

"Your Precious Love,"
Marvin Gaye & Tammi Terrell

"Surrender to Me,"
Ann Wilson & Robin Zander

Best Broadway Love Songs

5001

Love songs from Broadway musicals

✳ "Almost Like Being in Love" from *Brigadoon*
✳ "Can't Help Loving Dat Man" from *Showboat*
✳ "Do I Love You Because You're Beautiful," from *Cinderella*
✳ "Embraceable You" from *Crazy for You*
✳ "I Could Be Happy With You," from *The Boyfriend*
✳ "I Could Have Danced All Night" from *My Fair Lady*
✳ "I Have Dreamed," from *The King and I*
✳ "I Wanna Be Loved By You" from *Good Boy*
✳ "I'm in Love with a Wonderful Guy" from *South Pacific*
✳ "I've Never Been in Love Before," from *Guys & Dolls*
✳ "If I Loved You" from *Carousel*
✳ "Just in Time," from *Bells Are Ringing*
✳ "Love Song," from *Pippin*
✳ "Me and My Girl," from *Me and My Girl*
✳ "My Heart Is So Full of You," from *The Most Happy Fella*
✳ "On the Street Where You Live" from *My Fair Lady*
✳ "People" from *Funny Girl*
✳ "People Will Say We're in Love" from *Oklahoma*
✳ "She Loves Me," from *She Loves Me*
✳ "So in Love" from *Kiss Me Kate*
✳ "They Say It's Wonderful," from *Annie Get Your Gun*
✳ "This Can't be Love" from *The Boys from Syracuse*
✳ "Til There Was You," the *The Music Man*
✳ "Too Much in Love to Care," from *Sunset Boulevard*
✳ "Try to Remember" from *The Fantastics*
✳ "What I Did for Love," from *A Chorus Line*
✳ "Wonderful Guy," from *South Pacific*
✳ "You're the Top," from *Anything Goes*

Best Romantic Movies &
Best Romantic Movie Couples
500m

The Most Romantic Movies of All Time

*What are **your** favorite flicks?*

- An Affair to Remember
- The Bodyguard
- Bull Durham
- Casablanca
- Dirty Dancing
- Doctor Zhivago
- Flashdance
- From Here to Eternity
- Ghost
- Gone with the Wind
- Intersection
- An Officer and a Gentleman
- Prelude to a Kiss
- Shakespeare in Love
- Shadowlands
- Somewhere in Time
- Titanic
- Top Gun
- Untamed Heart
- The Way We Were
- When Harry Met Sally

Movies Starring the All-Time Great Romantic Couples

Who are your favorite on-screen lovers?

- Red Dust (Gable & Harlow)
- Hold Your Man (Gable & Harlow)
- Flying Down to Rio (Astair & Rogers)
- Top Hat (Astaire & Rogers)
- Maytime (MacDonald & Eddy)
- Sweethearts (MacDonald & Eddy)
- Love Finds Andy Hardy (Garland & Rooney)
- That Forsyte Woman (Garson & Pidgeon)
- To Have and Have Not (Bogart & Bacall)
- Fire Over England (Leigh & Olivier)
- Cleopatra (Taylor & Burton)
- The Long, Hot Summer (Newman & Woodward)
- Woman of the Year (Hepburn & Tracy)

Best Romantic Comedies

500n

- 10
- A Midsummers Night's Sex Comedy
- A Touch of Class
- All of Me
- All Night Long
- Almost You
- Annie Hall
- Arthur
- Best Friends
- Blind Date
- Blume in Love
- Born Yesterday
- Broadcast News
- Cactus Flower
- Continental Divide
- Crocodile Dundee
- Cross My Heart
- The Cutting Edge
- The Electric Horseman
- Father of the Bride
- Frankie and Johnny
- The Goodbye Girl
- Groundhog Day
- House Calls
- Housesitter
- It's My Turn

- Manhattan
- Micki and Maude
- Modern Romance
- Mr. Jones
- Mrs. Doubtfire
- Murphy's Romance
- Night Shift
- Overboard
- The Owl and the Pussycat
- Pillow Talk
- Play It Again, Sam
- The Princess Bride
- Quackser Fortune Has a Cousin in the Bronx
- Reuben, Reuben
- Risky Business
- Roxanne
- Shampoo
- Shirley Valentine
- Silver Streak
- Splash
- Starting Over
- The Sure Thing
- That Touch of Mink
- Tootsie
- Who Am I This Time?
- The Woman in Red

All true romantics have a good sense of humor!

Great Date Movies

500o

What movie most closely resembles your personal love story??

- A Star Is Born
- About Last Night
- The Accidental Tourist
- Act of Love
- The African Queen
- Aladdin
- Algiers
- All About Eve
- The American President
- Anna Karenina
- A Place in the Sun
- Basic Instinct
- Beauty and the Beast
- Braveheart
- Breakfast at Tiffany's
- Brief Encounter
- Butch Cassidy and the Sundance Kid
- Camelot
- Camille
- Carlito's Way
- Chapter Two
- Circle of Friends
- Color of Night

- Dances with Wolves
- Dance with Me
- Dark Victory
- Don Juan DeMarco
- Dying Young
- The Enchanted Cottage
- The English Patient
- Ever After
- Firelight
- Forget Paris
- Four Weddings and a Funeral
- French Kiss
- Gigi
- Grease
- The Heiress
- Holiday Inn
- Intermezzo
- IQ
- Key Largo
- The King and I
- The Lady in Red
- Last of the Mohicans
- Legends of the Fall
- Like Water for Chocolate

(More) Great Date Movies

500p

* *Lonesome Dove*
* *The Long Hot Summer*
* *Lovers—A True Story*
* *The Mask of Zorro*
* *Michael*
* *The Mirror Has Two Faces*
* *Moonstruck*
* *Mr. Skeffington*
* *Muriel's Wedding*
* *My Fair Lady*
* *Nine-1/2 Weeks*
* *Notorious*
* *Now, Voyager*
* *Oklahoma!*
* *On Golden Pond*
* *One Fine Day*
* *Only You*
* *Out of Africa*
* *Polish Wedding*
* *Pretty Woman*
* *Raintree County*
* *Rebel Without a Cause*
* *Roman Holiday*
* *Sabrina (with Bogart & Hepburn)*

* *Sabrina (with Julia Ormond & Harrison Ford)*
* *Saturday Night Fever*
* *Scent of a Woman*
* *Seems Like Old Times*
* *Sense and Sensibility*
* *Singin' in the Rain*
* *Six Days, Seven Nights*
* *Sleepless in Seattle*
* *Sommersby*
* *Speechless*
* *Splendor in the Grass*
* *Star Wars*
* *Suddenly Last Summer*
* *Summertime*
* *The Philadelphia Story*
* *The Wedding Singer*
* *To Have and Have Not*
* *Top Hat*
* *Up Close and Personal*
* *Waterloo Bridge*
* *West Side Story*
* *White Christmas*
* *Why Do Fools Fall in Love*
* *Wuthering Heights*

"Love conquers all"—even war—in Hollywood: in 1999 the Oscar for Best Picture went to *Shakespeare In Love*, not to *Saving Private Ryan*.

Gift Ideas (I)

501

Get her something that she's always wanted to have, but always held back on . . . because it was too expensive, too impractical, too weird or too self-indulgent.

502

Music boxes! Find them in gift shops, or get a cool catalog from The San Francisco Music Box Company. Call 800-227-2190. Their music boxes are beautiful, and they have *hundreds* of songs to choose from.

503

- ✦ The gift: A bottle of "Passion" cologne.
- ✦ The activity: A night of passion.
- ✦ The background music: "Passion," by Rod Stewart.

- ➻ The gift: Costume jewelry.
- ➻ The note: "The diamond is *fake*—but the love is *real*."
- ➻ The song: "Diamond Girl," by Seals & Crofts.

- ✳ The gift: A potted cactus.
- ✳ The note: "I'm stuck on you."
- ✳ The song: "Stuck on You," by Lionel Richie.

What's the difference between a "gift" and a "present"?
See index listing to find out.

504

Doesn't he deserve a trophy for being the "World's Best Lover"? Doesn't she merit a loving cup to celebrate her latest accomplishment?

Trophy shops have a wealth of ideas waiting for you. Just think of the romantic possibilities of plaques, medals, ribbons, nameplates, certificates and banners. And they all can be personalized, engraved, lettered or monogrammed.

Gift Ideas (II)

505

Romantic songs and romantic movies go together:

✳ Get the song "Some Enchanted Evening," by Jay & the Americans—
✳ And rent the movie *South Pacific*, featuring the song.
✳ Or—surprise your partner with tickets to the musical.

➤ Get the song "Summer Nights," by John Travolta & Olivia Newton-John—
➤ And rent the movie *Grease*, featuring the song.
➤ Or—surprise your partner with tickets to the musical.

506

Give her a *variety* of jewelry:

✳ Rings   ✳ Pins
✳ Bracelets   ✳ Ankle bracelets
✳ Necklaces   ✳ Toe rings
✳ Earrings   ✳ Hair accessories
✳ Watches   ✳ Belly button rings

Gift Giving for Dummies

507

Don't buy practical items for gifts. Appliances are wonderful, but *don't give them as gifts for birthdays, anniversaries or for any event that is in any way a romantic occasion!* (My father-in-law learned this lesson the hard way. For their very first Christmas together, he gave his wife . . . an electric broom. She still tells the story, thirty-seven years later.)

Exceptions to the "No Practical Gifts" Rule:

1) Gourmet kitchen utensils for cooks.
2) Garden implements for gardeners.
3) Tools for handymen.

508

Don't forget about charm bracelets. They bring good memories alive, and they provide a built-in gift idea for any occasion.

509

Gifts for *her:* Anything from Crabtree and Evelyn. Take my word for it. Visit a nearby bath shop, or find a Crabtree and Evelyn boutique, or call them at 800-CRABTREE; or visit www.Crabtree-Evelyn.com.

510

He was a golf fanatic. She was a chocoholic. She gave him a Ping putter with this inscription engraved on the shaft:

"I love you more than chocolate."

He gave her a dozen boxes of Godiva's chocolate golf balls. The enclosed note read:

"I love you more than golf."

Discuss with your lover the chapter "Memorize This List." It will inspire many great gift ideas.

Gift *Wrapping* for Dummies

511

Creative gift wrapping:

* Use Sunday comics for wrapping paper.
* Use cartons of Ben & Jerry's Ice Cream for boxes.
* Use *real flowers* instead of bows.

512

Be prepared to *gift-wrap* your gifts. Remember: The *presentation* is nearly as important as the gift itself. You do a great disservice to yourself as well as to your partner when you're too casual about how you prepare and offer your gifts and presents. Nicely wrapped gifts have *twice* the impact as those that are poorly presented. Thus, have extra wrapping paper, bows, ribbon and boxes around at all times.

513

Wrap your anniversary gifts in wedding paper.

514

Buy *several* heart-shaped boxes of Valentine chocolates. Dump out the chocolates and *save the boxes* for later in the year. (Note: It is nearly *impossible* to buy heart-shaped boxes at any time of the year other than early February.) Use these fancy heart-shaped boxes for wrapping birthday gifts and anniversary surprises.

Wrap all her gifts in her favorite color.

"The manner of giving is worth more than the gift."

~ Pierre Corneille

Television

515

When it comes to TV, less is more. Now, I don't expect you to reduce your TV watching to zero. (Heaven forbid!) But here's a realistic approach to reducing your TV habit and freeing up some significant time for yourself and your partner:

Without a doubt the most romantic TV show: Mad About You.

- ✦ Pick three shows that you often watch but which you could easily do without. Cut them out altogether.
- ✦ Don't watch *any* reruns!
- ✦ If you watch the news, do chores at the same time. The news doesn't need your full attention, and this kind of multi-tasking will further save you time.
- ✦ Never watch anything while it's being broadcast. Tape all the shows you want to watch on your VCR. First, this allows you to zap out the commercials, saving you about eleven minutes per hour of TV-viewing time. And second, this gives you control over *when* you watch TV.

Definition of a "Quickie":
Making love during a commercial break.

516

Are you tired of running to the video store for your fix of romantic movies? Why not simply watch the romantic classics on Romance Classics TV? (From the AMC/American Movie Classic people.)

517

Make a "Mission Impossible" tape.

- ■ "Your assignment, should you choose to accept it . . . is to meet a handsome, dark-haired stranger for a romantic dinner at the elegant Posh Café, tomorrow evening at 7 p.m. I suggest you take on the role of a mysterious and ravishing beauty . . ."
- ■ Leave the cassette tape in a Walkman with a note, "Play me."

Create a romantic surprise based on your lover's favorite TV show!

Radio

518

Call a local radio station and request a special love song to be dedicated to your partner. Make sure she's listening!

519

Schedule a weekly Saturday evening date to visit Lake Wobegon together, by listening to America's most romantic humorist and storyteller, Garrison Keillor. Tune in for two hours to *A Prarie Home Companion* on your local public radio station.

520

If your partner loves to sing in the shower or sing along while the radio blares in the car, here's a great gift for him/her: The Thompson Vocal Eliminator electronically removes virtually all of a lead vocal from a stereo record, cassette or CD, while leaving the backgound music. Call LT Sound at 770-482-4532; write to 7980 LT Parkway, Lithonia, Georgia 30058; or visit www.LTsound.com.

521

Many people have told me that their best romantic memories are car related. We all drove to and from our dates with the radio on. We all went parking on Lovers Lane with the radio providing mood music.

Re-connect with those romantic memories by creating a custom cassette tape of music that was popular during your dating years.

➤ Insert the tape in her car stereo. Set it so the first song begins as soon as she turns on the ignition. (What a great surprise!)
➤ Or go for a leisurely ride in the country and listen to the tape together. (What a great, nostalgic date!)

To help you create a soundtrack to your own personal love affair, bring home some new music once a month:

January: *Power of Love*, Luther Vandross

February: *Past Light*, William Ackerman

March: *Forever Friends*, Justo Almario

April: *Distant Fields*, Gary Lamb

May: *Lifestyle*, John Klemmer

June: *Livin' Inside Your Love*, George Benson

July: *Sun Singer*, Paul Winter

August: *Summer*, George Winston

September: *Heartstrings*, Earl Klugh

October: *Openings*, William Ellwood

November: *Feels So Good*, Chuck Mangione

December: *Something of Time*, Nightnoise

1-800-ROMANCE

522

* ❊ 800-762-6677—for balloon-o-grams
* ❊ 800-543-1949—for a romantic trip on a Mississippi riverboat
* ❊ 800-CRABTREE—for great bath accessories
* ❊ 800-214-9463—for wine with custom labels
* ❊ 800-444-3356—to have a custom romance novel written
* ❊ 800-SANDALS—for couples-only Caribbean vacations
* ❊ 800-888-4652—for all kinds of fun ink stamps
* ❊ 800-282-3333—to name a star after your lover
* ❊ 800-MARRIAGE—for *Marriage* magazine
* ❊ 800-919-3990—for Amor Music
* ❊ 800-322-0344—for gifts from The Smithsonian
* ❊ 800-829-2327—for the Vermont Teddy Bear Co.
* ❊ 800-LOVEBOAT—for Princess Cruise Line
* ❊ 800-888-0987—for games and puzzles
* ❊ 800-345-5655—for Harry & David gourmet foods
* ❊ 800-795-5683—to attend a Marriage Encounter weekend
* ❊ 800-3-STOOGE—for Three Stooges stuff
* ❊ 800-423-9494—for lingerie
* ❊ 800-888-8200—for *more* lingerie
* ❊ 800-323-9525—for *still more* lingerie
* ❊ 800-FARE-OFF—for the *Travel Smart* newsletter
* ❊ 800-233-4499—for worldwide adventure travel
* ❊ 800-JIGSAWS—for very cool jigsaw puzzles
* ❊ 800-637-0098—for gifts for lawyers
* ❊ 800-862-8537—for hot air balloon adventures in Europe

Chapter Theme Song:

"Had to Phone Ya," The Beach Boys

www.romance.com

523

- ✦ www.JewelryInfo.org—to learn how to choose *quality* jewelry
- ✦ www.StarRegistry.com—to name a star after your lover
- ✦ www.tunes.com—for music info from *Rolling Stone* magazine
- ✦ www.1800flowers.com—for flowers
- ✦ www.ProFlowers.com—for flowers
- ✦ www.ThreeStooges.com—for—*nyuk, nyuk, nyuk*—Stooge stuff!
- ✦ www.eps.org.uk—for info on The Erotic Print Society
- ✦ www.Perfumania.com—for a *huge* selection of perfumes
- ✦ www.VictoriasSecret.com—for lingerie
- ✦ www.EveryCD.com—for music CDs
- ✦ www.VirginMega.com—for music CDs
- ✦ www.Godiva.com—for world-class chocolates
- ✦ www.SharperImage.com—for all kinds of cool and techie stuff
- ✦ www.imdb.com—for The Internet Movie Database
- ✦ www.isbn.nu—for hard-to-find books
- ✦ www.addall.com—for out-of-print books
- ✦ www.bibliofind.com—for used books
- ✦ www.YourNovel.com—for a custom romance novel
- ✦ www.CreativeWorksStudios.net—to have a song custom written
- ✦ www.LandsEnd.com—for outdoorsy/casual clothes
- ✦ www.AuctionWatch.com—for all kinds of things being auctioned
- ✦ www.BestFares.com—for an international travel club
- ✦ www.CultureFinder.com—to see what's doing in lots of cities
- ✦ www.LuxuryLink.com—for auctions of high-end vacations
- ✦ www.InnCrawler.com—for bed and breakfasts
- ✦ www.BedAndBreakfast.com—for more B&Bs
- ✦ www.Virtual Florist.com—to send virtual bouquets and messages
- ✦ www.RosaScript.com—for original botanical artwork, customizable

And then there's always
www.1001WaysToBeRomantic.com

Concepts (I)

524

Major concept!

Do you know the difference between the "urgent" and the "important"? Mixing them up causes us to lose sight of our true priorities and the really important things in our lives.

The *urgent* is what demands your attention *right now:* Deadlines, details and short-term priorities. It *may* be what's important to you, but more often it reflects the priorities of *others*.

The *important* is what reflects *your* priorities and values. It is more long-term in nature and therefore easier to defer.

Love is *important*—car troubles are *urgent*. Beware of the *urgent* eclipsing the *important* in your life!

525

Are you stuck in a "romantic stalemate"— where each partner is holding back, waiting for the other to make the first move? Consider this: Making the first move isn't giving in— rather, it's the more assertive, more loving, and more risky thing to do. (Doesn't look like a sign of weakness to me!)

A "relationship" is an entity. It is a living, growing thing. This isn't just a poetic metaphor; I mean it literally. A *relationship* is something new that is created when two separate people decide to become a couple. The relationship is connected to and related to each individual, but it is still separate from the individuals involved. (There's *you*, there's *me*, and there's this mysterious, undefinable, invisible-yet-very-real thing that we call *us*.) And just as each individual person needs time, attention and care, so does the relationship.

526

Beware of the phenomenon of "Relationship Entropy"—the tendency of relationships to become more diffuse if not cared for and nurtured; the tendency for once-close lovers to drift apart if both of them don't work at it on a consistent basis. (File under "Better Relationships Through Physics Concepts.")

Concepts (II)

527

Occasional romance is "nice," but it's limited. *Romance-over-time* is what it's *really* all about. Why? Because consistency of romantic effort reflects your commitment to your partner. Because it shows that he/she is a top priority in your life.

528

Romantic love consists of a triad of passion, commitment and intimacy. Let's take a quick look at how these ingredients combine and recombine at different stages in a relationship.

Passion usually takes the lead during dating. Commitment may be non-existent, and intimacy is just a potential. As the relationship progresses, commitment and intimacy twist and turn around one another, building a framework for further relationship growth. Spurred on by passion, commitment often turns serious, and marriage results. Newlywed passion usually carries the relationship for a year or two, while commitment is assumed, and intimacy builds. When the inevitable challenges and temptations arise, it is hoped that the commitment is strong enough, and the intimacy deep enough, to sustain the relationship.

Passion, commitment and intimacy all come under fire from a variety of outside sources: Jobs, friends, money issues, children, etc. Some of the challenges come from *internal* sources: Insecurity, lack of self-esteem, fear, immaturity, lack of experience, etc.

The combined strength of the passion/commitment/intimacy will determine the fate of the relationship. If commitment is strong but passion weak, the couple will "hang in there" but will not be particularly happy. If passion and commitment are strong but intimacy is weak, the couple will stay together but fail to grow. The happiest couples are able to achieve a *dynamic balance* of passion, commitment and intimacy.

Feminine/organic metaphor:

Making romantic gestures is like watering the flower of your relationship. Don't let it wilt!

Masculine/mechanical metaphor:

Romance is like working on your car. Imagine this: You just got your dream car—a new red Ferrari F50. You fill it with gas, wax it up—and that's all you need to do in order to keep driving it for the next twenty years, right? *Wrong!* Relationships work the same way. They need to be fueled, tuned up, tinkered with and polished regularly.

Erotica (I)

529

In case you were wondering (and I *know* how you think): The most *sexually suggestive flower* is the Hibiscus. (And because I know how curious you are, Cala Lilies come in a close second.)

Osculate! Often.

530

Bob used to tease his wife, Tricia, saying she was "pretty as a playmate." She was flattered, but said she was too shy to be a *playmate*—but perhaps she'd be his *pin-up girl.* So Bob began calling her his "Pin-Up Girl." It was just a private little thing until . . . Tricia hired a local artist to paint a pin-up portrait of *her,* in the Vargas airbrush style from the 1940s. She surprised Bob with it on his fortieth birthday. To say that he was "surprised and pleased and amazed and thrilled" is an understatement!

"Love is its own aphrodisiac and is the main ingredient for lasting sex."

- Mort Katz

531

Create an "Erotic Fantasy Jar." On fifty little squares of paper describe some fantasies. Make some subtly erotic, make some blatantly sexy, make some for him, make some for her, make some quickies, make some long and luxurious, make some visual, make some auditory, make some tasty, make some favorites, make some surprises.

Once a week you take turns picking an idea out of the jar.

532

Don't leave lovemaking until just before sleeping! Why is it so often the last item on the list? (Why do so many people have their priorities so screwed-up? How could those silly household chores possibly be more important than being intimate with your lover?)

Chapter Theme Song:

"Bedroom Eyes," Eddie Rabbitt

Erotica (II)

533

One man in the Romance Class told us how an accidental wine spill resulted in an erotic tradition celebrated regularly with his wife. She'd spilled a glass of wine on her new silk blouse. Instead of being upset, she thought about it for a second, grabbed *his* wine glass, emptied it down the front of her blouse, and said, "If you want it, come and get it!" (They've since graduated to cordials!)

534

Do you *know* what your partner finds erotic? Or do you *assume* you know? Do you figure she likes what your *last* girlfriend enjoyed? Do you think he's just like the guy described in last month's *Cosmo?* Do you believe everything you read in *Penthouse Letters?*

* Talk about what each of you considers erotic.
* Set your inhibitions and judgments aside.
* Describe what you experience as sexy and erotic.
* Be open to new ways of looking at sexuality.

Gals—

Pose on a bed of *black* silk sheets wearing *white* silk lingerie.

Pose on a bed of *white* silk sheets wearing *black* silk lingerie.

535

When choosing erotic movies . . . it may be helpful to remember that men and women often have different definitions of "erotic." Women like the smoldering passion of *The Bridges of Madison County* or *Like Water for Chocolate*. For men, you can pretty much sum up their taste in erotic movies in two words: "Nude blonde." Think of the erotic thrillers *Basic Instinct* or *Body Double*.

536

Drip honey on various parts of your lover's body. Lick it off. (Wine and cordials work nicely, too.)

Happy Birthday! (I)

537

Send her a birthday card *every day for a month* preceding her birthday.

538

Find and record a bunch of "birthday" and "age-related" songs for him or her. Like "You Say It's Your Birthday" from the Beatles' "White Album." I've conducted a little musical research on your behalf, and here's what I've come up with:

* "Happy Birthday," Stevie Wonder
* "Happy Birthday," New Kids on the Block
* "Happy Birthday," Altered Images
* "Happy Birthday to You," Bing Crosby
* "Happy Birthday to You," Eddy Howard
* "Happy Birthday to You," Sunsetters
* "Young At Heart," Frank Sinatra
* "I Wish I Were 18 Again," George Burns
* "When I'm Sixty-Four," The Beatles

539

Original magazines from the week or month of his or her birthdate make great birthday gifts. (If, of course, your partner isn't overly sensitive about his/her age!) Try a local used bookstore.

540

If your partner is sensitive about his or her age, but you still want to find some way to celebrate, here's a solution: Count *blessings* instead of *years*. You could make lists on scrolls of things that the two of you are thankful for. You could focus on a different blessing at each celebration. You could take turns creating the list. You could celebrate several times a year.

If your lover is turning thirty, give him/her the soundtrack from the TV show *thirtysomething*. Then use the music as the soundtrack for the birthday party.

Fun and insightful: *Love Cards: What Your Birthday Reveals About You & Your Personal Relationships*, by Robert Camp.

Happy Birthday! (II)

541

Use *sparklers* instead of candles on his birthday cake.

542

Get him an actual newspaper from the day he was born! The Historic Newspaper Archives has newspapers from more than fifty U.S. cities, including *The New York Times*, *The Wall Street Journal* and *The Los Angeles Times*. These are authentic, well-preserved editions of the entire original newspapers. Call 732-381-2332; or visit www.Historic Newspaper.com.

543

If you're not satisfied with celebrating birthdays just *once* a year, you can always celebrate *half-birthdays* every six months!

A basic romantic concept: Birthday cards. Some twists:

* Send a card a day for a week, a month.
* Send as many cards as the number of years in his age.
* Send twenty-five cards—all on the same day.
* Hide cards in his briefcase, in the refrigerator.
* Create your own birthday cards.
  * Make them simple, with crayons or markers.
  * Make them elaborate, created on your computer.
* Write a birthday greeting on a cake—or on a pizza.
* Make a poster-sized card.
* Rent a billboard: Create a HUGE birthday card.
* Have the message written in beautiful calligraphy.

544

Convince her boss to call her at home at six o'clock on the morning of her birthday—to give her the day off!

Chapter Theme Song:
"Birthday," The Beatles

Money Makes the World Go 'Round

545

"How can I be romantic when money's tight?" many guys ask me. "I can't afford dozens of roses or expensive dinners or diamonds," they complain.

Actually, a shortage of money can be a *good thing* when it comes to romance. Why? Because it forces you to be more creative, to give more of yourself, to spend time instead of money. Love *never* dies because of lack of money, but it *often* dies because of boredom and neglect.

546

➤ A gift certificate to Tiffany's.
➤ A one-hour shopping spree with no budget limit!
➤ Dinner at every five-star restaurant in America.

547

Speaking of money . . . Did you know that you can write a check on *anything?* As long as you include all the important numbers on the item, it's legal, and the bank has to cash it!

➡ One guy presented his wife with a check written on a mattress!
➡ Another wrote a check on a pair of panties.

548

It was nearly midnight on a hot August night. They were watching TV together. Stu nudged his wife gently and whispered, "Let's make love outside on the back porch." "Not tonight! What if the kids hear us?" Peggy exclaimed. "C'mon, honey," he said, "Look, I'll give you a *hundred dollars* if you do!" he grinned wickedly. "Stop teasing!" she chided. He opened his wallet and waved a fistful of twenties at her. She hesitated. She smiled. She grabbed the money and headed for the porch.

Chapter Theme Song:

"If I Had a Million Dollars,"
by Barenaked Ladies

Love Makes the World Go 'Round

549

The "Romance Credit Card" is a cool concept created by a couple in one of my Romance Classes. Here's how it works:

You create your own "bank" which issues two types of credit: Money and time. On a quarterly basis the bank's officers (the two of you) meet to establish your credit limits. When money is tight, issue more *time*. When time is tight, make more *money* available.

Design, laminate and carry in your wallets the Romance Credit Card. It's a reminder that you have an obligation to spend time and money on your relationship on a regular basis. (Some couples keep their credit card balances on a chart on the refrigerator.)

550

Cynthia and Robert were sharing their answers for the "Memorize This List" chapter in this book. When Robert asked Cynthia what her favorite color was, she answered, "The rainbow." This might have stumped a lesser man, but being a creative romantic, here are some of the rainbow-related gifts Robert has given her:

* A crystal prism
* A poster showing a beautiful landscape with a rainbow overhead
* Many kaleidoscopes
* A box of Crayola Crayons (the big, 64-crayon box)
* A trip to Niagara Falls, where rainbows can be seen in the mist

(Robert is currently looking for a used spectrometer from a school or laboratory for Cynthia's next birthday.)

*Love may make the world go 'round, but it's **romantic love** that makes the ride worthwhile.*

Do It Outside

551

Watch a sunset together. It's a great way to change gears at the end of the day. It will slow you down and help you get reconnected with each other.

You may want to conduct some research to find the very best location from which to watch the sun set in your area. It might be an obvious hill, or it might be a subtle slope that you've never noticed before. Or it might be the roof of a building.

552

Go hiking. Go tobogganing! Go to a ballgame. Go to a state park. Go to an outdoor public garden. Go to an outdoor concert. Go on a picnic. Go for a ride in the country. Go for a walk. Go for it!

553

(Make love in your backyard at midnight.)

554

Go camping! Borrow friends' equipment for starters. If you enjoy it, buy your own stuff. (Make sure you include a *double* sleeping bag on your equipment list.)

555

When's the last time you played miniature golf? Go match your skill and have a good time.

Chapter Theme Song:

"Physical," Olivia Newton-John

Do It In Public

556

Do you praise her in public? When's the last time you told someone else how lucky you feel to have this woman in your life? Complimenting her in front of someone else will make her feel extra special.

557

Whisper sweet nothings in her ear while out in public.

➤ Whisper compliments; call her by her pet name.
➤ Whisper *shocking* comments and outright lewd suggestions! (The more formal the gathering, the more outrageous or suggestive your whispered messages should be. The juxtaposition of a stuffy event with the whispered raw passion of your feelings for her should add a little spark to the entire evening!)

558

Do you remember what teenagers used to call "PDAs"—Public Displays of Affection? Are you out of the habit of showing affection for your partner in public? Hold hands. Rest your hand on his shoulder. Entwine your arm with hers.

Chapter Theme Song:
"Tell Her (You Love Her Every Day),"
Frank Sinatra

Just Do It!

559

Have you ever dreamed of taking off with your partner for a fun-filled *four week vacation* touring all of Europe—but you only get *two weeks* paid vacation? Bummer.

Here's what you do: Go *anyway*. Don't let yourself be constrained by your employer's tightwad two-week vacation policy! Simply take an additional two weeks off *without pay*. I know that this is a radical thing for most people to *think* about, much less *do*—but I urge you to consider it. Create a savings plan that will allow you to do this. It might take a year, it might take five. But it will be well worth it!

560

Which ten ideas in this book do you think your lover would love most? Don't simply jot them down somewhere—write them directly into your appointment calendar, and schedule time to perform the gestures or buy the gifts.

Sally used to complain that Jack never complimented her. After pondering this, Jack realized, "It's not that I don't *love* you, or that I don't have nice things to say. It's just that I never think to say them *on my own*." With that insight, he instituted "Dial-A-Compliment" just for her. Sally could call him any time of the day or night and receive a spontaneous and heartfelt compliment!

561

Romantics are always "dating."

"Dating" is a *mindset* as much as it is an activity for singles. Married people who continue "dating" their spouses are among the happiest people in the world.

➤ Don't just go out to a movie on Saturday, like always. Call her from work on Wednesday and *formally* ask her out on a date.

➤ Many people with A+ Relationships have told me that they hold "date nights" on a weekly basis.

Chapter Theme Song:

"Do It," by Neil Diamond

Just a Little Bit Naughty

562

Exhibitionism for the Shy. What an enticing book title! What a cool concept! This awesome book demonstrates how to turn sexual modesty to your erotic advantage! As author Carol Queen says, "To discover a new world of erotic experience, you don't have to shed your inhibitions—you just have to exploit them creatively." This book is a serious exploration and guide book. (No sleazy pictures. In fact, no pictures at all!) In bookstores or call 800-289-8423, or visit www.GoodVibes.com.

563

For women only: When you're dressed up and out together, secretly hand him your panties under the table. Watch his expression.

*I'll be shocked if he's not **absolutely delighted!***

564

If your lover's not shy, you might want to try *nude sunbathing*. Its many practitioners praise the sense of freedom, healthfulness and back-to-nature benefits of baring it all in public.

❧ *Free Beaches,* a guide to nude beaches located around the world is available from The Naturist Society. Call 920-426-5009; write P.O. Box 132, Oshkosh, Wisconsin 54902; or visit www.naturist.com.
❧ Call the American Association for Nude Recreation at 800-879-6833; 1703 North Main Street, Kissimmee, Florida 34744; or visit www.aanr.com.

565

The Erotic Print Society sells classic and contemporary limited-edition prints, books and gifts. At www.eps.org.uk. Or at EPS, Dept. 1001, P.O. Box 10645, London SW10 9ZT, United Kingdom. Or call +44-(0)171-351 6955; or fax +44-(0)171-244 8999.

Chapter Theme Song:
"Feel Like Makin' Love," Bad Company

The Gift of Time

566

*Just **imagine** the possibilities!*

Your partner wants more of *you*, not more "stuff"!

Once every two months give her an entire day of your time. She gets total control over how to use that time. Now, ask her for the same, during the alternate months.

567

* You can *save* time by shopping via catalog.
* You can *reorganize* time by "chore-shifting."
* You can *create* time by "doubling up" on activities.
* You can *use time better* by buying a book on time-management.
* You can *release* time by hiring a housecleaning service.
* You can *make* time by adjusting your sleeping habits.
* You can *appreciate* time by simplifying your life.
* You can *find* time by planning better.

"Any time that is not spent on love is wasted."

- Torquato Tasso

568

"Double-up" on activities. Combine various activities and you'll find more time to be together:

* Meet for lunch. (You have to eat anyway, right?!)
* Eat dinner and watch a romantic movie on video.
* Do chores *together:* Go grocery shopping, take the car to the shop.

569

Two hours of peace and quiet: *Possibly the best gift you could ever give someone!*

Time for Love

570

Don't go grocery shopping on *Friday night!* Don't do laundry on *Saturday morning!* Those are *valuable times*—times you could be spending *together*.

Practice "chore-shifting."

- ✦ Find ways to shift chores to more efficient times.
- ✦ Do two chores at the same time.
- ✦ Do chores *together:* Doubling the person-power more than doubles the efficiency!

571

Once a week: Bring home Chinese take-out, or have pizza delivered. Streamline your dinner hour—then use the time you saved *romantically*.

Domino's to the rescue!

572

Learn to appreciate time; learn to redefine time; learn to put more love into the time you have. Read this book, it's fabulous: *Time and the Art of Living*, by Robert Grudin.

- ✳ Review your calendars and commitments together. Plan "dates."
- ✳ Plan surprises well in advance.
- ✳ Always have your "Gift Closet" well stocked.

573

Make time in the morning to make love. Get up an hour early!

Chapter Theme Song:
"Time After Time," Cyndi Lauper

For Singles Only (I)

574

You've been dating a while, you're considering "getting serious," but you're not sure that he's really everything you're looking for. How do you evaluate the relationship? With this simple formula:

70% + spark = Go for it!

In other words, if this person has at least 70% of the qualities you want your ideal partner to have, plus you have "spark" (passion and romance; you're soul-mates; you "click")—go for it! You *know* you're not going to get 100% (there ain't no Prince Charming!)—but you'd better not settle for less than 50%!

575

What's a "Ping"??

Listen for "Pings."

And what are Pings? They're any action or habit your partner has that you *just know you couldn't live with for the rest of your life.* For example:

✦ You're in the car, scanning radio stations for some classical music. You cringe when you hear "Stayin' Alive," but she squeals "Oh, I *love* the Bee Gees!" *(Ping!)*

✦ He told you to prepare for a "special night out" because he's got "box seat tickets." Expecting to attend the symphony and dine at the Posh Café, you spend hours getting ready, and dress in your classiest outfit. He shows up in jeans with two tickets to the Red Sox game. *(Ping!!)*

Note: One person's Ping may be another person's cherished quirk. Pings are relative things!

For Singles Only (II)

576

Guys: When giving jewelry, never, never, *never* package it in a ring box, unless it's an engagement ring. You're probably totally unaware of it, but those little square boxes spell one thing to women: M-A-R-R-I-A-G-E. Ask the jeweler to give you a different kind of box, or present the piece in a creative way. Why ask for trouble?

577

+ If you've talked about maybe moving in together, and you decide you want to go for it, place your apartment key in a gift box, wrap it up and give it to her.
+ Or—mail it to her with a note: "You already own the key to my heart . . . now I want you to have *this* key."

578

Advice for the guys:

◆ How to *catch* her: Learn to dance.
◆ How to *keep* her: Learn to cook.

If you don't believe me, guys, go ask some women.

579

Mail her a copy of your business resumé instead of a greeting card. Attach a note: "I'd like you to get to know me better." (Other fun stuff to send: A grammar school report card. A photo of yourself as a baby.)

For Marrieds Only (I)

580

On a Saturday afternoon, nonchalantly say to your partner, "If I had it to do all over again, I'd marry you *again*. As a matter of fact, let's do just that!" Then grab him or her and run down to your local church (where you've already planned things with the pastor), and hold a quick little re-dedication ceremony. Surprise! (You may want to use the song "Let's Get Married Again," by John Conlee.)

581

*If this doesn't bring tears to her eyes, **nothing** will!*

Guys: On your wedding anniversary, re-create her wedding bouquet. Since you probably don't know a chrysanthemum from poison ivy, show one of your wedding photos to your florist.

582

Dig out your wedding album. Have a new eight-by-ten-inch print made of the best photo of your bride. Wrap it up and give it to *yourself* for your birthday or for Christmas.

Read *The Case for Marriage*, by Maggie Gallagher & Linda Waite.

583

+ Have your wedding invitation professionally framed. Keep it on your nightstand.
+ For your tenth, twentieth and thirtieth wedding anniversaries, create a formal invitation to your spouse to join you for *another* ten years of marriage.

Chapter Theme Song:

"Darlin' Companion," Johnny Cash

For Marrieds Only (II)

584

✳ In the middle of a party or other social event, turn to her and whisper, "You're the *best*."
✳ While walking down the street together, turn to her and whisper, "I'm glad I married you."
✳ While driving somewhere together, turn to her and say, "I can't imagine my life without you in it."

585

Make an artistic collage of photos and memorabilia from your wedding.

586

Carry a copy of your wedding license in your wallet, right next to your driver's license.

587

Songs that celebrate love and marriage. Make a tape for an anniversary, a birthday or just to celebrate your love next Tuesday.

❤ "Love & Marriage" Frank Sinatra
❤ "I Married an Angel," George Siravo
❤ "Marriage Made in Heaven," Bob Crewe
❤ "Be My Wife," David Bowie
❤ "Happily Married Man," Duane Allman
❤ "Husbands & Wives," Neil Diamond
❤ "Longer," Dan Fogelberg
❤ "Make My Life with You," Oak Ridge Boys
❤ "Marriage," Ted Nugent
❤ "Never My Love," The Association
❤ "You'll Accomp'ny Me," Bob Seger and the Silver Bullet Band

"Happiness is being married to your best friend."

~ ANONYMOUS

Attend a Marriage Encounter weekend. Call 800-795-5683.

Join the Association for Couples in Marriage Enrichment. Call 336-724-1526.

Merry Christmas

588

✳ A gift-a-day for the twelve Days of Christmas.

✳ Or—go *all out* . . .

On the first day of Christmas, my true love gave to me—
 A red rose in a bud vase.
On the second day of Christmas, my true love gave to me—
 Two bottles of champagne.
On the third day of Christmas, my true love gave to me—
 Three French kisses.
On the fourth day of Christmas, my true love gave to me—
 Four nights of dancing.
On the fifth day of Christmas, my true love gave to me—
 Five golden rings!
On the sixth day of Christmas, my true love gave to me—
 Six bubble baths.
On the seventh day of Christmas, my true love gave to me—
 Seven movie passes.
On the eighth day of Christmas, my true love gave to me—
 Eight Beanie Babies.
On the ninth day of Christmas, my true love gave to me—
 Nine romance coupons for back rubs.
On the tenth day of Christmas, my true love gave to me—
 Ten shares of Microsoft stock.
On the eleventh day of Christmas, my true love gave to me—
 Eleven heart-shaped balloons.
On the twelfth day of Christmas, my true love gave to me—
 Twelve CDs by The Beatles.

Some Christmas tree ornament ideas:

Create a garland of one-dollar bills taped together.

Take the CD discs out of their cases and hang them on the tree as shiny ornaments.

Have a relevant, holiday-oriented comic strip laminated, and hang it on the tree.

Have a favorite poem or quote written in calligraphy, and turn it into an inspirational ornament.

589

One woman came to her marriage with a vast collection of very special Christmas tree ornaments. Her husband jumped on the bandwagon, and they now have a ritual "Search for This Year's Special Ornament."

Happy Hanukkah

590

In celebration of the "Festival of Lights":

* Light your home with hundreds of candles.
* Choose a menorah that holds special meaning for your partner.
* Write a poem about how he/she is the "light of your life."

591

Celebrate the eight days of Hanukkah:

Day 1: Give a gift that reflects your religious beliefs.
Day 2: Give a gift of one hour of your time.
Day 3: Give a gift that celebrates the number of years you've been together.
Day 4: Give a gift you've made by hand.
Day 5: Give a gift that acknowledges a private joke between the two of you.
Day 6: Give a gift that the two of you can share.
Day 7: Give a gift of music.
Day 8: Give an artistic gift.

An (im)modest suggestion for a Hanukkah gift: The book *Kosher Sex: A Recipe for Passion and Intimacy*, by Rabbi Shmuley Boteach.

592

Buy four dreidels. We're going to change the traditional children's game into a new *romantic* game. On each dreidel remove the traditional Hebrew letters *nun, gimel, he* and *shin*—and replace them with:

* M, Y, U, F— Which stand for *Me, You, Us* and *Family*.
* N, T, W, M—Which stand for *Now, Today,* this *Week,* this *Month*.
* D, M, P, C— Which stand for *Dinner, Movie, Picnic, Concert*.
* *You* decide how to label this one.

Here's how you play: Taking turns, one person spins one dreidel on each night of Hanukkah. The M-Y-U-F dreidel directs you to do something loving that focuses on whichever person the dreidel indicates.

Happy Anniversary

593

Identify that *one pivotal event* that brought the two of you together. Celebrate that event every year.

What brought the two of you together? Fate? Karma? Cupid? Cosmic coincidence?

594

Most couples celebrate their anniversary once a year. That's a nice, romantic thing to do.

A *few* couples celebrate their anniversary once a month. That's perhaps a little much, but it's very sweet, don't you think?

Then one day in a Romance Class I met a couple who claimed they'd celebrated 10,958 anniversaries! As they appeared to be in their mid-forties, I was politely skeptical—until they explained: They were married on August 25th—which is often written as 8/25. They translated that to 8:25 and were thus inspired to celebrate their anniversary *every day* at 8:25. And, of course (they explained matter-of-factly), it was obvious that they had to celebrate *twice* a day: First at 8:25 in the morning, and then *again* at 8:25 in the evening. (And I thought *I* was romantic!)

595

On their first wedding anniversary Michael sent Pamela a very romantic card. Pamela saved it and mailed it *back* to Michael on their *second* anniversary. Michael saved the card and mailed it back to Pamela on their *third* anniversary. This impromptu tradition began in 1949—and continues to this day. ("The cost of first-class postage is now more than the original cost of the card!" Pamela recently observed with a smile.)

Chapter Theme Song:
"Happy Anniversary," Little River Band

Happy Birthday

596

Declare it your lover's "Birthday *Month*," and do something special every day for the thirty days preceding THE day.

5/6

© 1987 Universal Press Syndicate

"What a coincidence! You forgot my birthday and I forgot how to cook."

597

How about a video celebration of the year he was born? You can get a thirty-minute taped newsreel, featuring world events, news, personalities, styles and major events from the year of your partner's birth (for the years 1929 through 1969). Cool, huh? Such a deal at only $14.95. Call Flik-Baks at 800-541-3533 or 310-823-5755; or visit www.flikbaks.com.

Custom-made

598

When you want to present your lover with some loving words rendered in artistic, beautiful, wonderful, elegant, fabulous calligraphy—call Maria Thomas, the most talented "artist of words" in America.

Call Maria or Caroline at 508-234-8827; or visit www.RosaScript.com. Or mail your copy to Rósa, P.O. Box 182, Whitinsville, Massachusetts 01588.

599

One of the Top Ten Coolest Ideas: Have an original song written and recorded for your lover!

Jim Rickert, "The Songsmith," will write and record original songs for you. The romantic possibilities are *tremendous!*

✦ The quickest and least expensive option is to choose one of his original melodies from a catalog of styles (rock, ballad, country, folk, reggae); then fill out a questionnaire that will allow him to customize the song with names, dates and personal references. Just $52.

✦ He can also write *new* lyrics for you, or set *your* words to music. This service starts at $87.

✦ He can also compose entirely *new* music from scratch for you, and record it simply or elaborately. From $175.

Normal turn-around time is only a few weeks. Call Jim at 617-471-8800; or write to The Creative Works, 49 Centre Street, Quincy, Massachusetts 02169; or visit www.CreativeWorksStudios.net.

600

If your lover is also a wine lover, why not surprise him or her with a great California wine bottled with *custom labels?* Be creative with words or artwork, and create a one-of-a-kind gift for your lover. Call Windsor Vineyards at 800-214-9463 or 415-435-3113, in Tiburon, California; or visit www.WindsorVineyards.com.

One-of-a-Kind

601

If she's a one-of-a-kind woman, why not present her with a one-of-a-kind piece of jewelry? Hire a jewelry designer, establish a budget, describe her personality and style and some of your own ideas for the piece, and let the designer give you some sketches. Then have your unique gift created for her, and present it to her with a flourish.

602

The reason why a dozen *roses* is so popular is because it works for virtually *everyone*. Roses are a great start—but how about creating a truly *personalized* bouquet?

✳ A bouquet of pencils—for a teacher, writer or journalist.
✳ A bouquet of wrenches—for a handyman.
✳ A bouquet of kitchen utensils—for a gourmet cook.
✳ A bouquet of Big Mac coupons for your junk food junkie.

603

Would you like your life to read like a romance novel? Well now it *can!* You can get a romance novel customized with you and your lover as the hero and heroine. Seven titles are available, including *Another Day in Paradise* and *Love's Bounty*. Each book will include more than twenty personal details about the two of you. Only $49.95. Call Beach House Presentations at 800-444-3356; or visit www.YourNovel.com.

604

Have a one-of-a-kind jigsaw puzzle created for your puzzle-lover. You might create a special message or propose marriage with one! Call the folks at J.C. Ayer & Co. at 781-639-8162, or visit www.ayerpuzzles.com.

Do-It-Yourself

605

Do-it-yourself: Custom-made Chinese fortune cookies! Buy a batch of them at a local Chinese/Oriental grocery store (or get some from your favorite Chinese restaurant). Pull out their fortunes with a pair of tweezers, and insert your *own* fortunes! From silly to sexy, from playful to profound, you decide!

*The more of **yourself** that you put into your gifts and gestures, the more they'll be appreciated.*

606

Make your own custom greeting cards. (Those store-bought cards are fine—I have a drawer full of them. But homemade cards are extra special.) You don't have to be artistic, just heartfelt. (Remember, she's with you not because you're Picasso, but because you're *you*.)

* Crayons and construction paper are just fine for this project.
* Create a giant, poster-sized greeting card!
* Design something cool with a graphics program on your computer.

607

What do *you* do with old greeting cards from your honey? You don't just toss them away, do you?! *Heaven forbid!* True romantics . . .

* Display them on mantles and tables.
* Set them on their desks at work.
* Have them mounted and framed.
* Put them in a scrapbook.
* Toss 'em in a file—to use in some creative way in the future.
* Paste 'em on a collage.
* And one crazy couple in my Romance Class actually wallpapered an entire room in their house with greeting cards!

"The most potent muse of all is our own inner child."

~ STEPHEN NACHMANOVITCH

Hide-And-Seek

608

Some hiding places for little love notes, Post-Its and small gifts:

* Under the pillow
* In the glove compartment
* In the medicine cabinet
* In the refrigerator
* Inside a book she's reading
* In her checkbook
* In his shirt pocket
* In her wallet
* In his briefcase
* In her purse
* In a pizza box
* Under his dinner plate
* In his sock drawer
* In his daily planner
* In the trunk of her car
* In his eyeglasses case

609

Truly mischievous romantics go to great lengths to hide gifts and notes. Herewith are some suggestions from the more off-the-wall students of my Romance Classes:

➤ Carefully open various product packages, insert the item, and carefully reseal the package. Favorite targets include cereal boxes, soup cans, ice cream cartons, bags of m&m's, candy bars, soda cans, and, of course, boxes of Cracker Jacks!
➤ Notes have appeared frozen in ice cubes, floating in punch bowls, hidden among bouquets and tied to balloons.
➤ Little gifts have been delivered via Federal Express.

You'll have as much fun as your partner will.

610

Want some suggestions for notes, gifts and trinkets to hide? Again, from Romance Class participants:

✦ Friendship rings
✦ Earrings
✦ Comic strips
✦ Hockey tickets
✦ Love Coupons
✦ Invitations to dinner
✦ Theater tickets
✦ Valentine conversation hearts

Creativity Exercises
611a

1. Give it a twist:
    Start with something basic, then give it a creative twist.

2. Change your routine:
    Shaking up your routine often leads to new ideas.

3. Consider every crazy idea that pops into your head:
    You won't use them all, but the process expands your thinking.

4. Give yourself a deadline:
    Sometimes working under pressure works!

5. Learn from your mistakes:
    Mistakes aren't really mistakes if they lead you somewhere useful.

6. Go with your strengths:
    Do what comes naturally, go with the flow.

7. Go counter to your natural strengths:
    Try something different.

8. Tap into your unconscious mind:
    There's a lot going on beneath the surface.

9. Challenge the assumptions:
    Don't assume you know it all!

10. Imagine how someone else would do it:
    How would Einstein create new ideas? Mozart? Walt Disney?

11. Use different "models" of thinking:
    Think organically; think like a cat; think like a millionaire.

12. Reframe the question:
    The question might be, "How can I be more loving?" Or it might
    be, "How can I be more spontaneous?"

13. Listen to your intuition/sixth sense/inner voice:
    Whatever you choose to call it, use it!

Cool book alert!

*The Everyday Work of Art: Awakening the
Extraordinary in Your Daily Life*, by
Eric Booth.

Exercising Your Creativity
611b

14. Admit that you're dissatisfied with the *status quo:*
    It will inspire you to find solutions.

15. Don't go it alone:
    Brainstorm romantic ideas with a group of friends.

16. Use random ideas to stimulate different avenues of thinking:
    Don't get locked into one mode of thinking!

17. Change your perspective:
    1) See the big picture, or 2) Look at the *details*.

18. Borrow (then customize) ideas:
    Borrow ideas from movies, books, products, other couples.

19. Face your fears:
    What's holding you back from being more creative? More loving?
    More spontaneous? More fun-loving?

20. Draw pictures, doodle, make diagrams:
    Use the visual, graphic side of your brain.

21. Try on a different persona:
    Think like a kid; think like a member of the opposite sex; think
    like your partner.

22. Withhold judgment:
    Generate lots and *lots* of ideas before you begin evaluating.

23. Have fun:
    Don't take it so seriously, play with ideas, be wacky.

Start with a classic romantic idea then "give it a twist."

Go Away!

612

Even if you're not newlyweds—*especially* if you're not newlyweds—visit www.world-party.com. It's the online guide to festivals and parties all over the world.

613

Combine your interest in bicycling with your passion for wine! Tour the California wine country *by bike*. Pedal at your own pace, and stop at as many as thirty-five wineries. These two firms offer five-day guided bicycle tours through the Napa Valley and Sonoma County:

* Backroads Bicycle Touring, 800-245-3874; and www.backroads.com
* Vermont Bicycle Touring, 802-453-4811

614

+ Tour a vineyard. Or two.
+ Visit a vineyard in *every state* that produces wine—all forty-two of them!

615

What's the difference between a **vacation** *and a* **honeymoon?**

A plain old vacation is *not* the same thing as a "second honeymoon"! There's a feeling of magic and romance around a second honeymoon. How do you create one?

You start planning about a year in advance (so the anticipation builds). You buy her a stack of bride magazines (that's where all the honeymoon destination ads are). You send travel brochures to him in the mail (with your personal notes and comments written in). You buy special clothes. If you do this *right*, it'll really spice up your life—for a year or more!

Bon Voyage!

616

When vacationing together, always take along a couple of little surprise gifts. It's inexpensive, gives you something to look forward to, lets you gift-wrap ahead of time, and allows you to surprise your lover at a moment's notice.

617

All kinds of travel tips and current information are available from special newsletters about specific destinations and topics. Here are two:

➤ *La Belle France: The Sophisticated Guide to France*
An eight-page monthly newsletter. A yearly subscription is $87.
➤ *Golf Odyssey: The Guide for Discriminating Golfers*
Twelve issues a year at just $79.

Both of these information-packed newsletters are available from Travel Guide Publications. Call 800-225-7825, or write to Post Office Box 3485, Charlottesville, Virginia 22903.

618

Imagine your own "Fantasy Vacation." What's your lover's idea of the Perfect, Ultimate, Wonderful, Fantasy Vacation? Let your imaginations run wild. Keep the dream alive over the years by collecting brochures, posters and books on your Fantasy Vacation location.

With the proper planning, a little creativity, a little time, a realistic savings plan and true dedication to your vision, you can make your Fantasy Vacation come true.

"Vacations are not about 'getting away'—but about getting 'in touch'."

~ A CHINESE FORTUNE COOKIE

Cars

619

Fill his car with balloons. Red ones.

FYI: It takes 217 balloons to fill a Honda Accord.

620

When was the last time you went out *parking*? (For most of us, it was waaay back in high school.)

Rediscover the sexual rush, the thrill of being caught, the just-plain *fun* of parking! Find the local "Lovers Lane" in your town, fill the back seat of your car with pillows, and make a date for late Friday night!

621

Hang a pair of your panties on his rearview mirror.

Go for a drive in a classic VW "Love Bug."

622

Hide little one-line notes all over his car: On the sun visor, in the glove compartment, in the ash tray, in the trunk, under the hood, on the mirror, on the seat belt.

623

Wash and vacuum her car until it sparkles like new.

Sports

624

Sports fans *love* sports memorabilia. Pennants, posters, T-shirts and caps from favorite teams; signed photographs and signed balls—all make great gifts. And of course, there's always season tickets!

© 1994 Wm HOEST ENTERPRISES INC
Distributed by King Features Syndicate

"OKAY, LORETTA, I'LL SHARE MY FEELINGS...
I WANT TO WATCH THE BALLGAME."

625

For your baseball fanatic: Have a local graphic artist create a custom baseball card featuring your partner. Write your own humorous "Vital Statistics," have his/her photo scanned in, and paste it onto cardboard. (Present it to your partner by slipping it carefully into an "unopened" package of baseball cards!)

626

While he's watching sports on TV, bring him peanuts and popcorn, beer and ice cream bars. When it comes to sports fanatics, the only reasonable philosophy to adopt is, "If you can't beat 'em, join 'em!"

Dining In

627

Choose a bottle of wine for its romantic label. Tracey and I recently shared a bottle of Il Cuore Cabernet Sauvignon 1996. The label is a colorful, geometric rendering of heart shapes. The back label explains: "The original artwork for Il Cuore was created by Dan Rizzie, whose bold cubistic works are in the permanent collections of both The Metropolitan Museum and The Museum of Modern Art in New York." The label also explains that Il Cuore is Italian for "the heart." Thanks to Aficionado Cellars in Graton, Sonoma County, California.

*Slow down! Every meal doesn't need to be "romantic," but every meal **can** be an opportunity to talk and reconnect.*

628

It's romantic—but commonplace—to eat dinner by candlelight. So here's a change of pace: Eat *breakfast* by candlelight.

629

Prepare *love food* for your partner on special occasions or when he or she needs a boost. Love food is "comfort food" served with an extra helping of love. Comfort food is a highly individual thing. It might be hot oatmeal with brown sugar, served late at night. It might be a cup of hot cocoa served on a cold winter afternoon. It might be two scoops of Ben & Jerry's Rocky Road ice cream. Does your lover know what *your* comfort food is? Do you know his/hers?

630

Make a toast to one another every time you hold a wine glass. Make eye contact. Take turns making the toast. Whisper it.

Dining Out

631

Did you know that there are *two* kinds of romantic restaurants?

1. The elegant/active/often-with-great-views restaurant.
2. The small/dark/cozy-with-tiny-tables restaurant.

Which kind of restaurant does she prefer? Don't take her to *one* when she's crazy about the *other*.

632

Arrange to have a small gift delivered to your table during dinner. Picture an elegantly wrapped box presented on a silver tray.

633

Arrange to have a dozen red roses delivered to your table.

Other patrons will think you're newlyweds!

634

Hire a musician to serenade your lover at your table. Have him play one of her very favorite romantic songs.

635

Get a menu from his favorite restaurant. Turn it into a "Certificate Good for One Romantic Dinner." Mail it to him at work.

Play "footsie" under the table at an elegant restaurant.

636

Sunday brunch! Check the Sunday newspaper for restaurant listings. Ask your friends for their favorite spots.

By the Number

637

- ✦ Send **20** stuffed animals to her on her **20**th birthday.
- ✦ Send **30** red roses to him on his **30**th birthday.
- ✦ Send **40** reasons why you love her on her **40**th birthday.
- ✦ Send **50** classic love songs to him on his **50**th birthday.
- ✦ Send **60** greeting cards to her on her **60**th birthday.
- ✦ Send **70** sunflowers to him on his **70**th birthday.
- ✦ Send **80** love quotes to her on her **80**th birthday.
- ✦ Send **90** balloons to him on his **90**th birthday.
- ✦ Send **100** Hershey's Kisses to her on her **100**th birthday.

638

- ➻ Send him one birthday card for each year of his age—send them *one a day for as long as it takes*.
- ➻ Send him one birthday card for each year of his age—send them *all at one time!*

639

Variations on a Theme:

Present those 9 Beethoven symphonies with 9 red roses, 9 balloons and 9 little love notes.

- ➤ Does he *love* Beethoven? Get him recordings of all **9** symphonies.
- ➤ If it's Mozart he loves, you'll have to buy **42** symphonies.
- ➤ And if it's Haydn he loves, you're *really* in trouble, because Haydn composed an incredible **108** symphonies!

By the Book

640

Wouldn't it be cool to *publish a book for her?!* Perhaps a book of poems you've written for her. Maybe a collection of love letters. Maybe it's a book of memories the two of you have shared. Maybe it's a fictional story based on your life together. (Maybe it's an *erotic* novel!)

Armed with any computer and PageMaker or Quark software, anyone can write and design a professional-looking book. Next, design a cover (maybe hire a professional graphic designer) then call a local printer and have one copy printed up. If it's a Memory Book for your twenty-fifth wedding anniversary, or a big fiftieth Birthday Book, you may want to have copies printed for everyone who attends your party.

641

Read aloud to one another. It's a wonderful, quiet way to share time and a story. (Think of the comfort and closeness you create when reading aloud to a child.) Some favorite read-aloud books from Romance Class participants include:

* *Illusions*, by Richard Bach
* *The Lord of the Rings*, by J.R.R. Tolkien
* *The Prophet*, by Kahlil Gibran

642

Of *course* there's amazon.com and barnesandnoble.com. But additional web resources for popular books and harder-to-find books include: www.isbn.nu; www.addall.com; www.powells.com; www.fatbrain.com. And a resource that lets you search the inventories of thousands of used bookstores is www.bibliofind.com.

*Reading some good **erotic** literature aloud might be defined as "foreplay."*

Engaging Ideas

643

One guy in the Romance Class was inspired to present his girlfriend with one red rose . . . *which had a diamond ring hidden inside the unopened bud.* The rose sat on her desk for two days, where she admired it and smelled it often, before it bloomed, revealing the ring! (She nearly fainted.)

FYI

The ancient Romans believed that diamonds were splinters from falling stars with which Eros' arrows were tipped.

The ancient Greeks believed that diamonds were the tears of the gods.

644

And then there's always the classic "Diamond-Ring-in-the-Box-of-Cracker-Jacks" trick.

645

Apply for the job of "Husband"! Write an "Engagement Resumé" outlining your "goals," your desirable qualities, your qualifications and relevant experience.

646

A call for equal rights (for men)!

Engagement Rings for Men! Why should *women* be the only ones to get engagement rings??

From a modern woman's point of view: Engagement rings are public statements that you're "spoken for" or "taken." Why should *he* be running around "free"?

From a man's point of view: You just dropped several thousand dollars on a diamond—wouldn't you like her to put her money where her mouth is, too?

(A report from the "Practice What You Preach Department": Yes, my wife gave me an engagement ring. In fact, I have *three* rings. They're three coordinating bands that symbolize Love, Peace and Happiness.)

Chapter Theme Song:
"With This Ring," The Platters

Will You Marry Me?

647

Here are some of the more creative and unusual ways that some Romance Class participants have gotten engaged:

* Skywriting proposals
* Sky banner proposals
* Custom jigsaw puzzle proposals
* Videotaped proposals
* Proposals on billboards
* Proposals inside custom-made Chinese fortune cookies
* Audiotaped proposals
* Telegrammed proposals
* Using lit candles to spell-out "Will you marry me?"
* Painting the proposal on the roof, then taking her flying!

Winner, Quirkiest Proposal Award:

He giftwrapped a stack of twelve bridal magazines and said to her, "You're going to need these!"

648

A touch of class for men: Send a clever telegram to her parents, asking their permission to marry their daughter.

649

Some couples consult astrologers for the best dates and times to get engaged. (Couldn't hurt. Might help.)

Astrology?! Hey, don't knock it! With a 51% divorce rate, we need all the help we can get!

650

Gals: Make a photocopy of your hand and new engagement ring. Attach a note saying "I've got a piece of the rock." Mail it to him to show your appreciation.

651

She received an unexpected gift for no special occasion. A beautifully wrapped box from Tiffany's. She opened it to find a sterling silver tray—engraved with "Sally, will you marry me?"

Chapter Theme Song:

"Will You Marry Me?" Paula Abdul

Marriage Matters

652

One husband in the Romance Class always introduces his wife in this manner: " . . . And I'd like you to meet my *bride*, Alice." (Alice, his sixty-four-year-old wife of forty years, always blushes.)

653

Get a subscription to *Marriage Magazine*, one of America's great little secrets. I find every issue to be both inspiring and practical. Call for a subscription: 800-MARRIAGE.

654

Ten great books on marriage:

1. *The 7 Marriages of Your Marriage*, by Mel & Patricia Krantzler
2. *The Book of Marriage*, by Hermann Von Keyserling
3. *Growing a Healthy Marriage*, edited by Mike Yorkey
4. *Heart Centered Marriage*, by Sue Patton Thoele
5. *Love Between Equals: How Peer Marriage Works*, by P. Schwartz
6. *Marital Myths*, by Arnold Lazarus
7. *Marriage & Personal Development*, by Rubin & Gertrude Blanck
8. *Married People*, by Francine Klagsbrun
9. *The Mirages of Marriage*, by William Lederer & Don Jackson
10. *The Triumphant Marriage: 100 Extremely Successful Couples Reveal Secrets*, by Neil Clark Warren

655

Have your wedding vows penned in beautiful calligraphy. Have them framed. Hang them in your living room.

Chapter Theme Song:

"Forever's as Far as I'll Go," Alabama

Monogamy—*Not* Monotony

656

Have you ever noticed that most of the best movie romance occurs between *single* people? Contrary to popular belief, this is *not* because the romance ends with marriage; it's because it is simply so much easier to catch infatuation on film than it is to catch the depth, meaning and subtleties of a long-term, A+ Relationship on film.

"In real life, of course, marriage, with its subterranean motifs and trade-offs, is more fascinating and unfathomable, hence more tantalizing, than a score of love affairs. But in movie life, surfaces—faces, in fact—must tell the story, and once those faces become familiar or imply the virtues of endurance rather than the sparks of strangeness, romance loses its neccssary tension." From *The New York Times*, "The Love That's Forever: Making Matches," by Molly Haskell.

For a rare treatment of mature love, see the great movie **On Golden Pond.**

657

Create your own personal "anniversary ritual" that you re-enact every year together in a private little ceremony. You might play special music for background; you might light candles; you might read aloud to one another your original wedding vows; you might write a poem every year.

658

Get a large wardrobe box from a local moving company. Wrap the box with wrapping paper in your partner's favorite color and a giant bow. Place the box on your front porch. Hop inside. Have a friend close the lid, finish the wrapping, ring the doorbell and run.

Chapter Theme Song:
"Married," Liza Minnelli

(More) Kid Stuff

659

Buy some crayons. If you're right-handed, take a crayon in your left hand. Write a short note to him as if you were in first grade.

660

Wind-up toys are very cool: Monsters that walk and shoot sparks, creeping bugs, racing cars, crawling babies, lumbering robots. Use your creativity and wrap a little wind-up toy with a clever note. Call Lilliput at 800-TIN-TOYS, or write to 321 South Main Street, Yerington, Nevada 89447.

661

Notes to accompany stuffed animals . . .

* Teddy bears: *"I can't bear being away from you . . . "*
* Stuffed pigs: *"I'm hog-wild over you!"*
* Stuffed lions: *"I'm roarin' to get you!"*
* Stuffed tigers: *"You're Grrrrrrreat!"*
* Stuffed monkeys: *"Let's monkey around! "*

662

Go fly a kite!

Ride on a carousel.

Play a board game.

Share your favorite jokes.

Blow bubbles.

Toss a Frisbee.

Watch cloud formations.

Wish on a falling star.

➻ Visit a playground, swing together, play on the teeter-totter.
➻ Visit a playground—at midnight, under a full moon, with a bottle of fine champagne.

(More) Funny Stuff

663

Send comics to him or her at work. Work-related, hobby-related or relationship-related. He'll appreciate the fact that you thought about him.

The New Yorker is a great resource for relationship-oriented cartoons.

664

➤ Present him with a *written bill* for the next dinner you prepare for him: "Jean-Ann's Café: Bill for Services: Salad: 1 kiss. Entree: 8 kisses. Dessert: 3 kisses. Total bill: 12 kisses. (Tipping *is* encouraged.) You may want to take advantage of our Frequent Diner Program. See the manager. Thank you, come again!"

➤ Present her with a bill for the next time you change the oil in her car: "John's Garage: Bill for services: 6 quarts of oil: 1 kiss each. Oil filter: 1 kiss. New wiper blades: 3.5 hugs. Labor: 4 kisses. Total bill: 11 kisses. No checks accepted. Note: Special rates for customers who sleep with the mechanic!"

665

Get a favorite comic blown up to poster size. (Head for your local copy shop.) Mount it on cardboard. Send it to her at work or prop it up on the front porch.

666

For your comic strip lover: Check-out www.Comics.com for info on the Sunday Comic Store.

(More) Cool Stuff

667

Give your lover a bouquet of edible flowers!

- ✦ Anise hyssop flowers
- ✦ Arugula flowers
- ✦ Borage
- ✦ Calendula
- ✦ Chamomile
- ✦ Chive flowers
- ✦ Chrysanthemums
- ✦ Daisies
- ✦ Dandelion flowers
- ✦ Day lilies
- ✦ Hollyhocks
- ✦ Honeysuckle
- ✦ Lavender
- ✦ Marigolds
- ✦ Mustard flowers
- ✦ Nasturtium flowers
- ✦ Pansies
- ✦ Rose petals
- ✦ Squash blossoms
- ✦ Violets

668

Cool, huh?!

Musical greeting cards! Yes, open one up and it plays an electronic tune for you. Very cool. Look in card shops and gift stores.

669

You can get a complete lobster feast shipped to you anywhere in the USA! Call The Clambake Company, on (where else?) Cape Cod, at 508-945-7771; or visit www.clambake-to-go.com.

They'll send you an entire lobster feast including the pots and utensils— air expressed overnight! The traditional New England seafood dinner-for-two includes: two 1-1/4 pound lobsters; 1-1/2 pounds of steamers; a pound of mussels; two ears of fresh corn; four to six red bliss potatoes; two chunks of onion; and two links of sweet Italian sausage.

(More) Concepts

670

*Time is **not** money.*

"Time is money." You've heard it a *thousand* times. A call for efficiency. A time management maxim. An excuse for workaholics.

Well, it's a *lie*. Time is *not* money!

You can *save* money, but you *can't* save time—it's slipping by all the time, regardless of what you do. Also, you can create *more* money—by working harder or longer or smarter. But you *can't* create more time. *That's it. Sorry. Nope. No more. No—you can't live on "borrowed time"—It doesn't work that way.*

So I suggest that you *save the money* (perhaps for a big gift or special event)—but *spend the time* now, while you still have it.

671

*Romantics are **not** martyrs.*

Romantics do not put their partners first by ignoring their own needs and wants. Rather, they put their *relationship* first, and they do things that enhance the couple as a whole. You see, self-sacrifice always backfires because it builds resentment in the giver and creates guilt in the receiver. Romantic gestures performed out of love provide benefits to both the giver and the receiver.

672

Your physical surroundings affect your emotional well-being. While many of us would agree with this, the Chinese art of *feng shui* takes it to quite another level. Feng shui regards homes, buildings and rooms as "energy systems" that affect *qi*—our basic life energy. It makes sense to me that we should do everything possible to create personal environments that support our lives and our loves. Here are two books to help you learn more: *Feng Shui: Art and Harmony of Place,* by Johndennis Govert. *Interior Design with Feng Shui,* by Sarah Rossbach.

(More) Do-It-Yourself

673

Learn to play the guitar just well enough to accompany yourself as you sing a favorite love song. Now serenade her!

Responses to the most common excuses for not doing this:

- ❖ Excuse: "I'm not musical." Answer: Practice, practice, practice!
- ❖ Excuse: "I can't sing." Answer: Then don't! But play an instrumental version of the song on guitar.
- ❖ Excuse: "I'd be too embarrassed." Answer: C'mon! Challenge yourself. Stretch yourself.

674

Make a "This Is Your Life" videotape. Interview his friends and family, neighbors, high school teachers, college buddies, fraternity brothers, colleagues and co-workers. This idea is an especially great idea for a special birthday.

675

Make a custom certificate for your lover. You can get blank certificate forms at a stationery or paper store. It doesn't have to be artistic and perfect; don't forget, *it's the thought that counts!* Here are some certificates that were created by Romance Class participants:

- ➥ A certificate "For Putting Up with Me Over the Years"
- ➥ An award "For Meritorious Conduct in Bed"
- ➥ An acknowledgment of "The World's Best Wife"
- ➥ A ribbon "For Hugs & Kisses Above and Beyond the Call of Duty"

Chapter Theme Song:

"Handy Man," James Taylor

(More) Custom-Made

676

Compose an original song for your lover. You may get some help from a local musician, but the *essence* of the song should be yours.

* Present him/her with the score, rolled into a scroll and tied with a red ribbon.
* Sing the song to him/her.
* Hire a band to perform the song for him/her at a party.

677

How about a custom jigsaw puzzle to challenge your puzzle-lover? High quality, custom work is priced at about $1.50 per square inch, by the folks at J.C. Ayer & Co. Call 'em at 781-639-8162 or visit www.ayerpuzzles.com.

678

Make a "Commemorative Scroll" to celebrate some special occasion: Your lover's birthday, your wedding anniversary, some other special date, or maybe a special *year*.

☞ Research the major happenings of that date or year. Consider these categories: In the news, quotable quotes, famous people, world events, scientific breakthroughs, advertising and commercials, TV shows, popular music, movies, books, Broadway, sports, art, politics, daily life, religion, miscellany.

☞ Some resources to help you:
  * *American Chronicle*, by Lois & Alan Gordon
  * *The Timetables of History*, by Bernard Grun
  * *Daily Celebrity Almanac*, by Bob Barry

This commemorative scroll can be handwritten, designed on computer, or rendered in calligraphy. Tie it with a bow and present it. You may want to make a special presentation of it: Read it aloud to your partner.

One-of-a-kind items are among the most cherished gifts.

(More) Surprises

679

Buy tickets well in advance to the theater, symphony, ball game or concert. Don't tell her what the tickets are for. Simply tell her to mark her calendar. The mystery surrounding the event will be almost as much fun as the event itself. Guaranteed.

680

Surprise her by bringing dinner home from the best restaurant in town.

681

Surprise him by making his favorite homemade dessert.

682

While the two of you are out grocery shopping or running errands together, have a friend deliver a gourmet dinner to your home. Have him or her set the table with your best china, candles and flowers, and turn the stereo on to play some soft jazz.

683

If the two of you have to be *apart* for a birthday, anniversary or Christmas: Wrap a new mobile telephone as your gift. Give instructions that the gift must be opened at a *precise time* that you name. Then, call your partner on the new phone *exactly one minute* before it's to be opened, and let the gift ring until he/she unwraps the box and answers the phone. (Note: Make sure you synchronize your watches!)

Many men understand the fun and romance of presenting an engagement ring as a surprise. How can you surprise her now?

(More) Flowers

684

One gal in a Romance Class gives her guy *pressed* flowers. She explained that, *"Flat* flowers are more versatile than *real* flowers: You can slip them in between the pages of a book he's reading; you can hide them in his work files; and you can *mail* them!"

685

Give him one giant sunflower. Attach a note: "You are the sunshine of my life." Also attach a copy of Stevie Wonder's song "You Are the Sunshine of My Life."

686

Always ask *specifically* for fresh flowers. A good, fresh rose should last nearly a *week*, while an older one can wilt in less than a day.

687

+ Every home needs one elegant crystal vase.
+ And a bud vase.
+ And it wouldn't hurt to have a special vase for flowers at work.

Chapter Theme Song:
"Send One Your Love," Stevie Wonder

(More) Romance on a Budget

688

Timing is *everything*, when it comes to saving a few bucks. You could save 20 to 50 percent on virtually every gift you buy if you shop smart.

➤ Hit the stores immediately after Christmas.
➤ Shop at end-of-the-season sales.
➤ Look for overstock sales.
➤ Scan catalogs regularly, looking for deals.

*Romantics aren't spendthrifts!
(But there is a difference between
being frugal and being cheap.)*

689

Most cities have "City Coupon Books" that include hundreds of discount coupons for restaurants, shops and services. These coupon books usually cost just a few bucks, and can save you *hundreds* of dollars. They're also a good incentive to get the two of you out of the house, and get out of that rut you've been in!

690

Rediscover coffeehouses and small clubs. They're an inexpensive and entertaining change of pace. (Folk music never really dies, it just continually ebbs and flows.)

FYI, lingerie catalogs often have great
end-of-season sales.

691

"TKTS" in New York City is the place to get half-price tickets for Broadway shows on the day of performances! Located in Times Square, it's the best deal in town. (Be prepared to stand in line—a *long* line. It's a "scene" in itself!)

(More) Bubble Baths

692

Run a bath for her while she's out running errands. Put a candle, a glass of wine, and a bottle of fancy bubble bath on the kitchen table—along with a note saying, "I'll put the groceries away for you. Go relax. You deserve it. I love you."

693

Towel her dry after she showers. S-L-O-W-L-Y.

694

If your lover loves nothing more than a luxurious soak in a steamy, hot, elegant tub, then consider taking him/her on vacation to one of these first-class hotels—where they really understand the romance of baths.

* Post Ranch Inn, Big Sur, California. Picture sunken marble tubs in rooms at the edge of 1,000-foot cliffs overlooking the Pacific Ocean. Call 800-527-2200.
* Chateau de Bagnols, Bagnols, France. Featuring huge old tubs in a Renaissance castle near Lyons. Call 011-33-4-74-71-4000.
* Park Hyatt Hotel, Tokyo, Japan. Imagine sitting in a deep, hot tub that overlooks the city of Tokyo. Call 800-233-1234.
* Mandarin Oriental Hotel, San Francisco, California. How's this for luxury with a view? A bathroom on the 48th floor, with floor-to-ceiling windows overlooking the Golden Gate Bridge. Call 415-276-9888.

Thinking of You

695

Buy some small, red, heart-shaped ❤ stickers and place one on the face of your wristwatch. It's a reminder to think of your lover every time you check the time. If you're like most of us, that's about a thousand times a day! ❤

Tuck a little gift into the inside zippered pocket of her favorite purse.

696

Make a donation to her favorite charity—instead of going on your next expensive date. You can show her that you care about *her*—*and* at the same time show you care about the whales or the birds or the environment or whatever her favorite cause is.

Ask yourself what's **important** to your partner—then make gestures that reflect it.

697

Wonderful insights can be gained by asking each other quirky questions:

1. If you could be a comic strip character, who would you be?
2. If your name were to appear in the dictionary, how would you define yourself?
3. If you could create the perfect job for yourself, what would it be?
4. Who are your heroes? (Fictional and real.)
5. If you had three wishes, what would they be?
6. Could you live for a year in a tent with your partner (without going crazy)?
8. If you could accomplish one crazy stunt that would land you in the *Guinness Book of World Records*, what would it be?
9. Would you rather be really *smart*, or really *good looking?*
10. If you could be a super hero, who would you be?
11. If you were Rick, in the movie Casablanca, would you have let Ilsa leave at the end?
14. What one part of your body would you like to change?

Think Different*

698

Do something *totally out of character.*

- ❤ **Always late?**—Be on time.
- ❤ **Not creative?**—Think-up something original and unexpected!
- ❤ **Forgetful?**—Remember her birthday *every day for a month!*
- ❤ **Watch TV every night?**—Go out to dinner instead.
- ❤ **Two left feet?**—Take dance lessons together.

699

Are you stuck in a rut? Are you taking each other for granted lately? Try "reframing." Reframe, or redefine, how you see your partner.

- ❤ Start thinking of her as *your lover* once again.
- ❤ Start treating him as your *best friend*—which he *was,* once upon a time. Remember??

700

Act out different fantasies of meeting for the first time:

- ✳ Meet in a bar after work.
- ✳ Meet while grocery shopping.
- ✳ Meet in line, waiting at the bank.
- ✳ Meet over lunch at work.

701

Spend an "all-nighter" together: Make love, watch videos, go out to an all-night diner, go for a moonlit stroll, make love again. Then sleep all day the next day to recover.

*Think "different"—and you'll **never** run out of romantic ideas!*

*Yes, this page is upside-down on purpose.

*Thanks to Apple Computer.

*Yes, this page is upside-down *on purpose.*

Choreography
702

*This choreography technique is **not** taught at Arthur Murray!*

"Choreograph" your lovemaking to your favorite music! This may sound artificial and contrived, but several people in my Romance Class have told me that they often do this, although they never thought of it as "choreography."

I don't mean that you plan *every* movement, but rather that you match some favorite music to the general mood and pace of your lovemaking.

- For example, some people like to start slowly and gently, and build to a fast-paced climax. Their musical choreography could look like this: Start with a little George Winston; move to some Al Jarreau; mix in some Glenn Miller; and finish up with Maynard Ferguson.

- Others like to start out fast and passionately, and wind down to a gentle conclusion. Their musical choreography could look like this: Start with the soundtrack from *Nine-1/2 Weeks*; move to the soundtrack from *When Harry Met Sally*; and end with the soundtrack from *Out of Africa*.

- One couple prefers Mozart symphonies. "Beethoven is great music, but too frenetic for our lovemaking," Judy B. explains. "Mozart is great—especially *The Jupiter Symphony*, No. 41. It has four movements, which correspond with our pattern of lovemaking.

  1) "The first movement, *Allegro Vivace* is strong and passionate, this gets us going. It runs 11:50—good for energetic foreplay.

  2) "The second movement, *Andante Cantabile*, slows the pace, which allows us to talk a little and build the intimacy more. This runs a good 10:53.

  3) "The third movement, *Menuetto: Allegretto*, picks up the speed again, which moves us from quiet intimacy into a more intense passion. This one is *quick*, at 5:13.

  4) "The last movement, *Molto Allegro*, races to a roaring and passionate conclusion. Just perfect at 8:37."

- What music would *you* use to choreograph your lovemaking?

Creativity

703

Keep a journal. It will benefit you in lots of ways. Many Romance Class participants have observed that creative ideas often flow while they're writing in their journals.

704

Guys: Learn a little sleight-of-hand well enough to make her diamond engagement ring "appear" out of thin air!

George was a bibliophile. He *loved* browsing in bookstores. On his forty-third birthday he happened to be wandering by his favorite local bookstore—and stopped suddenly on the sidewalk. The window display held hundreds of copies of a book titled: *Happy Birthday, George!* Looking closer he saw that the author was his wife! He ran into the store, where the clerk handed him a copy of the book. George discovered that the *Happy Birthday, George!* book was really a different book with a custom-made book jacket slipped over it.

Shaking his head in wondrous surprise, George turned the book over and read on the back cover: "Happy Birthday, oh wonderful husband of mine! This book is Surprise #1. Surprise #2 is a $100 gift certificate for books. Enjoy! Surprise #3 is waiting patiently to enjoy lunch with you at the Posh Café. Happy Birthday!"

705

Use a thesaurus to help you express your love—and to help you rev up your love letters.

* Tell your mate that you—love, adore, admire, cherish, desire, want, need, prize, esteem, idolize, revere, treasure—him/her.
* Describe how you're—crazy about/mad for/nuts about/smitten with/stuck on/sweet on/wild about—your mate.
* Tell your lover that you're—enchanted by/captivated by/enamored of/fond of—him/her.

Are you—infatuated, crazy, frantic, frenetic, frenzied, intoxicated, mad—with love for him/her?

Cruisin'

706

- ❏ Abercrombie & Kent Int'l.: 800-323-7308; www.abercrombiekent.com
- ❏ American Canadian Caribbean Line: 800-556-7450; www.accl-smallships.com
- ❏ American Hawaii Cruises: 866-546-2929; www.cruise-hawaii.com
- ❏ Carnival Cruise Lines: 800-227-6482; www.carnival.com
- ❏ Celebrity Cruises: 800-437-9111; www.celebritycruises.com
- ❏ Clipper Cruise Line: www.clippercruise.com
- ❏ Club Med Cruises: 800-258-2633
- ❏ Costa Cruise Lines: 800-332-6782; www.costacruises.com
- ❏ Cunard Line: 800-728-6273; www.cunardline.com
- ❏ Disney Cruise Line: 800-939-2784; www.disneycruise.com
- ❏ First European Cruises: 888-983-8767; www.firsteuropean.com
- ❏ Holland America Line: 800-426-0327; www.hollandamerica.com
- ❏ Norwegian Cruise Line: 800-327-7030; www.ncl.com
- ❏ Princess Cruise Line: 800-LOVE-BOAT; www.princesscruise.com
- ❏ Regal Cruises: 800-270-7245; www.regalcruises.com
- ❏ Royal Caribbean Int'l.: 800-327-6700; www.royalcaribbean.com
- ❏ Star Clippers: 800-442-0551; www.star-clippers.com
- ❏ Windjammer Barefoot Cruises: 800-327-2601; www.windjammer.com
- ❏ Windstar Cruises: 800-626-9900; www.windstarcruises.com

Have you ever seen the sun set over the Caribbean from the deck of a cruise ship?

Lovin'

707

Make love in *slow motion*.

708

Things to Never, Never, *Never* Do While Making Love:

* Never, never, *never* answer the phone.
* Never, never, *never* call her by a former lover's name.
* Never, never, *never* glance at your watch.
* Never, never, *never* interrupt yourselves for a whining pet.
* Encourage open-mindedness, but *never* push too far.
* Never, never, *never* leave too little time.
* Never, never, *never* say anything negative about your partner's body.
* Never, never, *never* criticize his/her technique (but *do* discuss it later).
* Never, never, *never* get into arousal without dealing with birth control first.
* Never, never, *never* criticize your lover in any way.
* Never, never, *never* lose your sense of humor.
* Never, never, *never* talk about work or children in bed.
* Never, never, *never* fake orgasm.
* Never, never, *never* leave the bedroom door unlocked if kids are in the house.

709

Make love by catering to her sexual desires 100 percent—and putting your sexual desires on hold until tomorrow.

Leave a rose on her pillow.

Leave a sexy love note on his pillow.

Leave your worries at work.

Leave yourself plenty of time

Chapter Theme Song:
"Lovin' You," Bobby Darin

Please, Mr. Postman

710

You can get your Valentine card postmarked from one of these romantic cities or towns:

- ❤ Valentine, Texas 79854
- ❤ Valentine, Nebraska 69201
- ❤ Loveland, Colorado 80537
- ❤ Loving, New Mexico 88256
- ❤ Bridal Veil, Oregon 97010
- ❤ Loveland, Ohio 45140

Just put your card, addressed and stamped, inside another envelope addressed to the postmaster of the town of your choice. Attach a note requesting that your Valentine be hand-stamped and mailed.

Items to insert inside love letter envelopes: Confetti, a lock of your hair, feathers, stickers, heart-shaped paper cut-outs.

711

Carry stamps in your wallet at all times. (Preferably several Love Stamps!)

712

The following is part of a "Junk Mail Campaign" that one Romance Class participant created for her husband. She designed it to look like a Publishers Clearinghouse mailing. Clever, huh?

YOU MAY ALREADY BE A WINNER! The Publishers Clearinghouse Lovestakes has chosen *YOU* to be the recipient of AT LEAST 1,000,000 kisses—that's **ONE MILLION** kisses (and hugs!) Nothing to buy! No coupons to fill-out! What do you have to do in order to qualify for ONE MILLION kisses and hugs?!—Just bring home one bottle of champagne this Friday. That's all!

But—if you want to qualify for the BIG BONUS PRIZE of 1,000 nights of passionate lovemaking, you'll have to bring home one red rose per week for the next year. A SMALL PRICE TO PAY, WOULDN'T YOU SAY—FOR 1,000 NIGHTS OF PASSIONATE LOVEMAKING!!

This offer expires *tomorrow*—so act *TODAY!*

Chapter Theme Song:
"Please Mr. Postman," The Marvelettes

You've Got Mail*

713

With a nod to America Online . . . Stay in touch with your lover through Email. Always use the latest electronic communications technology to break down the artificial barriers between "work time" and "personal time." Email is great for keeping a conversation going with your partner all day long.

Treat email as an *extra* method for staying connected. Email doesn't take the place of real love letters via "snail mail."

714

✦ Type this: colon, close parenthesis :) and you get a smiley face when you look at the page sideways.
✦ Type this: semi-colon, hyphen, close parenthesis ;-) —a wink!
✦ Type this: colon, hyphen, open parenthesis :-(—a frown.

These are called emoticons or "smileys," and they're used by frequent Emailers to enhance the emotional content of their Emailed notes.

715

It's getting easier and easier to send audio files via Email. With the proper software your lover will be able to hear your voice as well as read your words. This technology is especially great if you're in a long distance relationship.

Use your lover's pet name as your email password.

716

Create your own custom-made electronic greeting cards. Using PowerPoint or similar software you can use scanned in pictures and animation to create lively, funny and entertaining E-cards.

*This chapter dedicated to Meg Ryan and Tom Hanks.

Mindset of a Romantic

717

Romantics have a good sense of humor.

There's no such thing as a "humorless romantic." While the *foundation* of romance is a serious love, the *nature* of romance is lighthearted.

Mindset of a Romantic:

Creative
Quirky
Flexible
Observant
Childlike
Thoughtful
Fun
Wacky
Curious

718

Romantics "work at it."

Yes, relationships require work. But it's not "work" like nine-to-five work. It's more like an artist working on a painting. Painting requires skill, time, effort, planning, frustration and sweat sometimes—but the work is so rewarding that the artist doesn't view it as "work." Working on a loving relationship is like that.

719

Romantics not only *work at it*, they "play at it," too!

Being romantic is a lot of *fun*. (In case you haven't guessed by now!) Being romantic involves your creativity, self-expression and your passionate spirit. Remember my earlier definition of romance as "adult play"?

720

Romantics live in the moment.

"Carpe diem"—seize the day! Seize the moment. Don't let another ten minutes go by without making some expression of your love for your partner. (Yes, I mean that *literally*. If you're at home reading this, set the book down, saunter over to him or her, and wrap your arms around your lover. If you're out somewhere, call on the phone. Go do it. *Carpe diem*.)

Thinking Like a Romantic

721

Romantics are *magnets* for romantic ideas.

Romantics find romantic ideas *everywhere*.

- ❋ Romantics keep an eye on the concerts and shows scheduled to appear in their area.
- ❋ Romantics read the newspaper not only for the *news*, but for romantic opportunities.
- ❋ Romantics notice articles *and* ads in newspapers and magazines.
- ❋ Romantics save miscellaneous articles for future reference.
- ❋ Romantics notice unique gifts when shopping for other things.

722

Romantics are flexible.

- ❖ What would *you* do if you'd planned a romantic picnic, and it started raining? One couple held their picnic *in bed!* Another couple grabbed two umbrellas and headed for the park *anyway!*
- ❖ If your partner showed up at your office wearing a trench coat *and nothing else*—what would you do?
- ❖ Would you be comfortable taking the afternoon off work on the spur of the moment to spend it with your partner?

723

Employing the concept of "Couple-Thinking" will automatically turn anyone into a romantic. Couple-Thinking is a technique in which you *first* think of yourself as a member of a couple, and second as an independent individual. (Men, and our culture in general, put too much emphasis on rugged individualism, and not enough emphasis on relationship-building and connection-making.) [Note: I am *NOT* suggesting that you martyr yourself on the altar of Relationship.]

Idea inspired while eating Alpha-Bits:

For each letter of the alphabet, write down three possible romantic gifts or concepts. Use this list for generating romantic ideas.

Romantics have a portion of their brains assigned to the task of recognizing romantic opportunities when they appear. Other people screen them out.

Love Is . . .

724

Love is . . . eliminating *all* interruptions so you can really be alone together. Disconnect the phone; unplug the TV; ship the kids to the neighbors; disconnect the doorbell.

725

➻ Love is . . . framing a favorite greeting card she's given you.

➻ Love is . . . reading aloud to each other before bed.

➻ Love is . . . having a poem delivered to your table at a restaurant.

➻ Love is . . . sending a postcard every day that you're away from her.

➻ Love is . . . believing in one another.

Love is . . . waking her gently with soft caresses and kisses.

726

✳ Romance is the expression of love.

✳ Romance is the icing on the cake of your relationship.

✳ Romance is *always* about love, but only *sometimes* about sex.

✳ Romance is a state of mind.

✳ Romance is also a state of being.

✳ Romance is what you *do*. (Love is what you *feel*.)

✳ Romance is the language of love.

Chapter Theme Songs:

"Love Is Alive," Gary Wright

"(Love Is) Thicker than Water," Andy Gibb

"Love Is Strange," Mickey & Sylvia

"Love Is a Many Splendored Thing," The Four Aces

"Love Is . . ."
727

* "Love is a little haven of refuge from the world."
  ~ BERTRAND RUSSELL

* "Love is the fairest flower that blooms in God's garden."
  ~ ANONYMOUS

* "Love is a flower and you its only seed."
  ~ AMANDA McBROOM

* "Love is a verb."
  ~ CLARE BOOTHE LUCE

* "Love is an energy which exists of itself. It is its own value."
  ~ ANONYMOUS

* "Love is an irresistible desire to be irresistibly desired."
  ~ ROBERT FROST

* "Love is being stupid together."
  ~ PAUL VALERY

* "Love is more easily demonstrated than defined."
  ~ ANONYMOUS

* "Love is not love until love's vulnerable."
  ~ THEODORE ROETHKE

* "Love is patient and kind; love is not jealous or boastful."
  ~ 1 CORINTHIANS 13:4

* "Love is the great asker."
  ~ D.H. LAWRENCE

* "Love is the greatest refreshment in life."
  ~ PABLO PICASSO

* "Love is the only disease that makes you feel better."
  ~ SAM SHEPARD

* "Love is trembling happiness."
  ~ KAHLIL GIBRAN

"Love is blind."

~ GEOFFREY CHAUCER

"Love is blind. That is why he always proceeds by the sense of touch."

~ FRENCH PROVERB

Love is merely an empty concept unless you bring it alive through action.

*"Love is patient, Love is kind,
it does not envy; it does not boast,
it is not proud.
It is not rude, it is not self-seeking,
it is not easily angered,
it keeps no record of wrongs.
Love does not delight in evil
but rejoices with the truth.
It always protects, always trusts,
always hopes, always perseveres."*

~ I CORINTHIANS 13:4-7

The Way to a Man's Heart*

728

➤ When in doubt, buy her chocolate.
➤ When in doubt, order him pizza.

729

You can spice up *any* meal at home—from gourmet extravaganzas to TV dinners—by adding candlelight and soft music. Don't wait for "special occasions" or weekends to bring out the romance.

730

Or—Shape the entire pizza into a heart-shape.

Or—Cut each and every slice of pepperoni into a tiny heart-shape.

Or—Use the mushroom toppings to spell out both of your initials.

Get the pizza chef to arrange the pepperoni in the shape of a heart.

731

If your lover is a tea lover, get her a subscription to the *Upton Tea Quarterly* newsletter. It includes listings and information on hundreds of varieties of fine loose tea. Write to Upton Tea Imports, 231 South Street, Upton, Massachusetts 01748.

732

What's her all-time favorite meal? Learn to make it! Get help from friends, neighbors or relatives—whatever it takes.

733

Create an "At-Home Date": Includes dinner and dancing. Formal attire required.

*Also the way to a *woman's* heart!

Recipes for Romance

734

Spread whipped cream or chocolate syrup on selected body parts and invite your lover to enjoy dessert.

735

The way to his stomach often involves directions to his favorite restaurant. Do you know his all-time favorite restaurant; favorite diner; favorite fast food joint; favorite fancy restaurant; favorite pizza parlor?

736

Create a personalized "Wine-of-the-Month Club" for her.

Embark on a series of "Restaurant Discoveries": Each week go to a different restaurant within a 100-mile radius of your house. Choose a restaurant "theme" that appeals to both of you.

✦ You might choose a type of *food:* French, Thai, Mexican, Italian, Chinese, etc.
✦ You might choose a type of *restaurant:* Diners, elegant bistros, casual cafés, pizzerias, etc.

737

♥ Take a wine-tasting class together.
♥ Attend wine tastings at local wine shops.
♥ Host wine-tasting parties for your friends.
♥ Get a subscription to *The Wine Spectator.* Call 800-395-3364.

(Not) For Newlyweds Only!

The Newlywed Cookbook, by Robin Vitetta-Miller

Aphrodisiacs

738

You know, of course, that green m&m's are *aphrodisiacs*, don't you? With that as a start . . .

✦ Carefully open a one-pound bag of m&m's and empty it out. Refill it entirely with green m&m's. Seal it up so it looks like new.
✦ Give him a heart-shaped box full of green m&m's.
✦ Fill his box of Cheerios with green m&m's.

739

Someone in every Romance Class asks, "What about *aphrodisiacs*!?"

Wondrous claims have been made about a great variety of foods, from oysters and chocolate to basil and green m&m's. Personally, I feel that it's the *mood and environment* surrounding the presentation of the food that determines the potential amorous conclusion of the evening.

But by all means, try some exotic recipes. (Couldn't hurt—might help!)

And regardless of whether or not certain foods can *chemically* make one more interested in love, you can definitely use food to *psychologically* affect one's mood for love! There's always the scientifically proven "placebo effect," which indicates that the mere *belief* in the power of an agent can bring about the believed-in effect. This means that virtually *any* food could potentially be an aphrodisiac.

740

If you'd like to prepare some real gourmet meals that have real aphrodisiac potential, you *must* get the book *InterCourses: An Aphrodisiac Cookbook*, by Martha Hopkins and Randall Lockridge. This the most amazing, elegant and erotic cookbook you've ever seen! The photos *alone* will inspire some fantasy ideas that have never before occurred to you. I *guarantee* it!

Henry Kissinger once said, "Power is the ultimate aphrodisiac." Does that mean only world leaders are leading sexy lives? Not at all! We all have tremendous potential in our *personal* power, the power of *charm*, the power of *romance*, the power of *imagination* and the power of *love*.

Chapter Theme Song:

"(You're My) Aphrodisiac," Dennis Edwards

(More) Recipes for Romance

741

Picnics. (I checked, and nowhere is it written that you can't have picnics indoors, in the nude, in front of a fireplace, in your office, in bed, on the roof of your apartment building, or at midnight.)

742

Bake a giant chocolate chip cookie for him. (And I mean GIANT— at least *two feet* in diameter.)

743

If you're especially inept in the kitchen, you've got a great opportunity to surprise your partner. *Cook a gourmet meal!* Send your partner out for the afternoon. Enlist the help of a friend who cooks. Prepare your lover's favorite dish. *Voilà!*

744

Create your own special mixed drink and name it after your partner. ("A Peter Colada." "A Catherine Cooler.")

745

❤ Carefully open a packet of tea. Remove the tea bag and replace it with a little love note. Seal the packet to make it look untouched.

❤ Create custom "Love Quote Tags" and attach them to the end of the string on each tea bag.

*"Blockbuster Recommends"... The classic film **Tom Jones**. (Watch for the pub scene. Wow!)*

FYI—
The most popular soft drink in Brazil, Guarana, is also a recognized and legendary aphrodisiac(!)

Classic Romance

746

What could be more classic than a fine gold locket with your photo inside? (Maybe a photo of the two of you.)

747

Revive chivalry. Women love a real gentleman.

- Open her car door for her. Hold her dinner chair. Help her on with her coat.
- Older women will love the revival of manners.
- Some younger women will need to be encouraged to see these gestures as tokens of respect and affection, and not as messages that men feel women are inferior and helpless.

748

Arthur Murray Dance Studios: 305-445-9645; www.ArthurMurray.com.

Go out dancing! Ballroom dancing is enjoying a resurgence unlike anything since World War II. Glenn Miller, Benny Goodman and the Big Band sound are once again being heard in dance halls, restaurants, clubs and church basements throughout the land. Sign up for ballroom dancing lessons, it may be the single best romantic decision you make this decade.

749

Go for a horse-drawn carriage ride through the city—or the country.

Classical Romance

750

My panel of experts has compiled its official list of The Most Romantic Operatic Arias:

* "Deh Vieni, Non Tardar," from *The Marriage of Figaro*
* "Che Gelida Manina," from *La Bohème*
* "Parigi, O Cara," from *La Traviata*
* "Recondita Armonia," from *Tosca*
* "Bimba, Bimba, Non Piangere," from *Madama Butterfly*
* "The Flower Song," from *Carmen*
* "Sì, mi chiamano Mimì," from *La Bohème*
* "Celeste Aïda," from *Aïda*
* "Amor Ti Vieta," from *Fedora*
* "Mon Coeur S'ouvre à Ta Voix," from *Samson and Dalilah*
* "Quando, Rapito In Estasi," from *Lucia di Lammermoor*

751

Most Romantic Piano Concertos (just take my word for it):

✦ Mozart's Piano Concerto No. 21 in C
✦ Beethoven's Piano Concerto No. 5 in E flat
✦ Schumann's Concerto in A Minor for Piano & Orchestra
✦ Grieg's Concerto in A Minor for Piano & Orchestra

752

Be prepared with a Romantic Music Library. True romantics have everything from Beethoven to The Beatles, from Mozart to Meatloaf; from jazz to rock to country to R&B to folk to acoustic to show tunes.

Does your partner like the power and passion of Beethoven? Or the beauty and grace of Mozart? Or the depth and elegance of Bach?

Classic

753

Serenade her. Sing her favorite love song, or "your song" to her. You don't need to have a great voice. Your sincerity will more than make up for your lack of perfect pitch.

- Sing along with The Beatles or Celine Dion on CD.
- Get a good friend to accompany you on guitar.
- If singing truly embarrasses you, hire a local singer/guitar player to serenade her for you.

754

A true classic is the lazy-Sunday-afternoon-canoe-ride on a calm, beautiful pond, lake or river.

- Version 1: "Just Do It!"—Toss on your jeans and T-shirt, grab a bottle of wine and some cheese, and hop in an old rowboat and *go!*
- Version 2: "Your Sunday Best"—Dress up in your best clothes, pack a great picnic basket, rent a nice canoe, and enjoy!
- Version 3: "A Victorian Afternoon"—Rent costumes! Tails and top hat for him, hoop skirt and parasol for her! Guaranteed to cause a stir at the shore.

755

One guy in the Romance Class wrote to his wife: "Honey, I love you as much as I love the Super Bowl!" (She cried with relief and happiness.)

Write a classic, romantic, passionate, handwritten, heartfelt love letter. Most adults haven't written a love letter since *high school.* (Why not?? Have we lost our youthful idealism, or have we just gotten lazy?)

No excuses! Sit down for twenty, maybe thirty minutes, and simply *put your feelings on paper.* Don't try to be eloquent or "poetic." Just be yourself. The effort and intention are more important than the precise words you use.

Classy

756

Dress up for dinner at home. Tuxedo for him, evening gown for her.

757

Hire a pianist to play during a romantic dinner at home.

758

Anything from Tiffany's.

759

Take a leisurely stroll through a local park or public garden.

760

Learn calligraphy so you can create *incredible* love letters for him/her.

761

Get a pair of crystal champagne flutes. Use them *often!*

762

Hire a limousine for an elegant evening out.

763

Have dinner-for-two prepared in your home by the best chef in town.

*Save that Tiffany's box! That distinctive "Tiffany's turquoise" box is guaranteed to get your lover's heart racing, **regardless** of what's inside!*

FYI—
Shakespeare-in-the-Park in New York City's Central Park. Call 212-260-2400.

Picture This

764

Have a special photograph blown-up to *poster size*. You might choose a wedding photo, or a really funny photo of the two of you.

765

➤ You do, of course, carry a photo of her in your wallet, *don't you?*
➤ And you have an eight-by-ten of her on your desk at work, *right?*

766

Tape funny photos of the two of you to the refrigerator door, then add funny cartoon balloons.

Make a life-size cardboard cut-out of yourself, and give the gift of "yourself"!

767

Turn your drawer of miscellaneous photographs and slides into a "Video Photo Album." Gather your favorite photos, choose some favorite music, and have a local production studio turn them into a keepsake videotape.

768

Find your old high school yearbook picture. Add funny captions. Mail it to her. (If yours is as awful as *mine* is, it could be the funniest thing you ever give her!)

769

How about an original, signed photograph of your honey's hero, favorite movie star, sports star or celebrity?

Picture Perfect

770

Have his portrait painted from a photograph.

771

Capture your memories and the good times . . . Or, as they say at Kodak, "For the times of your life"—take up photography. Whether you use a sophisticated 35mm or a disposable camera, it'll add fun to your outings, and provide you with scrapbooks full of good memories.

772

You do, of course, have a photo of your wife on your desk, *don't you?!*

* If you don't, here's what I want you to do: Get a nice eight-by-ten photo made, frame it, giftwrap it, and *give it to yourself*. Open it over breakfast with your wife, then take your gift to work with you. You'll leave her with a great memory.
* Note: Place the photo *front-and-center* on your desk, not off to the side. Her smiling face will help you keep your priorities straight when you start to get stressed-out over some seemingly important work problem.

773

Spend an entire afternoon together taking instant pictures of each other with a Polaroid camera. One couple simply documented their experience of a dinner date. Another couple spent the afternoon in bed. One couple focused on close-ups, and another couple focused on the artistic settings.

Commission a photographer to shoot a formal portrait of the two of you.

"Love does not consist in gazing at each other but in looking outward together in the same direction."

~ ANTOINE DE SAINT-EXUPERY

Flower Power

774

- On Monday place a single red rose on the kitchen table. No note. No explanation.
- On Tuesday place one lily on the coffee table.
- On Wednesday place one daisy in the bathroom sink.
- On Thursday place one geranium on his/her pillow.
- On Friday place one forget-me-not in the mailbox.
- On Saturday place one sunflower on the kitchen counter.
- On Sunday present your lover with a **huge** bouquet made specifically with the kinds of flowers you've been giving all week.

775

My twenty-year survey reveals that 99.9998 percent of all women *love* flowers. Basically, you can't go wrong with flowers.

The remaining 0.0002 percent of women have the belief that, "It's wasteful to buy flowers that are simply going to die in a few days." It's not really that they don't *like* flowers, it's that they don't like being *wasteful*. Tip: Get these gals *flowering plants* instead of *cut flowers*.

776

Get to know your local florist. Become a "regular"—you'll get better service and fresher flowers!

777

Use a flower as a "private signal." One couple in the Romance Class told us that for years they've used the "Flower-on-the-Pillow" as a signal that they're interested in making love that night. Sounds good to me!

Chapter Theme Songs:

"Blue Gardenia," Nat King Cole

"Passion Flower," Duke Ellington

"Wildflower," The Carter Family

More Power!*

778

Look, guys, this *ain't* brain surgery! You want more *sex*? Then be more *romantic*. It's as simple as that.

779

If you want your lover to wear lingerie more often, *why do you think that you have the right to slouch around in your ratty boxer shorts or dirty sweat pants?!* Take a hint! Get a nice bathrobe, or silk pajamas, or a lounging jacket, or a Japanese kimono!

780

Listen to her! Don't problem-solve; don't give advice; don't agree or disagree. Just *listen*. Validate her. Honor her.

Often, when men think women are looking for *answers*, they're simply looking for *compassion and understanding*.

781

Pick up a copy of *Cosmopolitan* or *Glamour* or *Ms.* or *Redbook* or *Shape* or *Self* or *Vogue* or *Ladies Home Journal*. (How do you expect to know what women are thinking about and talking about if you don't peek at their magazines occasionally?)

*Thanks to Tim Allen and *Tool Time!*

Greg & Tracey

782

Tracey had fallen in love with Natalie Cole's album *Unforgettable*. One day in the Sunday *New York Times* I saw an ad for Natalie Cole in concert at Radio City Music Hall. So of course I immediately called for tickets. I told Tracey to mark her calendar for a surprise date—two months in the future. A month later it occurred to me that with many events—like Christmas—the *anticipation* is just as much fun as the event itself. So I told Tracey about the concert. She was thrilled! There was, however, one *little* piece of information that I held back: The fact that we had *front row seats!* She didn't discover this until we were seated at the concert.

The "wedding vow" lyrics from the song performed during our wedding ceremony:

So here we stand together,
    and here we make a stand,
To offer love to Holiness,
    in faith to understand . . .
That if living is for loving,
    and if only Truth is true,
Then I dedicate myself to loving you.
~ Brit Lay, "Wedding Song," *Illusions & Dreams*

(To get this CD, see the index listing for "Wedding Song.")

783

Last year I substituted Tracey's regular Christmas stocking with *real silk stockings*. (Ho-ho-ho!!)

784

I created *The LifeChart* to celebrate my Tracey's birthday several years ago. On poster paper I drew a timeline representing her life—from birth to the present. Along the line are noted events from her life: Significant, outrageous, funny and serious. (I interviewed her parents and friends for items that I had no way of knowing.) Parallel timelines indicate a few events from my life, and some world events, for putting her life into perspective. It became an instant heirloom.

- ❤ Maybe I'll update it every ten years for our anniversary. That would make a nice ritual, don't you think?
- ❤ And then maybe on our fiftieth anniversary I'll have the whole thing rendered in calligraphy. (But will I be able to wait that long??)

Heart & Soul

785

For your next vacation do something different, spiritual and rejuvenating. Spend a week on a spiritual retreat at a quiet sanctuary or monastery.

✳ Green Gulch Farm Zen Center, Muir Beach, California. Buddhist workshops and meditation periods in Japanese-style surroundings on the picturesque Pacific coast. Call 415-383-3134.

✳ The Mountain Retreat, Highlands, North Carolina. Atop a breathtaking 4,200-foot peak overlooking the Blue Ridge mountains, you and your lover can experience retreats and workshops hosted by the Unitarian Universalist Association. Call 828-526-5838.

✳ Marie Joseph Spiritual Center, Biddeford, Maine. Followers of all faiths are welcomed by the sisters of the Presentation of Mary to join in daily prayers and experience the peaceful environment on the beautiful Atlantic shore. Call 207-284-5671.

786

Read an inspirational passage every morning and evening. Some suggestions for inspirational readings:

➤ *The Prophet*, by Kahlil Gibran
➤ *The Bible*, by You-Know-Who
➤ *A Course In Miracles*, Foundation For Inner Peace
➤ *The Quiet Answer*, by Hugh Prather

A great resource: *Vacations that can Change Your Life*, by Ellen Lederman. This ultimate vacation guide features more than two hundred life-changing destinations including holistic, spiritual, healing, health-promoting, self-improvement and learning vacations.

Chapter Theme Song:

"Heart and Soul," Jan & Dean
"Heart and Soul," Huey Lewis & The News
"Heart and Soul," Johnny Maddox
"Heart and Soul," The Cleftones

Moon & Stars

787

Especially for diamond-lovers, sci-fi fans and astrology nuts!

Diamond Astrological Pins! Jewelry designer A.G.A. Correa has created an incredible collection of constellation pins. Based on star charts, the pins are not only elegant, they're *accurate*: Each diamond is proportional to the magnitude of its corresponding star. All of the signs of the Zodiac are available, plus other constellations. Prices vary depending on the number of stars in each constellation and on their magnitude. Prices range from around $1,000 to $4,000. Write to Post Office Box 401, Wiscasset, Maine 04578, or call 800-341-0788.

788

Inspired by the classic romantic song "Fly Me to the Moon," one gal is planning to take her husband to the moon. Literally! She figures that regular commercial flights should be running by the year 2025. Anticipating that the tickets will probably be rather expensive, she put $5,000 into an annuity fund in 1990. Here's her rationale: "We skipped our annual vacation for one year to set this money aside. No big deal. And I figure that $5,000 at a modest return of seven percent per year will yield $53,382 in the year 2025."

When was the last time you took a quiet, romantic moonlit stroll?

789

You may not be able to give her the moon and the stars, but you *can* name a star after her! The International Star Registry will provide you with a beautiful certificate that notes the star's coordinates and its new name, plus star maps and stargazing information. At only $48 per star, this makes a great, unique gift for that person you're starry-eyed over. Call the International Star Registry at 800-282-3333, or write to 34523 Wilson Road, Ingleside, Illinois 60041, or visit www.StarRegistry.com.

Science Fiction

790

If your lover is a *Star Wars* fanatic, take a vacation in Tunisia, where key scenes from *Star Wars* (Episodes One and Four) are set, including Luke's homestead and the Cantina. Call TunisUSA for info on their Star Wars tours: 800-474-5500.

791

Rent *all* of the *Star Trek* movies and watch them over a weekend. Rent all of the *Star Wars* movies. Rent all of the *Alien* movies. Rent a dozen classic sci-fi movies from the 1950s and 1960s.

Trekkers celebrate James T. Kirk's birthday: March 21, 2228 A.D.

792

Consider a stargazing vacation at the Star Hill Inn, located in Sapello, New Mexico. The Star Hill Inn has been a well-kept secret of amateur astronomers and star-gazers for several years. At 7,200 feet above sea level, and far enough east of Santa Fe to be unaffected by the nighttime glare, the inn caters to its clientele with an observation deck, star maps and a well-stocked astronomy library. Call 505-425-5605; or visit www.StarHillInn.com.

Visit Forbidden Planet Bookstore, the greatest sci-fi bookstore in the world. Call 212-473-1576 or browse at 840 Broadway in Manhattan.

793

Is he a *Doctor Who* fan? Sign him up to be a member of The Companions of Dr. Who. Write to P.O. Box 56764, New Orleans, Louisiana 70156.

If your lover would love to watch a space shuttle (or other rocket) launch, call NASA for timetables and other info (or visit www.nasa.gov):

- ➟ 321-867-4636—will get you launch information.
- ➟ 321-449-4444—will get you a base pass so you can watch a rocket launch from close-up!
- ➟ 202-358-0000—will get you NASA Public Information.
- ➟ 321-452-2121—will connect you with the Kennedy Space Center.

Wonderful Weekends

794

Love is timeless. And to *prove* it, cover up all the clocks in your house for the weekend. Turn them to the wall or cover their faces. You'll discover that time seems to pass more leisurely when you don't know exactly what time it is.

795

Surprise your partner with an *unexpected* three-day weekend. Arrange it ahead of time with his or her boss and staff. This may take some time to coordinate just right, but the payoff is well worth it!

Just picture the scene: It's a typical Friday morning. You both get up at your usual time. You shower and get dressed. Over breakfast you turn to your unsuspecting partner and say, "Oh, by the way, we've both got the day off work today. What would you like to do?"

After your partner recovers from the shock—and showers you with kisses and thank-yous—you get to plan the day together. What are you going to do?? Go back to bed and sleep til noon? Go back to bed and make love? Go for a drive? Go shopping? Go out for lunch?

796

The surprise get-away weekend is a romantic classic. Find a quaint bed and breakfast or picturesque inn. Pack bags for both of you, and whisk your partner away upon his or her arrival home from work!

797

What if you have a house full of kids? Try the "Distraction Diversion": Rent *several* of your kids' favorite movies; buy a ten-pound bag of popcorn and a bunch of juice boxes. The kids sit hypnotically in front of the TV while the two of you escape upstairs for some "quality time" together.

*FYI—The weekend is twenty-nine percent of a week. This is a **lot** of time! Don't waste it doing chores!*

Chapter Theme Song:
"Weekend in New England," Barry Manilow

Mark Your Calendar

798

Surprise your partner by celebrating some oddball special occasions that you know he or she will appreciate. Create a fun ritual or get a funny little gift to mark the event.

✦ Cat in the Hat Day is March 2nd.
✦ International Lefthanders Day is August 13th.
✦ Trivia Day is January 4th.
✦ Bad Poetry Day is August 18th.
✦ Do It! Day is September 7th.
✦ Punsters Day is November 7th.

You can find something to celebrate every day of the year in *Celebrate the Day*, by John Kremer.

799

Print up a batch of custom business cards, patterned after a doctor's appointment card. Something like this:

YOUR NEXT APPOINTMENT WITH YOUR WIFE IS ON:

_____

THE EVENING'S ACTIVITIES WILL BEGIN WITH

_____

CONTINUE WITH

_____

AND CONCLUDE WITH

_____

NO CANCELLATIONS. ONLY ONE RESCHEDULING IS PERMITTED.
PROPER ATTIRE IS REQUIRED.

Even natural-born romantics mark our calendars. Sometimes the ole memory slips!

Fill-out several cards: Make one classically romantic, one outrageous, one sexy, one easy, one hard, one inexpensive, one expensive, one time-consuming, one quick, etc. Mail 'em one at a time to your lover.

February 14th

800

Don't buy roses for Valentine's Day!

It's common, expected and expensive. Buy *different* flowers. Flowers in her favorite color. Flowers that match his eyes. Flowers that send a message. Flamboyant flowers. Tiny, delicate flowers. Lots and *lots* of flowers. One single flower.

801

Keep your eyes open for pre-Valentine's Day articles in magazines and newspapers. Rip out the articles, circle the best ideas, and plan accordingly. (And don't forget to *keep those articles for future reference!*)

Rose Is Rose reprinted by permission of United Feature Syndicate, Inc. © 1990.

802

Use kids' valentines: A whole box full of silly puns and clichés, all for just a couple of bucks.

* Mail a boxful of 'em.
* Fill his briefcase full of them.
* Tape them all over her car.
* Fill the sink with them.
* Fill her pillow with them.
* Mail one-a-day for a month.

Valentine's Day

803

Valentine's Day is *not* the most romantic day of the year. You *still* have to recognize it and act on it—send flowers and/or chocolate and/or cards and/or jewelry and/or perfume and/or romantic gifts—but you *don't* get any extra credit for it, guys. Valentine's Day is one of those *Obligatory Romance* days.

804

Turn Valentine's Day into a *real* holiday: Take the day off work. Then spend the day in bed together. Go to the movies. Go out to dinner. Go dancing. Take a drive. Make love. Go for a stroll.

805

* Mail him a Valentine's Day card. Mail him twenty!
* Make your own, *custom* Valentine card.
* Write your own romantically poetic card.
* Or use some verses from a favorite love song.
* Make a *huge* card. Use colored markers and draw a card on poster paper or on a refrigerator-size cardboard box!
* Send a *musical* greeting card.

Tip: If Valentine's Day falls on a **weekday**, *simply shift your personal celebration to the nearest weekend.*

806

■ Send her a box filled with those Valentine Conversation Heart candies. A **BIG** box.

■ Use Valentine Conversation Heart candies to spell out a romantic message to her. Leave it on the kitchen table or paste it to a piece of construction paper.

■ Replace all the Cheerios with Valentine Conversation Hearts.

For Lovers—Of Books

807

❋ Give him a first-edition book by his favorite author.
❋ Give her a book signed by her favorite author.

Attend a booksigning by his favorite author.

Have the cover of her favorite book made into a poster. Have it framed for her office.

Buy him every book written by his favorite author.

Visit the hometown of, or museum/library dedicated to, her favorite author.

Vacation at locations featured in his favorite books.

808

Write your *own* book!

■ A love story (non-fiction)—about the two of you.
■ A "Romance" novel—based loosely on the two of you.
■ A mystery, a science fiction saga, a Western.
■ A picture-book—with photos or sketches of your life together.

809

If he already has that special book in hand, and you'd like to make it even *more* special, you could have it bound in leather for him. Paperbacks can be made to look like family heirlooms, and old, ratty books can be beautifully restored. Call the Argosy Bookstore at 212-753-4455, or drop in at 116 East 59th Street, New York City 10022.

810

For fans of Ernest Hemingway:

✦ Visit the Hemingway Museum in Piggott, Arkansas.
✦ Visit Hemingway's birthplace, Oak Park, Illinois. Call 708-848-2222.
✦ Attend the legendary "Hemingway Look-Alike Contest" at Sloppy Joe's Bar in Key West, Florida, in July. Call 305-294-1136.

Chapter Theme Song:

"Storybook Lovers," The Four Seasons

Sex—By the Book

811a

Humbly submitted for your perusal, some *erotic fiction:*

* *The Best American Erotica 1993*, edited by Susie Bright
* See above, also available: *1994, '95, '96, '97* and *'99*
* *Little Birds,* by Anaïs Nin
* *Delta of Venus,* also by Anaïs Nin
* *Lady Chatterley's Lover,* by D.H. Lawrence
* *Tropic of Cancer,* by Henry Miller
* *Tropic of Capricorn,* also by Henry Miller
* *Yellow Silk,* edited by Lily Pond & Richard Russo
* *The Literary Lover*, edited by Larry Dark
* *Erotica: An Illustrated Anthology of Sexual Art & Literature,* edited by Charlotte Hill
* See above, also available: *Erotica II* and *Erotica III*
* *Herotica: A Collection of Women's Erotic Fiction*, edited by Susie Bright
* See above, also available: *Herotica 2* and *Herotica 3*

Libido magazine—"Erotica for people who like to read." Call 800-495-1988.

811b

Modestly submitted for your perusal, some *sexy non-fiction:*

* *Full Exposure: Opening Up to Sexual Creativity and Erotic Expression*, by Susie Bright
* *The Sexual State of the Union*, by Susie Bright
* *Human Sexuality Today*, by Bruce King
* *The Kama Sutra*
* *101 Nights of Grrreat Sex* or *101 Grrreat Quickies* by Laura Corn
* *Red Hot LoveNotes for Lovers*, by Larry James
* *The Joy of Sex,* by Alex Comfort
* *Is Sex Necessary?* by James Thurber and E.B. White
* *Sex: If I Didn't Laugh I'd Cry*, by Jess Lair
* *The Couples' Guide to Erotic Games*, by Gerald Schoenewolf

A hot and helpful book:
Passion Play: Ancient Secrets for a Lifetime of Health and Happiness Through Sensational Sex,
by Felice Dunas.

Married . . . With Children
812

Guys: Give your *wife* a gift on your *kids'* birthdays. (Why should the kids get all the gifts? Your *wife* is the one who did all the work!)

813a

Sometimes you really need to *escape* from the kids. Time *alone* together is required in order to build intimacy.

➤ Hang a "Do Not Disturb" sign on your bedroom door when you want a little privacy. Enforce this directive strictly! (Teach your rugrats to read "Do not disturb," before "Once upon a time.")

➤ Declare every Wednesday to be Mom's and Dad's "date night." Just go off by yourselves for a couple of hours. Maybe just take a walk or go out for coffee. It makes a great, rejuvenating break in the middle of the week.

813b

Sometimes its great to *include* your children in your romantic adventures. (How *else* are they going to learn how loving adults are supposed to act?!)

➥ Take vacations at family-oriented resorts. When there are lots of things for the kids to do, it takes the pressure off you. The kids will have a better time and so will you.

➥ Declare every Thursday to be "family night." Make a special point to have dinner together. Play a board game. Pile onto the couch and watch a movie together. Take a walk together. Read aloud from a favorite book.

Chapter Theme Song:

"Eyes of a Child," The Moody Blues

Kid Stuff

814

Instead of having the babysitter come in while the two of you go out, *have the babysitter take the kids out—while you two stay home!* Send all of them to a movie—a *double feature*. ("Now, what was it we used to do with all this peace and quiet? *Oh, yes . . . !*")

815

Send your kids to summer camp. It just might revitalize your marriage unlike any specific romantic gesture *ever* could! Some resources:

- ❐ American Camping Association: 800-428-CAMP; www.ACAcamps.org/
- ❐ National Camp Association: 800-966-CAMP; www.SummerCamp.org/
- ❐ Tips on Trips and Camps Service: 800-519-8477; www.TipsTripsCamps.com/

*True romantics retain a **childlike** mindset. Therein lies wonder, joy and a natural, uninhibited way of expressing love.*

816

Guys: Add Mother's Day to your list of *Obligatory Romance* dates to observe. Mark it on your calendar *now*.

817

Make special "Love Coupons" to help each other deal with the kids:

- ✳ An "I'll get up in the middle of the night with the baby" coupon.
- ✳ An "It's my turn to stay home with the next sick kid" coupon.
- ✳ A coupon for "Five 'taxi trips': Hauling the kids to soccer practice."
- ✳ An "I'll cook the kids' dinner" coupon.

Chapter Theme Song:
"I Won't Grow Up," from *Peter Pan*

Rituals of Romance

818

For your next anniversary: Write a short, sweet poem titled, "Another Wonderful Year with You." Then for the following year, write *another* poem (same title). This ritual gives you a built-in gift every year!

For your twenty-fifth or fiftieth anniversary you might collect the poems into a book, or have them all framed, or have them rendered in elegant calligraphy.

Rituals heighten the meaning of special events in our lives.

819

One couple in the Romance Class told us that they celebrate the changing of the seasons by taking a walk together on the first day of summer, autumn, winter and spring—*regardless* of the weather.

820

Another couple plants a new rose bush on their anniversary to celebrate another year together.

821

One man brings his wife a cup of tea before bed every night—*whether she wants one or not.*

822

➤ Write a toast, just for the two of you. Use it whenever having wine.
➤ Write *two* toasts: One for *private* use, and one for *public* use.
➤ Write a new toast once a year.
➤ Write a toast that incorporates lyrics from her favorite love song.

Romantic Rituals

823

Some couples have *morning* rituals:

- They spend ten minutes talking in bed before rising.
- They read an affirmation aloud to one another.
- They make a point of kissing before parting.

824

Some couples have *evening* rituals:

- They go for a walk after dinner together.
- They meditate silently together.
- They take turns every other night giving each other backrubs.

825

And, there are Sunday morning rituals:

- Attending a church service together.
- Reading the Sunday funnies aloud to each other.
- Sunday brunch.

826

My wife and I have a little "car ritual" we've performed for as long as we've known each other: I always open the car door for her (regardless of which one of us is driving), and she always leans over and unlocks my door from the inside. I never really thought of it as a "ritual" until recently. It's just a little thing we *always* do that helps us not take the other for granted.

Chapter Theme Song:
"Cherish," The Association

Oldies But Goodies

827

Romantic inspiration from the famous Burma Shave roadside ads. (Ask a senior citizen to explain it to you.) Hang a series of four brief-and-clever signs in your house.

☞ WELCOME HOME—LET'S MISBEHAVE—THE KIDS ARE OUT—BURMA SHAVE!

☞ TO LOVE YOU—ONE NEEDN'T BE BRAVE—JUST KINDA CRAZY—BURMA SHAVE!

☞ BE MY WIFE!—FULFILL MY DAYS—JUST SAY YES—BURMA SHAVE!

828

Hold your own "Oldies But Goodies" nights at home. Here are some different themes that Romance Class participants have tried:

➜ *The 1920s:* Complete with flapper outfits and jazz.

➜ *WWII:* Complete with military uniforms, USO posters and patriotic music.

➜ *The 1960s:* Love beads, Woodstock, old jeans and tie-dyed T-shirts!

➜ *The Victorian Era:* With rented costumes, minuets and horse-drawn carriage rides!

829

Creating a nostalgic mood will help you remember (then recreate!) those favorite romantic memories. Amor music offers a collection of popular music from the 1930s, '40s, '50s and '60s—all by the original artists. Choose from swing, jazz, love songs, rock 'n roll, Latin and international music. Each CD is packaged in a beautifully decorated round can.

Look in stores or call Amor Music at 800-919-3990 or visit www.AmorMusic.com.

Some Oldies But Goodies:

"I Can't Give You Anything but Love" (1928)

"All of Me" (1931)

"I'm Getting Sentimental Over You" (1932)

"Let's Fall in Love" (1933)

"I'm in the Mood for Love" (1935)

"In the Still of the Night" (1936)

"My Funny Valentine" (1937)

"Some Like It Hot" (1939)

"You Made Me Love You" (1941)

"People Will Say We're in Love" (1943)

"As Time Goes By" (1943)

"Sentimental Journey" (1945)

"Some Enchanted Evening" (1949)

"Love Is a Many Splendored Thing" (1955)

"Moon River" (1961)

"Growing old is mandatory, but growing up is optional."

~ ANONYMOUS

Oldies But Goodies: Movies
830

Movies from the 1930s:

* *Gone With the Wind*
* *Camille*
* *The Awful Truth*
* *Wuthering Heights*
* *The Thin Man*
* *City Lights*

Movies from the 1940s:

* *Casablanca*
* *The Shop Around the Corner*
* *Adam's Rib*
* *The Philadelphia Story*
* *Now, Voyager*
* *To Have and Have Not*

Movies from the 1950s:

* *The African Queen*
* *Roman Holiday*
* *An Affair to Remember*
* *Magnificent Obsession*
* *South Pacific*
* *Pillow Talk*

Movies from the 1960s:

* *Doctor Zhivago*
* *Breakfast at Tiffany's*
* *West Side Story*
* *David and Lisa*
* *Splendor in the Grass*
* *Two for the Road*

Movies from the 1970s:

* *The Way We Were*
* *Annie Hall*
* *Robin and Marian*
* *Love Story*
* *The Goodbye Girl*
* *Mahogany*

Movies from the 1980s:

* *An Officer and a Gentleman*
* *Crossing Delancey*
* *When Harry Met Sally*
* *Moonstruck*
* *Arthur*
* *Dirty Dancing*

Movies from the 1990s:

* *Shakespeare in Love*
* *You've Got Mail*
* *Ghost*
* *Titanic*
* *Pretty Woman*
* *Sleepless in Seattle*

Hold an at-home "Romantic Oldies But Goodies" movie festival, organized by decade. Great for recreating memories.

Movie Madness

831

Present her with a framed movie poster from her all-time-favorite movie! Vintage or current, romantic, dramatic or funny! Prices vary depending on availability, size, age and condition. Call Jerry Ohlinger's Movie Material Store at 212-989-0869. They have a vast assortment of stuff from the 1930s to the present. Visit their amazing shop at 242 West 14th Street, New York, New York 10011.

832

Or create themes for your At-Home Video Film Festivals. Choose your lover's favorite "type" or genre of movie:

- ✦ Comedy
- ✦ Science fiction
- ✦ Silent films
- ✦ Elvis movies
- ✦ All of the Pink Panther movies
- ✦ All of the Beatles' movies
- ✦ All Neil Simon movies
- ✦ All Woody Allen movies
- ✦ James Bond movies
- ✦ All of John Wayne's films

833

Don't neglect the many classic film series hosted by local colleges and universities, YMCAs, museums and classic theaters.

834

And don't forget about drive-ins! They're a great way to inspire some nostalgia and ignite some passion.

What is your partner's favorite movie of all time? (What insights does this reveal about his/her personality?)

Mad About You

835

She hung a thirty-six-inch-wide strip of butcher paper on the wall. She then painted her body with water-based red tempera paint, then struck a pose and pressed her painted body against the paper—creating a very personalized and definitely one-of-a-kind work of art. She let it dry, rolled it up, tied it with a red ribbon, and gave it to her husband for Valentine's Day. He still talks about it to this day.

836

He always did have a tendency to "overdo" things. One year he rented a limousine for her birthday. She enjoyed it so much that the following year he rented the limo *again* . . . but this time he rented it *for an entire week!* So in addition to their fancy night on the town, she got chauffeured to the supermarket, to the dry cleaner, to church; the kids got chauffeured to school, to soccer practice, to the playground. A memorable experience for one and all!

837

It was Sally's birthday, but her husband David hadn't acknowledged it all day, and Sally's disappointment was starting to turn into anger. Then David asked her to run some errands for him while he went out to play golf, and her heart just sank. She gave up.

While walking dejectedly through the mall she did a double-take at a store mannekin who looked remarkably like David. Then the mannekin *winked* at her. It was David, who stepped out of the store window and kissed her. Dressed in a tuxedo, he led her to the dress department, where he bought her an elegant evening gown. Then, in their formal attire, they went out to the best French restaurant in town.

*Remember when you were "mad about" each other? You **can** recreate that feeling!*

Chapter Theme Song:
"Mad About You," Belinda Carlisle
"Mad About You," Sting

Great Escapes

838

Don't just "go to the islands"—*rent a private island* for a truly amazing fantasy vacation or honeymoon!

* Turtle Island, Fiji—The location for the film *The Blue Lagoon*. Call 877-288-7853 or visit www.TurtleFiji.com.
* Little Palm Island, Florida—An exotic honeymoon hideaway in the Keys. Call 800-343-8567 or visit www.LittlePalmIsland.com.

839

Visit Liverpool, England, for a "Magical Mystery Tour" of The Beatles' hometown. Walk down Penny Lane, see the Cavern Club, visit the multi-media exhibit, and ponder the Eleanor Rigby statue (dedicated to "All the lonely people.") And, of course, there's The Beatles Shop, which is chock-full of memorabilia and music.

840

The romance of the open road . . . the vacation that never ends . . . the RV lifestyle! (Some people think that "RV" stands for "Recreational Vehicle." *I* say it stands for "Romantic Vehicle.")

Call 800-327-7778 for CruiseAmerica, which rents all makes and sizes of RVs—so you can try different units before buying one.

841

Go for a "mystery drive" in the country. Keep to the back roads and ignore the map. Agree to have lunch at the first charming inn or classic diner you pass. If you stumble onto a quaint bed-and-breakfast, stay the night! (You do, of course, have "His" and "Hers" overnight bags stored in the trunk, don't you?!)

Escape from the mundane.

Escape from the clock.

Escape from stress.

Escape from the kids.

Escape from the Rat Race.

Escape from boredom.

Getting Away From It All

842

The top five "romantic images," from polling thousands of Romance Class participants:

1. Candlelight dinner
2. A classic wedding ceremony
3. Cuddling in front of a roaring fireplace
4. Walking on a beach
5. An ocean cruise

When you're ready to take the ultimate in romantic vacations and you want to book a cruise, my suggestion is to talk to lots of people and see whom they recommend. Norwegian Cruise Line keeps popping up at the top of the list. For destinations, schedules, info on their ships and services: 800-327-7030; www.ncl.com.

Some of my most romantic memories involve cruises.

843

Before going on vacation, get stacks of brochures, posters and books about your upcoming destination. Mail them to your partner on a regular basis. It will help build the anticipation for your vacation.

Great travel resource: *The Modern Bride Guide to Honeymoons and Destination Weddings*, by Geri Bain.

844

Two opposite approaches to spending money on vacations:

✦ Spend *as little as possible* on accommodations, and *as much as possible* on dining out! Some folks appreciate a great meal more than anything. This approach allows them to indulge without guilt!

✦ Pamper yourselves with *the most luxurious room* you can find, and save money by *cutting other corners*, like eating frugally and avoiding costly tourist traps. Some folks create a "love nest" out of their vacation room and settle in for a week of loving, reading, cuddling and relaxing.

An Anniversary Checklist

845

I pose this question in my Romance Classes: "Just who made up this anniversary gift list, anyway?" Well, no one has been able to answer the question definitively, so I figure *my* gift list is as good as anybody's!

*Nobody knows **why** these lists always jump by five-year intervals following number fifteen! (It's up to **you** to fill in the in-between years!)*

How are you going to celebrate your next anniversary?

Year	Traditional	*MODERN*	Godek's
1	Paper	Clocks	Lingerie
2	Cotton	China	Lingerie
3	Leather	Crystal/glass	Lingerie
4	Fruit/flowers	Appliances	Software
5	Wood	Silver/silverware	Books
6	Candy/iron	Wood	Lingerie
7	Wood/copper	Desksets	Wine
8	Bronze/pottery	Linens/laces	A cruise
9	Pottery/willow	Leather	CDs
10	Tin/aluminum	Diamond jewelry	Jewelry
11	Steel	Fashion jewelry	Silk
12	Silk/linen	Pearls	Perfume
13	Lace	Textiles/furs	Umbrellas
14	Ivory	Gold jewelry	Lingerie
15	Crystal	Watches	Computers
20	China	Platinum	Champagne
25	Silver	Silver	Jacuzzis
30	Pearl	Diamond/pearl	Diamond
35	Coral	Jade	Sculpture
40	Ruby	Ruby	Stocks
45	Sapphire	Sapphire	Emerald
50	Gold	Gold	Rolls Royce
55	Emerald	Emerald	Gold
60	Diamond	Diamond	Paris vacation

1001 WAYS TO BE ROMANTIC

A Romantic Basics Checklist

846

Here, in checklist form, are all of the "Romantic Basics." These items are described and expanded upon elsewhere in this book, but here's a quick-and-handy reference page for you.

- ❐ Roses
- ❐ Chocolate
- ❐ Champagne
- ❐ Lingerie
- ❐ Love songs
- ❐ Love poetry
- ❐ Ballroom dancing
- ❐ Dinner out
- ❐ Dinner at home
- ❐ Formal dates
- ❐ Love Coupons
- ❐ Classic gold chain
- ❐ Massages
- ❐ Romantic fantasies
- ❐ Sexy fantasies
- ❐ Diamonds
- ❐ Cruises
- ❐ Vacations
- ❐ Honeymoons
- ❐ Birthdays
- ❐ Special holidays
- ❐ Heart-shaped box of candy

- ❐ Flowers
- ❐ Perfume
- ❐ Jewelry
- ❐ Greeting cards
- ❐ Love letters
- ❐ Love notes
- ❐ Breakfast in bed
- ❐ Movie at a theater
- ❐ Movie at home
- ❐ Little surprises
- ❐ Homemade cards
- ❐ Candy
- ❐ Candles
- ❐ Having sex
- ❐ Making love
- ❐ Wine
- ❐ Drive-in movies
- ❐ Bed and breakfasts
- ❐ Hotel suites
- ❐ Anniversaries
- ❐ Valentine's Day
- ❐ Crystal champagne flutes

*How would you **personalize** this list?*

Generating Ideas

847

Set a goal of generating or discovering one new romantic idea each day for a year. (Your commitment will help draw ideas to you.) Keep your notes, articles, comics, ads and miscellaneous reminders in a shoebox under your bed.

You have tremendous, untapped reservoirs of creativity inside!

848

Train your subconscious mind to find romantic ideas *for* you. Hey, why should your subconscious mind be doing nothing but daydreaming all day long while the rest of your mind is doing all the work? Scientists say that we only use about 10 percent of our brains: This is a way to boost your brain efficiency to 25 percent or better!

Seriously, you *can* assign a small portion of your brain the task of being constantly on the lookout for romantic ideas. The goal is to retrain your mind to stop *filtering out* those ideas, and start letting them come to the attention of your conscious mind. What starts happening is that romantic articles and gift ideas will start "jumping out at you." Guaranteed.

849

Practice creating "Variations on a Theme" for generating romantic ideas. Start with any idea and build on it, expand it, extend it.

- Start with "greeting cards": Buy one; buy a *hundred!* Make some yourself. Send one-a-day for a week, send one-a-day for a *month!* Frame some cards that she's given you.
- Start with "candy": What's her favorite? Buy ten pounds of it. Fill her shoes with candy; fill her purse, her glove compartment, her pillow. Send it to her at work. Spell out words with it. Create trails throughout the house with it.

Romantic Brainstorming

850

Hold a "Romantic Idea Brainstorming Session" with a group of friends. Serve pizza and beer. Hand out pads of paper and markers. Use a large pad on an easel to compile ideas.

The goal is to generate *as many ideas as possible* in one hour: Serious and silly, practical and unrealistic, expensive and inexpensive, thoughtful and outrageous, sweet and sexy.

851

Generate romantic ideas using your partner's likes, passions and favorite things. What's his or her favorite color, favorite author, poet, artist, movie, TV show, song, singer, wine, perfume, restaurant, ice cream, sport or flower? Use this knowledge as a springboard for creating romantic ideas that you *know* will be unique and special.

852

Tap into the strength of your own personal style and your special talents. Do you have a flair for writing, dancing, building things, organizing, cooking or drawing? Use these talents and abilities to enhance the romance in your life!

Sit down and take an inventory of your own personal talents, interests, skills, aptitudes and passions. Write a list. Use it as an idea-generator.

853

Institute the "Buddy System." Team-up with a good friend and act as each other's personal "Romance Coach." Encourage each other, trade ideas, remind each other of important dates, compare notes, and share new discoveries.

Chapter Theme Song:
"One Hundred Ways," Quincy Jones

A Kick in the Pants

854

Do you take your partner for granted? *Well stop it!* Taking your partner for granted is not only the death of romance, but could well be the death of your relationship.

*I **dare** you to be romantic!*

855

Take a risk—be romantic. *I dare you.*

Being truly romantic is a risky thing to do. I respect this difficulty and at the same time encourage you to leap off the cliff. Being truly romantic involves opening yourself up and revealing your feelings. Let's face it, nobody wants to be burned, and it's hard to risk a broken heart when you've been through a number of relationships.

- ❤ But if you're not going to open up to your lover, who else is there?
- ❤ And if you're consciously choosing *not* to open up, you might want to ask yourself what you're afraid of, or what you're hiding.
- ❤ And if you're not going to be romantic and open up, then what's the point of being in a relationship in the first place?!

856

Go for it!

Change one bad habit. Just *one!* (You'll be helping *yourself* as well as pleasing your partner!) Lose those ten pounds you've been meaning to shed. Stop smoking. Eat more healthfully. Dress better. Exercise more. Listen better. Be more courteous. Slow your pace.

Motivating Your Partner
To Be More Romantic

857

Do things that your *partner* will interpret as loving gestures. Do these things *without an attitude*, without expecting anything in return, and without any wise comments.

Most people respond in kind. It might take a week or two, but most people *do* come around. Now don't forget that love is worth working on, and that these things take time.

*The **nice** approach.*

858

Don't try to get him to be more romantic to you. Instead, aim at changing his *level of awareness* about the need for more romance/intimacy/communication in your relationship. Successful long-term changes in behavior usually follow a change in awareness. If you start with behavior modification, you'll probably only produce *short-term* results. Some techniques for raising awareness include:

* Simply talking (heart-to-heart)
* Model romantic behavior ("Monkey see, monkey do!")
* Getting like-minded friends to set him straight
* Good psychology/relationship books
* A class or seminar on love and relationships
* Couple's counseling

*The **psychological** approach.*

859

If you have a *really reluctant* partner, I recommend that you play a lighthearted game that I call, "I'll do *this* for you if you'll do *that* for me." You might trade meals, chores, sex, erotic fantasies, back rubs, babysitting, naps or balancing the checkbook. This simple and fun approach often works to recharge a relationship when the more sophisticated "pshycholgical" approaches fail.

*The **give-and-take** approach.*

Motivating the Romantically Impaired

860

A major reason why some people aren't romantic is that *a lack of it doesn't affect them*. If you want him to be more romantic, but he's satisfied with the status quo ... "Well, tough luck—that's *your* problem!" he says/thinks.

The solution? Simple: *Make it his problem*. People only really solve problems that they see as *problems that relate to themselves*.

How do you "make it his problem"? Well, you start by telling him up front *what* you want (more romance), and *how* you want it (circle your favorite items in this book!). You need to be specific, positive and loving in your approach.

It might help both of you to remember that problems (especially *relationship* problems) are actually opportunities in disguise! I've seen couples use this technique to transform frustrating D- Relationships into happy, solid B+ Relationships. (You can do it, too!)

*No, the Romantically Impaired are **not** entitled to use parking spaces for the handicapped.*

861

Seven Ways to Woo a Workaholic Away from Work:

1. Promise your partner the best sex of his/her life—
2. Follow through on your promise!
3. (If you can't beat 'em, join 'em!): Create a business together.
4. Make a "Mission Impossible" audio tape that leads him/her to a mystery date with you.
5. Book a hotel room—within walking distance of his office—and invite him over for an afternoon "meeting."
6. Meet him for lunch; dress very sexy. Then coyly ask him if he'd like another lunch date next week.
7. Have a courier deliver a steamy love letter to her office.

Attitude Adjustment Section

862

Be spontaneous. Be silly. Lower your inhibitions. Express your love. If you do these things, you'll *automatically* be romantic.

863

Try being totally positive, accepting, supportive and nonjudgmental for one entire week. No complaining, nagging, preaching, etc. It may change your life!

864

- Loosen your purse strings.
- Loosen your schedule.
- Loosen your tie.
- Loosen your *attitude*.
- Loosen your inhibitions.

"Is not this the true romantic feeling—not to desire to escape life, but to prevent life from escaping you?"

- THOMAS WOLFE

865

Want to keep your marriage fresh and vital? *Live as lovers*. Not just as husband and wife, mother and father, workers and housekeepers, caregivers and bill payers. First and foremost *you are lovers*. Remember that's how you *started* your relationship. You *can* recapture the glow, the passion and the excitement. It's largely a mindset, followed by a few active gestures.

For one week, make this your affirmation, your mantra, your prayer: *Live as lovers*. Post notes to yourselves, remind each other, and practice!

License to Love

866

Create a custom cassette tape of romantic love songs for her.

➤ Choose a dozen great songs and record them on a cassette tape.
➤ Listen to the tape together in the car. Sing the solos to her. Sing the harmonies together. Sing the duets at the top of your lungs!

867

Drive by his parking lot at work. Attach balloons to the side mirror. Tape streamers to the back windshield. Leave a love note on the front seat.

Surprise her with a personalized license plate!

■ Most states charge somewhere between $50 and $100 a year.
■ Many of the most popular and common names and phrases are already taken, so you'll have to use a little creativity. Consider these possibilities, and use them to spark your own ideas:

✱ Her initials
✱ Both of your initials
✱ Her birthdate
✱ Your anniversary date
✱ Your pet name for her

✱ "Code phrases"
  ✴ ILY
  ✴ IMWLD4U
  ✴ 4EVER
  ✴ UNME

Note: The most populous states usually have the most digits in their license plates, giving the creative copywriter more flexibility. (One innovative man in the Romance Class registered his wife's car in a neighboring state [New York] so he could use *seven* digits to spell out his wife's name.)

868

Pun alert!

➥ Jim's wife is a graphic artist. He created for her an "artistic license" which hangs on her office wall.

➥ Harriet's husband writes poetry in his spare time. For his birthday she created a "poetic license" which he carries proudly in his wallet.

Baby, You Can Drive My Car

869

Place a little love note or poem under the driver's side windshield wiper of his or her car.

*True romantics let **nothing** stand in their way: If it's rainy or snowy, place the love note in a Ziploc bag!*

870

Other items to put under the windshield wiper:

* A single rose
* A candy bar
* Wildflowers
* A little book
* A poem
* A pizza coupon
* A cartoon
* A Love Coupon
* A short note

871

Buying a new car? Arrange to have it delivered one day *earlier* than she expects it, park it in the driveway, and wait for her to notice it.

872

Wrap the car with a big red bow!

Write and design a fake traffic ticket; place it under the windshield wiper. Possible violations include:

* Leaving the scene of a love affair
* Speeding down the highway of life
* Driving me crazy

Possible options for making restitution include:

* Taking the judge out to dinner
* Bribing the officer with sexual favors
* One sensual backrub

Chapter Theme Song:
"Drive My Car," The Beatles

Little Love Stories (I)

873

She gave him the key to her apartment in a velvet jewelry box. On the card she wrote: "You hold the key to my happiness, and now you hold the key to my home. You've unlocked my heart. Please don't break it."

874

During their seven years of dating he'd given her many flowers. During their long-awaited wedding ceremony she surprised him with a roomful of flowers—the very flowers he had given her. She'd had *every flower he'd ever given her* carefully and lovingly dried or pressed.

875

At a farmhouse in Iowa: A wire fence runs along the western side of the Smiths' house. One morning Sara notices hundreds of red ribbons hanging like streamers from the fence. She asks Fred about it, but gets only a mischievous grin in return. Later that day when the wind starts blowing and the ribbons start flapping, Sara sees that they are tied in a pattern that spells out "I LOVE MY SARA."

Little Love Stories (II)

876

Charlie and his girlfriend Randi were aboard Continental Airlines flight 191 from Newark to San Francisco. Shortly after takeoff the pilot made this announcement: "I have an important message for the passenger in seat 3-B. Will you marry the gentleman in seat 3-A? If the answer is *yes*, press the Call Button for the flight attendant." As Randi burst into tears, Charlie kept saying "Push the button!" When she did, a flight attendant came up with a silver tray, champagne and the ring!

877

Mary was a Beanie Baby *fanatic*. Her husband, Bob, hired a custom doll-maker to create a "Beanie Bob" for her.

Bob credits the comic strip Bizarro, by Dan Piraro, for this idea.

878

Tom arrived home from running errands one Saturday morning to find his wife, Susan, gone. His daughter handed him a note from her:

"Go to the drug store. See the pharmacist." Even though his first reaction was, "Why? Who's sick?" he went along. What else *could* he do but follow instructions? When he started up the car, a tape of romantic music started playing. ("Ah, ha! I think something's going on here!") The pharmacist had a card for him: "Happy Anniversary!—Now, head for the liquor store!" A bottle of champagne was waiting for him there, along with *another* note: "Ready to celebrate? Not yet! On to the men's shop first!" A monogrammed shirt was his surprise there. The note was no longer a surprise: "Almost done! But first, please stop at the grocery store." A picnic basket packed with goodies was ready for him there.

The last note simply had an address on it. It led him to a romantic little bed and breakfast, where Susan was waiting for him. The rest, as they say, is history.

"Love creates an 'us' without destroying a 'me'."

~ Leo Buscaglia

Notes from an A+ Relationship

879

While *everyone* knows that commitment is important in a relationship, only folks with A+ Relationships are *specific* about their commitments. These are the dozen best relationship commitments generated during twenty years of my Romance Classes:

1. Commit yourselves to your relationship.
2. Commit to spending 10 percent more time together.
3. Commit yourselves to being less judgmental.
4. Commit yourselves to living up to your wedding vows.
5. Commit yourselves to having more fun together.
6. Commit yourselves to practicing your religious beliefs on your partner.
7. Commit yourselves to seeing your partner's negative behaviors as calls for love.
8. Commit to communicating your feelings fully.
9. Commit yourselves to your partner's happiness.
10. Commit yourselves to feeling your feelings of love.
11. Commit yourselves to acting on your feelings of love.
12. Commit yourselves to listening to the voice of love inside you.

880

☞ Touch your partner—with your eyes.
☞ Touch your partner—with your words.
☞ Touch your partner—with gifts and presents.
☞ Touch your partner—with your thoughts, prayers and wishes.
☞ Touch your partner—with your actions.

Did you know—?

Having an A+ Relationship can help you live a longer and healthier life? This is not simply common sense, but has been proven *medically.* See these two books by Dean Ornish, M.D.

Love & Survival: The Scientific Basis for the Healing Power of Intimacy

Love & Survival: 8 Pathways to Intimacy & Health

How to spot people who have an A+ Relationship: Look for the sparkle in their eyes.

Recipe for an A+ Relationship

881

Overview: Recipe takes 2 individuals and turns them into 1 couple.

Background: Gather ingredients over time, and practice cooking for twenty to thirtysomething years.

Ingredients:

1 cup attraction
1 cup compatibility
2 nuts
1 quart honesty combined with 2 quarts compassion
1 pint each of faith, hope and charity: Combine and mix vigorously
1 dash thoughtfulness
1 pinch
2 pints cooperation combined with 2 pints compromise
2 quarts forgiveness
2 gallons sense of humor
2 pounds sex (raw)
Plus an endless supply of love, sex and romance, in the ratio 2:1:3

Preparation:

Combine all ingredients (in any order!) and stir like crazy. Leave medium lumps. (If too smooth, days will be boring; but if lumps too big, problems will be too big to swallow.) Heat with passion but never bring to a boil!

Spice to your personal taste.

Serving:

Yields 50 or more years of marriage.
Divide into 50 years and serve separately.
Sub-divide each year into 365 days; savor each day individually.

Note: Each day tastes different. *This is normal.* Some days are sweet. Some days are sour. Some days are smooth. Some days are chewy and difficult. Some days are spicy. Some days are hard to swallow. But every day is *exactly what you need,* and the portions are just right for your needs.

Note: The first two years tend to be spicy. The middle years tend to be nutty. The later years tend to be savory. But they're all *delicious!*

Important! Pass down this recipe to your children and to future generations.

Romance Across America

882

→ Visit all fifty states—one or two a year for as long as it takes.
→ Camp in every national park in the country.
→ Then, start on the state parks.

883

Go whitewater rafting! Adventurous folks at these firms will get you started downstream:

➤ Appalachian Wildwaters: 800-624-8060; www.awrafts.com
➤ USA Raft: 800-USA-RAFT; www.USAraft.com
➤ Outback Expeditions: 800-343-1640

884

Bicycle across the United States! The 4,500-mile TransAmerica Bicycle Trail follows side roads and uncrowded state routes through rural America. The trail goes from Yorktown, Virginia to Astoria, Oregon, and takes from fifty to ninety days to complete. For more information, call Adventure Cycling at 800-755-2453 or 406-721-1776, or write P.O. Box 8308, Missoula, Montana 59807, or visit www.adv-cycling.org.

885

Attend one of America's many *hot air balloon festivals*.

❖ The U.S. National Hot Air Balloon Festival: Early August, in Indianola, Iowa. Call 515-961-8415.
❖ The "Greit Oktoberfest Balloon Rallye": Late August/early September, in Dansville, New York.
❖ The International Balloon Fiesta: Mid-October, in Albuquerque, New Mexico. Call 800-284-2282.

When you're in Rochester, New York:

Dine at Café Cupid. (A *stunningly* romantic little place!) 754 East Ridge Road, in Irondequoit.

Shop at the coolest gift shop in America, The Parkleigh, 215 Park Avenue in Rochester. Call 800-333-0627, or visit www.Parkleigh.com.

When you're in Fort Wayne, Indiana:

Visit the butterfly aviary at the Fort Wayne Children's Zoo.

When you're in Phoenix, Arizona:

Visit the Hall of Flame Museum of Firefighting. Call 602-275-3473.

When you're in Springfield, Massachusetts:

Visit the *Titanic* Museum (the *ship*, not the movie). Call 413-543-4770.

When you're in Atlanta, Georgia:

Take your chatterbox to visit the Telephone Museum. Call 404-223-3661.

Romance Around the World

886

Some recommendations from Romance Class participants:

* The most romantic restaurant in Vienna: Steirereck
* The most romantic restaurant in Amsterdam: De Goudsbloem
* The most romantic restaurant in Rome: Girone VI
* The most romantic restaurant in Stockholm: Min Lilla Tradgard

887

* The most romantic hotel in Paris: La Tremoille
* The most romantic hotel in Vienna: Romischer Kaiser
* The most romantic hotel in Rome: Sole al Pantheon
* The most romantic hotel in Amsterdam: Pulitzer
* The most romantic hotel in Copenhagen: Skovshoved
* The most romantic hotel in Madrid: Santa Mauro

888

If your lover loves the beach, plan a vacation to one of the great beaches of the world. Choose a beach based on the kind of beachy activity he/she likes to indulge in:

A+ for *unspoiled:*

* Barbuda, West Indies
* Kea, Greek Islands

A+ for *lazing:*

* Isla de Cozumel, Mexico
* Molokai, Hawaii
* North Island, New Zealand

A+ for *beachcombing:*

* Mindoro, Philippines
* Sanibel Island, Florida

Gather lots of info for your romantic trip!

Austria: www.anto.com

Belgium: 212-758-8130; www.visitbelgium.com

England: 212-986-2266; www.usagateway.visitbritain.com

Cyprus: 212-683-5280; www.cyprustourism.org

Denmark: 212-885-9700; www.visitdenmark.com

Finland: 800-346-4636; 212-885-9700

France: 310-271-6665; www.francetourism.com

Germany: 800-637-1171

Greece: 213-626-6696

Iceland: 212-885-9700

Ireland: 800-223-6470; www.ireland.travel.ie

Italy: 310-820-0098

Netherlands: 888-464-6552; www.goholland.com

Norway: 212-885-9700; www.norway.org

Poland: 212-338-9412; www.polandtour.org

Portugal: 800-767-8842; www.portugal.org

Sweden: 212-885-9700; www.gosweden.org

Switzerland: www.myswitzerland.com

The Right Stuff

889

Psychological experiments have shown that most people can turn a new behavior into a habit in three weeks. *Their* experiments involved *boring* activities like exercising or waking up an hour earlier than usual. *My* suggestion (as you might have guessed) is that you conduct your own experiment in turning romantic behavior into a habit.

Here's a possible approach to your Experiment In Romance: For three weeks—that's twenty-one straight days—practice these behaviors:

◆ Say "I love you" to your partner at least five times a day.
◆ Find at least one romantic idea in the newspaper every day.
◆ Call your partner from work at least three times a day.
◆ Reduce your TV-watching by one hour per night. Do something *together* with that time.
◆ Make love at least twice a week.
◆ Circle ten ideas in this book that you think your partner would enjoy. Discuss them with him/her.
◆ Surprise your partner in some *small way* every other day.

At the end of three weeks you'll be a more romantic person. You may not become Valentino, but you *will* be more aware of the importance of romance in your life, you'll be more in touch with your own feelings of love, and you'll be in closer touch with your lover.

Not a bad habit, huh?!

"The greatest acts of love are done by those who habitually perform small acts of kindness."

~ ANONYMOUS

The Write Stuff

890

Some books on love, relationships, men and women, etc.

Love Is Letting Go of Fear, by Gerald Jampolsky
Living, Loving & Learning, by Leo Buscaglia
✦ *Notes on Love and Courage*, by Hugh Prather
The Oxford Book of Marriage, edited by Helge Rubinstein
Love, by Leo Buscaglia
The Psychology of Romantic Love, by Nathan Branden
You Just Don't Understand, by Deborah Tannen, Ph.D.
Loving Each Other, by Leo Buscaglia
✦ *Rediscovering Love*, by Willard Gaylin
The Tao of Relationships, by Ray Grigg
✦ *Love and Will*, by Rollo May
Iron John, by Robert Bly

891

Some *fun and funny* books about relationships, love and/or sex:

✳ *Dave Barry's Guide to Marriage and/or Sex*, by Dave Barry
✳ *Sex: If I Didn't Laugh I'd Cry*, by Jess Lair
✳ *The Dieter's Guide to Weight Loss During Sex*, by Richard Smith
✳ *Why Did I Marry You, Anyway?* by Arlene Modica Matthews

892

Be prepared: Write it down! Make a list of at least ten little things you *know* your partner would love. Would she love a massage? Would he love a special dessert? Would she love to have her car waxed? Would he love a new CD?

Don't put this off until later—write this list by the end of the day today. Then keep this list with you as a reminder. Commit yourself to accomplishing one item per week over the next ten weeks.

A Bookstore Coupon

Good for a one-hour shopping spree
in the bookstore of your choice.
Good for up to $50.

Real Men *Are* Romantic

893

Do something *with* her that you normally hate doing (and do it cheerfully without complaint). Go dress shopping with her; go out to a movie with her; attend the ballet with her; do some gardening with her.

894

Do something *for* her that you hate doing (and do it cheerfully and without complaint). Go grocery shopping, wash the dishes, weed the garden, get up in the middle of the night with the baby.

Proof that Real Men *are* romantic:

Clint "Dirty Harry" Eastwood directed and starred in *The Bridges of Madison County*, one of the most romantic movies of all time.

895

Shave on Saturday night.

896

Do you treat your employees better than you treat the woman in your life? A lot of men do. (What *is it* with you guys?!)

Here's a hypothetical role-playing exercise for you: View your lover as a customer, client, or employee. Good managers think of ways to motivate their employees, they don't simply order them around or take them for granted. And salesmen are always considerate of their customers... After all, customers are very important. Well, isn't she just as important?!

"If God made anything better than women, I think he kept it for himself."

- KRIS KRISTOFFERSON

897

Be *extra* nice to her during her menstrual periods. (Mark the dates on your calendar as a reminder.) And thank heaven that *you* don't have to experience cramps!

Real *Women* Are Romantic

898

Do you want to give him flowers—but you're concerned that he'll feel uncomfortable because it's not "manly" enough?

✦ Reconsider your assumptions. A big, burly construction worker in my Romance Class once told me that his girlfriend had sent flowers to him at his work site! After the required good-natured ribbing from the guys, he found that many of them complained that their gals had never sent flowers to *them!*

✦ Send a variety of flowers—all in his favorite color. (Sixty-two percent of American men say their favorite color is blue). Here are some blue flowers: Forget-Me-Not, Balloon Flower, Catmint, Delphinium, Lobelia, Sea Lavender, Spiderwort and Virginia Bluebells.

✦ Present the flowers in a "manly" vase—like a distributor cap or a toolbox. Or how about placing three small roses in the finger holes of his bowling ball?

*Seventy-four percent of American men have **never** received flowers from a woman. Eighty-two percent of them say they would appreciate the gesture.*

899

Do something *with* him that you normally hate doing (and do it cheerfully and without complaint). Accompany him fishing, bowling, bird-watching, running or camping. Or simply watch "The Game" on TV with him.

I highly recommend a thoroughly enchanting and practical book, *The Goddess' Guide to Love*, by Margie Lapanja.

900

Do something *for* him that you normally hate doing (and do it cheerfully and without complaint). Iron his shirts; wash his car; cook his favorite, hard-to-make dinner; run some errands; perform that little sexy fantasy you know he loves so much.

Guy Stuff

901

Guys, I don't *blame* you for being freaked out by the whole Valentine's Day thing. The problem is not with *you*—it's with our screwed-up culture.

The problem, you see, is with Cupid. Cupid represents romantic love, right? Now Cupid is a cute, naked little cherub who flits around and boinks people with his little arrows. *How cute!* So along comes February, and the store windows are full of flitting Cupids and are, of course, swathed in pink and red. What's the problem with this? The problem is that the images are either infantile or feminine.

The ancient Romans understood love better than we do. Cupid was originally the Roman god of romantic love. His mother, Venus, was the goddess of love. So the Romans had both feminine *and* masculine images for the concept of love. Pretty smart, huh? You may also be interested to know that Cupid was an adolescent—not a chubby cherub. (Picture one of those classic marble sculptures: Heroic pose, bulging muscles and a bow big enough to bring down a *bear*, much less two lovers!)

All of which is to say . . . that there *is* a masculine side to romantic love. It's just that our culture has few good male role models. Our culture also promotes simplistic, stereotypical thinking ("Men are logical, women are emotional,") which makes it doubly difficult for us guys to get in touch with that side of ourselves.

What to do? Well, you could celebrate Valentine's Day in a *masculine* way on *even* years, and celebrate in a *feminine* way on *odd* years. (So, for example, on even years you'd go on a bowling date, give tools for gifts, dine at a pub and then have sex. Then on odd years you'd stay at a bed and breakfast, give perfume, dine at a French café, make gentle love.)

Best guy quote from a Romance Class:
*"I'm not **dumb**—I'm just **confused**."*

*Real Men love the **Three Stooges**, right? So get him a gift from the "Soitenly Stooges" catalog! Call 800-3-STOOGE, or visit www.ThreeStooges.com.*

Gal Stuff

902

Many men would consider this the *Ultimate Gift:* A "Fantasy Photo" of you. You can get a sensual, provocative and stunning "Fantasy Portrait" made of yourself by contacting a photographer who specializes in the growing art form often called "Boudoir Photography."

Many of these photographers are women with a talent for making their subjects feel comfortable, and then bringing out the subtle, sexy side of your personality, and capturing it on film. "Lingerie" portraits seem to be most popular, followed by "Fantasy Outfit" shots, "Pin Up Girl" poses and "Playmate/Nude" photography.

Look for professional studios in your area, check references, or call:

* Fantasy Photography by Daphne, in Arlington, Massachusetts, at 781-641-2100.
* Lucienne Photography, in New York City, at 212-564-9670.

903

F.M. shoes.

904

Take a quick look through *Playboy* or *Penthouse*—see for yourself what *men in general* find sexy. Then ask your guy *specifically* what he finds sexy. You might be surprised at what you learn about him! You might also open up the door to more frank discussions about sexuality and sensuality.

Gals: Respect him. Give to him. Trust him. Care for him. Share with him. Laugh with him. Love him. Romance him.

Guys: Know her. Love her. Appreciate her. Remember her. Talk to her. Listen to her. Cherish her. Romance her.

Everyone: Enjoy yourself. Express yourself. Reveal yourself. Share yourself. Know thyself. Love yourself. Develop yourself. Risk yourself. Be yourself. Give yourself.

Characteristics of True Romantics

905

Romantics are cheerleaders.

Romantics are the biggest fans of their lovers. They provide enthusiastic support, constant encouragement and unconditional love. (They don't succeed 100 percent of the time, naturally, but they're always in there trying.)

Guys, kiss her in a special way: Cup your hands and hold her face gently in your hands when you kiss her.

906

Romantics are creative.

Romantics see their relationships as opportunities to express their creativity, as arenas for self-expression, as safe havens for experimenting and as places for growth.

907

Romantics are mind-readers.

Those who are tuned in to their lovers—those who *listen really well*—develop a kind of "sixth sense" about what their lovers would love. One of the best things about long-term relationships is that you can develop this sense. And as it develops, your relationship deepens and your intimacy grows.

* What kind of special *gift* do you know would please your partner?
* What little *gesture* do you know would bring a smile to his/her face?
* What special *meal or dessert* could you prepare that you know he/she simply loves?
* What has he *really wanted* for a long time, but held back from buying? Get it for him!

Have you *complimented* her lately?
Have you *thanked* him recently?
Have you *encouraged* her lately?
Have you *surprised* him lately?
Have you *acknowledged* her accomplishments?
Have you *marveled* at his talents lately?

Characteristics of Crazy Romantics

908

Slow-dance at a restaurant—*when there's no music playing*. (When one man from the Romance Class did this with his girlfriend, he reported that they were applauded by the other patrons, and given a complimentary bottle of champagne by the management!)

909

Snuggle up to a roaring fire in the fireplace—in the middle of *August*.

Don't forget to open the flue!

910

Cool things you could rent from a rental store. Great for theme dates, surprise parties or fantasies acted out in great detail!

* An automatic bubble machine
* A "fogger" that makes special-effects fog
* Various costumes
* A jukebox
* A Victorian carriage and horse
* A pinball machine

911

On a budget? Create a "Disney World Vacation-At-Home"! Shop at a Disney Store for paraphernalia such as Mickey ears, stuffed animals, wind-up toys, balloons, puppets and posters. Rent the most romantic Disney movies: *Beauty and the Beast, Lady and the Tramp, The Little Mermaid* and *Pocahontas*.

Chapter Theme Song:
"Crazy," Patsy Cline

Speaking of Love

912

Let other *things* speak for you.

Romantics *do not* constantly buy gifts and presents for their partners. But they *do* give "things." Little things. Private things. Goofy things. Meaningful things. Things like comic strips, love quotes, a "perfect" cup of coffee, flowers, greeting cards, penny candy, magazine articles, little toys.

913

Let other *people* speak for you.

You don't have to be *eloquent* in order to be *romantic*. You don't have to write great poetry—or even mediocre love letters. And, you don't have to be particularly well-spoken. But you *do* have to express your feelings *somehow*. One great strategy is to *borrow* the romantic words of the great poets, songwriters and wordsmiths of the world.

Let these people speak for you: William Shakespeare, Billy Joel, Paul McCartney, Charlie Brown, Susan Polis Schutz, Elizabeth Barrett Browning, Kahlil Gibran, Stevie Wonder and Emily Dickinson.

Now, I *don't* suggest that you try to take credit for composing "How do I love thee? Let me count the ways." Your expression isn't diminished in the least when you borrow others' words. Simply add to the note something like, "Stevie Wonder expressed my love for you when he sang 'You Are the Sunshine of My Life.'"

914

Let your *touch* speak for you.

Sometimes words are simply inadequate to express the incredible feelings of love inside of you. At those times a simple touch can express volumes. A caress, a squeeze, a hug. Sometimes the simplest things are *just right*.

"No sooner met but they looked;
no sooner looked but they loved;
no sooner loved but they sighed;
no sooner sighed but they asked one another
the reason;
no sooner knew the reason but they sought
the remedy;
and in these degrees have they made a pair of
stairs to marriage . . ."

~ WILLIAM SHAKESPEARE, *AS YOU LIKE IT*

Chapter Theme Song:
"Let's Talk About Love," Celine Dion

Speaking of Romance

915

Guess which major magazine this quote is from:

"... we *need* romance and sentimentality in our lives ... Note that I say 'we need'—*all* of us, men and women, right down to the most macho truck driver or professional mud wrestler. There was a general supposition a couple of decades ago, when women first banded together to seek 'liberation,' that one of the first casualties would be 'romance,' particularly in its more obvious and exploitative forms. Would Betty Friedan really expect a box of chocolates on February 14? Would Kate Millett wait for flowers? Would women, once they had become astronauts, weight lifters, firepersons, and entrepreneurs, and after becoming dependent on the Pill and sisterhood, still crave romance? And was not romance itself merely another of those many cultural traps that men had perfected for women over the centuries? As anyone could have predicted, romance won out, in fact was never in danger at all."

Where did this item appear? *Cosmo?* Nope. *Glamour?* Nope. *Reader's Digest?* Nope. *Penthouse?* Yup! By Michael Korda.

916

A word to the wise: *Don't equate romance with sex.* Romance is intertwined with both love *and* sex, so there's plenty of opportunity for misunderstandings between lovers.

Romance is *really* love-in-action. But sometimes actions that *look* a lot like romance are used for *seduction.* And sometimes actions that *look* a lot like romance are used for peace offerings. And sometimes actions that *look* a lot like romance are used for barter.

When it comes to romance, the **passion** is more important than the **happy ending**. Think:

Romeo and Juliet
Titanic
The Bridges of Madison County
Gone With the Wind

What's in a Name?

917

Name your boat after her.

918

If her name is April, May or June, declare the corresponding month "her" month, and do something special for her every day that month. (*Every* woman is "one-in-a-million," but few are "one-in-twelve"!)

919

✦ What's in a name? Make special use of her name-flower if she's a Rose, Daisy, Ivy, Lily or Iris.

✦ What's in a nickname? Use Buttercups, Poppies and Sweet Peas.

✦ If your pet name for her is Angel: Make angels in the snow; celebrate August 22nd—it's "Be an Angel Day"; visit Los Angeles, the "City of Angels"; record these songs for her: "Angel of the Morning," by Merrilee Rush; "I Married an Angel," by Larry Clinton; "Earth Angel," by The Penguins; and "Heaven Must be Missing an Angel," by Tavares.

920

Most couples have private "pet names" for one another. Many pet names lend themselves to specific gifts. From some of my Romance Class participants here are some pet names and their corresponding gifts:

✛ Big Bear: A five-foot-tall teddy bear
✛ Macho Man: A "muscle T-shirt" and the Village People's CD
✛ Bunny: Bunny motif clothing, posters, figurines
✛ Sweetie: Candies of all kinds
✛ Cookie: A cookie-a-day, for nine years—so far!
✛ Tiger: 1) A stuffed "Tigger," 2) Calvin & Hobbes books

Her name in a song:

"Diane," The Bachelors

"Wendy," The Beach Boys

"Janet," The Commodores

"Joanna," Kool & the Gang

"Kathleen," Willie Nelson

"Tracy," The Cuff Links

His name in a song:

"Ben," Jackson 5

"Daniel," Elton John

"Henry," New Riders of the Purple Sage

"Jeremy," Pearl Jam

"Rudy," Supertramp

If you ever have occasion to discover a new planet or comet, name it after your lover.

The Meaning of a Name

921

Do you know the *significance* of your lover's name? Here are a few samples taken from a "baby name" book:

* Ada is Teutonic for "joyous."
* April is Latin for "open, accepting."
* Barbara is Roman for "mysterious stranger."
* Catherine is Greek, meaning "pure."
* Cheryl is French for "beloved."
* David is Hebrew for "beloved."
* Diane is from the Latin Diana, meaning "Goddess of the Moon."
* Dominique is French, meaning "she who belongs to God."
* Erik is Scandinavian for "ever-powerful."
* Frederick is Germanic, meaning "peaceful."
* Gary is Germanic for "spear carrier."
* Gregory is Greek, meaning "vigilant, watchful."
* Helen is Greek for "light."
* Jean derives from Jane, Hebrew for "God is gracious."
* Jennifer is Welsh, for "fair one."
* John is Hebrew for "God is merciful."
* Judy is Hebrew, meaning "admired and praised."
* Kelsey is derived from Gaelic, meaning "female warrior."
* Kevin is Irish for "handsome, gentle, lovable."
* Linda is Spanish, meaning "beautiful."
* Marjorie is derived from Greek, meaning "pearl, precious one."
* Neil is Gaelic, meaning "champion."
* Raymond is Old English for "wise guardian."
* Richard is Old German for "powerful ruler."
* Sally is Hebrew for "princess."
* Susan is Hebrew, for "lily."
* Thomas is Aramaic, meaning "the twin."
* Tracey is derived from Gaelic, meaning "fighter, or reaper."
* Warren is Germanic for "defender, or protective friend."
* Wendy was invented by J.M. Barrie for the heroine of *Peter Pan!*

I heard a rumor that one couple, inspired by the comic strip "Zits," has legally changed their name to one word, **Tomandsusan.**

Get a book of baby names and discover what your lover's name means. Then use that meaning as a theme for romantic gifts and gestures:

For Linda: Find poems and songs that use the word *beautiful.*

For Neil: Play for him "We are the Champions" by Queen.

For Susan: Give her many lilies.

Chapter Theme Song:
"The Name Game," Shirley Ellis

And Now For Something Completely Different*

922

Are you stuck in a boring routine every evening? (Home from work; run some errands; grab some dinner; pay some bills; watch some TV; crawl into bed exhausted.) *Radically change your routine:*

➤ Meet after work at the local art museum; eat at the café there; spend the evening browsing with the high-brow.
➤ On a Tuesday night, order a quick pizza for dinner, then head for an early movie.
➤ Meet at the mall; go window shopping; dine at your favorite fast food joint.

923

There's no better way to loosen up than to get in touch with the child inside yourself. That little kid is playful, creative, curious, spontaneous, trusting and imaginative! Stop being such an *adult*, and recapture those childlike qualities. Suggested reading:

✦ *The Tao of Pooh*, by Benjamin Hoff
✦ *The Missing Piece*, by Shel Silverstein
✦ *I'm OK—You're OK*, by Eric Berne
✦ *A Book of Games*, by Hugh Prather

*For your Monty Python fan:

Serve Spam, eggs, Spam and Spam for breakfast.

Plant some shrubbery.

Promise that you'll never, "Run away!"

Visit www.PythonShop.com

924

Is your honey a *Wizard of Oz* fanatic? Well, take her to the Judy Garland Museum and see rare photos, video documentaries, rare recordings and memorabilia. It hosts a Judy Garland Festival every year, too. The Yellow Brick Road is in Grand Rapids, Minnesota. Call 218-326-6431.

What Is Your Quest?

925

If the two of you decided to undertake a quest to share **one million kisses** over the course of your lives, *how often* would you have to kiss?

1,000,000 kisses!?

Note: For the sake of practicality I'm making these assumptions: You each sleep six hours per night—so you can't kiss during that time. And between work, commuting and separate chores, you'll spend an additional sixty hours per week apart. Given all that, here's how often you'd have to kiss if you wanted to share 1,000,000 kisses:

✳ Over ten years you'd have to kiss once every 2.06 minutes.
✳ Over twenty years you'd have to kiss once every 4.12 minutes.
✳ Over thirty years you'd have to kiss once every 6.18 minutes.
✳ Over forty years you'd have to kiss once every 8.24 minutes.
✳ Over fifty years you'd have to kiss once every 10.3 minutes.
✳ Over sixty years you'd have to kiss once every 12.36 minutes.

Note #1: You're welcome, of course, to bunch your kisses together so that you'll have time to attend to other matters in your life.

Note #2: Sorry, but the judges have ruled that *extra long* kisses still only count as one kiss each. (That goes for French Kisses, too.)

926

If your quest is to fill the house with the wonderful aroma of flowers, be aware that your favorite flowers aren't necessarily the most *fragrant* ones. Create a bouquet of especially fragrant flowers, and your romantic gesture will take on a whole new dimension.

Especially *fragrant* flowers:

Freesia
Roses
Casablanca lilies
Rubrum lilies
Stock
Stephanotis
Lilacs
Gardenias
Hyacinths

927

Go in search of "The Perfect Pizza." It could take you months or years, and you might gain ten pounds—but if your lover is a pizza *fiend*, it will all be worth it!

Getting to Know You

928

Interview his mother, father, siblings, friends and colleagues—to learn about his unique quirks, likes, dislikes, hobbies and passions.

929

What's the difference between "sexy" and "sleazy"? What's the difference between "cute" and "coy"? I'll bet *your* definitions differ from your partner's. But you'll never know unless you talk about it.

930

* Play "Show and Tell": Pick a beloved object. Talk about its history and why it's special to you. (An old baseball glove; a doll from childhood; something given to you by a grandparent; a stuffed animal; a trophy; a piece of jewelry, etc.)
* Another Show and Tell game: Visit *places* that have special meaning to you.

"Getting to Know You" Questions:

Do you believe in love at first sight?

What three adjectives best describe you?

How did you *know* you two were in love?

Which comic book character would you be?

What animal would you be?

How are you just like your mother? Father?

What was your favorite childhood game?

Are you a *lucky* person?

When do you feel most creative?

What would you do if you won the lottery?

Do you dream in color?

931

Grab some books on astrology and see what the stars have to say about your and your partner's personalities. My favorite is *Star Signs*, by Linda Goodman. The fun thing about this book is that it describes every possible pairing of the twelve signs of the zodiac.

Staying in Touch

932

Real communication between lovers is one part talking and nine parts listening. Listen, for a change. You'll learn a lot about your partner.

- ➤ Listen for the feelings behind the words. We don't always say what we mean, but the emotional content is still there if we tune in to it.
- ➤ Listen without interrupting. (Quite a challenge—especially if you've been together for many years!)

933

Respond with love, *regardless* of what your partner says or does. Why? Because behaviors such as complaining, worrying, shouting and nagging are all *disguised calls for love*. (When a child exhibits these kinds of behaviors we instinctively understand that it comes from fear, and has nothing to do with us personally. Unfortunately, we rarely grant adults this courtesy.) Try to respond to what's *really* going on, not simply to what's on the surface.

Hearing and listening are very, very different! Hearing is automatic (you even hear things in your sleep!)—while listening requires conscious choice. Listening is a gift of love you give to your partner.

934

Give your partner more reassurance. Reinforce her good qualities. Compliment his talents and abilities. Reinforce all the good qualities *that attracted you to your partner in the first place.*

- ✦ Tell him what you really appreciate about him.
- ✦ Remind her that you really *do* adore her.
- ✦ Concentrate on the *positive* when talking to him.
- ✦ Focus on who she *really is*, instead of on your unrealistic fantasy of "The Perfect Partner."

935

Make a "Just Married" sign. Tape it to the back windshield of your car before taking a Sunday afternoon drive. People will honk and wave. Pretend you're newlyweds!

(Maybe even stay in the bridal suite of a local hotel!)

936

*While most people **sign** their letters with X's and O's, one man wrote a **whole letter** with X's and O's—with a secret message embedded among the kisses and hugs!*

```
XOXOXOXOXOXOXOXOXOXOXOXOXOXOXOXOXOXO
OXOXOXOXOXOXOXOXOXOXOXOXOXOXOXOXOXOX
XOXOXOXOXOXOXOXOXOXOXOXOXOXOXOXOXOXO
OXOXOXOXyXOXOXOXOXOXOXOXOXOXOXOXOXOX
XOXOXOXOXOXOXOXOXOXOXOXOXOXOXOXOXOXO
OXOXOoXOXOXOXOXOXOXOXOXOXOXOXOXOXOXOX
XOXOXOXOXOXOXOXuXOXOXOXOXOXOXOXOXOXO
OXOaOXOXOXOXOXOXOXrXOXOXOXOXOXOXOXO
XOXOXOXOeOXOXOXOXOXOXmXOXOXOXOXOXO
OXyXOXOXOXOXOoXOXOXOXOXOXOXOXnXOXO
XOXOXOXeXOXOXOXOXaXOXOXOXOXOXOXOXOX
OXOXnXOXOXOXOXOXOXOXOXOdOXOXOXOXOX
XOXOXOXOXOXOXOXOXOXOXOXOXOXOXOXOXOXO
OXOXOXOoXOXOXOXOXOXOXOXOXOXOXOXOXOX
XOXOXOXOXOXOnOXOXOXOXOXOXOXOlOXOXOXO
OXOXOXOXOXOXOXOyOXOXOXOXOXOXOXOXOX
```

937

Write a personal message *somewhere* on your body (with washable ink)— and let him discover it.

Chapter Theme Song:
"Message in a Bottle," The Police

Massages

938

Before you leave on a trip, leave a bottle of scented massage oil on the nightstand, along with a note saying, "I'm going to use this on you as soon as I return."

939

Touch is healing.

Massages come in two varieties: Sensual and sexual. Learn the subtle—but important—differences. A *sensual* massage is soothing, healing and relaxing. It often lulls your partner to sleep. A *sexual* massage is stimulating and arousing. It often leads to lovemaking. True romantics know when each type of massage is appropriate.

940

Some recommended books on massage:

☞ *The Massage Book*, by George Downing
☞ *Erotic Massage: The Tantric Touch of Love*, by Kenneth Ray Stubbs
☞ *Erotic Massage: Body Magic*, by Janet Wright
☞ *The Art of Erotic Massage*, by Andrew Yorke
☞ *The New Sensual Massage*, by Nitya Lacroix
☞ *Massage: Principles & Techniques*, by Gertrude Beard & E. Wood

ABC

941a

A is for Attitude, Available, Accept, Ardor, Accolades, Admire, Aphrodisiacs, à la Mode, Anniversary, Ambrosia, Ardent, Athens, Australia

B is for Boudoir, Bed & Breakfast, Buttercups, Beaches, Blue, Books, Boston, Balloons, Bicycling, Broadway, Brandy, Bubble baths, Bahamas

C is for Champagne, Creativity, Candlelight, Candy, Chocolate, Convertibles, Casablanca, Cognac, Caviar, Chivalry, Crabtree & Evelyn

D is for Diamonds, Dancing, Daffodils, Dating, Dolls, Dirty Dancing, Dinner, Divine, Dearest

E is for Enthusiasm, Energy, Excitement, Emeralds, Earrings, Elvis, Erotic, Exotic, Expensive, Escapes

F is for Flirting, Fantasies, Feminine, Faithful, France, Flowers, Fruits, French kissing, Foreplay

G is for Garters, Gardenias, Godiva, Get-Aways, Gifts, Glenn Miller, Gourmet, Greece, Gondolas

H is for Hearts, Humor, Hugs, Hideaways, Horses, Honeymoons, Hawaii, Hershey's Kisses, Hyatt, Holidays

I is for Intimacy, Intrigue, Italy, Inns, Islands, Ingenuity, Ice Cream, Ice Skating, Interdependent, Imaginative, Invitation, Incense

J is for Jewelry, Java, Jasmine, Jello, Jazz, Journey, Joyful, Jacuzzi

K is for Kissing, Kinky, Kittens, Koala Bears, Kites

L is for Love, Lingerie, Laughing, Love Letters, Lilacs, Lace, Leather, Leo Buscaglia, Lobsters, Lovemaking, Limousines, Love songs, London

Chapter Theme Song:
"ABC," The Jackson Five

DEF

941b

M is for Monogamy, Marriage, Masculine, m&m's, Massage, Movies, Mistletoe, Music, Mozart, Moonlight

N is for Negligee, Naughty, Nibble, Nighttime, Nubile, Novelty, Nurture, Nymph, Naples, Nightcap, Nape, Nepal, Necklace

O is for Orgasm, Opera, Orchid, Outrageous, Outdoors

P is for Passion, Perfume, Poppies, Poetry, Persimmons, Paris, Polkas, Panties, Pizza, Photos, Pearls, Picnics, Playfulness, Purple, Parking

Q is for Quiet, Quaint, Quality, Queen, Quebec, Question, QE2, Quiche, Quiver, Quilts

R is for Rendezvous, Roses, Rubies, Red, Reading, Rome, Rituals, Riviera, Restful, Rapture, Rings, Rio, Rainbows

S is for Sex

T is for Tea, Talking, Teasing, Tulips, Titillating, Theater, Tickets, Togetherness, Toasts, Toys, Trains, Trinidad, Travel, Tenderness

U is for Umbrellas, Uxorious, Undress, Undulate, Urges, Unexpected, Union, Under the Spreading Chestnut Tree

V is for Violets, Virgins, Vibrators, Venice, Venus, Valentines, Vegetables, Victoria's Secret

W is for Wine, Wisteria, Walking Hand-in-Hand, Weddings

X is for X-Rated, Xerographic, Xylophones, Xmas

Y is for Yachts, Yes, Yellow, Yin & Yang, Young-at-heart

Z is for Zany, Zanzibar, Zeal, Zodiac, Zurich

"Do you know your ABCs?" Ask your partner to pick a letter. Then read the list of corresponding words. He or she has twenty-four hours in which to get a romantic gift or perform a romantic gesture based on any one of these key words.

XYZ

942

Always kiss each other hello and goodbye. **B**e there for each other—always. **C**reate an environment of love. **D**o it. **E**scape from the kids. **F**ight fair. **G**ive of your time. **H**andle with care. **I**nspire your partner with your love. **J**udge not. **K**eep your good memories alive. **L**isten to her. **M**ake love with your partner's needs foremost. **N**ever go to bed angry. **O**ffer to handle an unpleasant chore. **P**raise him. **Q**uality Time isn't just for the kids. **R**espect her feelings. **S**ay what you feel when you feel it. **T**ell her you love her every day. Every day. **U**nderstand your differences. **V**alentine's Day is every day. **W**alk together; talk together. E**X**cite your partner as only you know how. **Y**ou can never say "I love you" too often. **Z**ero-in on his little passions.

Choose a letter. Follow the corresponding piece of advice this week. Choose a different letter next week.

943

Give your partner a "Romantic ABCs Coupon":

Write the letters of the alphabet on twenty-six slips of paper. The coupon-holder picks one letter out of a hat. The coupon-giver will create a day of romance with gifts and gestures that all begin with that letter.

FYI

944

The song list from the best cassette tape of romantic music I've ever created for my wife, Tracey:

1. "I Won't Last a Day Without You," by Paul Williams
2. "Coming Around Again," by Carly Simon
3. "Closer to Believing," by Greg Lake/Emerson, Lake & Palmer
4. "Saving My Heart," by Yes
5. "If I Had a Million Dollars," by Bare Naked Ladies
6. "I'm Gonna Be (500 Miles)," by The Proclaimers
7. "Symphony No. 35, *Haffner*," by Wolfgang Amadeus Mozart
8. "In the Mood," by Glenn Miller
9. "Kalena Kai," by Keola Beamer
10. "Crazy," by Patsy Cline

945

There are *three* kinds of people in the world: "Past-Oriented" people, "Now-Oriented" people" and "Future-Oriented" people. Your "romantic style" is often determined by your "time orientation."

❖ *Past-Oriented* people tend toward the sentimental and nostalgic. They're into scrapbooks and saving things.

❖ *Now-Oriented* people are spontaneous and often extremely creative. They're into last-minute activities and adventures.

❖ *Future-Oriented* people are planners and listeners. They're into surprises and grand gestures.

946

It's getting harder and harder to find classic 45 RPM records, and it's almost *impossible* to locate old 78s! Find a local used record shop or call House of Oldies at 212-243-0500; or visit them at 35 Carmine Street in New York City; or visit www.HouseOfOldies.com.

FYI, romance is habit-forming.

Gift Ideas

947

Doesn't he deserve a trophy for being the "World's Best Lover"? Doesn't she merit a loving cup to celebrate her latest accomplishment?

Trophy shops have a wealth of ideas waiting for you. Just think of the romantic possibilities of plaques, medals, ribbons, nameplates, certificates and banners. And they all can be personalized, engraved, lettered or monogrammed.

948

Buy her an *entire* outfit. Include: Beautiful lingerie, a gorgeous dress, a matching scarf, pin or necklace, and shoes! Spread 'em out on the bed. Wait for her jaw to drop.

949

Satin sheets.

Treat her like a queen and she'll treat you like a king.

950

Gentlemen: Approach the subject of lingerie *gently*.

✤ Your *first* lingerie present should *not* be a peek-a-boo bra. (Have a little class, huh?!)
✤ You might start by giving her a say in the matter: Attach a one-hundred dollar bill to a lingerie catalog along with a note saying "You choose." Or make a custom "Lingerie Coupon."
✤ How about just paging through some lingerie catalogs together and talking about what each of you likes and dislikes?

Coupon Ideas

951

A basic romantic concept: Love Coupons. Here's a twist: Love Coupons made from the little slips of paper from Hershey's Kisses. Each coupon is redeemable for one kiss.

952

Here are some *twists* on the concept of "Coupons":

- Coupons made out of your business cards
- Coupons made on restaurant menus
- Coupons made on pillow cases
- Coupons made into bookmarks
- Coupons inserted into computer documents
- Coupons made from magazines

953

Another twist on the Love Coupon idea: "Dollar Bill" coupons: Make a simply sketched "one-dollar bill"; put your picture in the center; make a hundred photocopies; cut them out; make a stack. Then give them to your lover, along with a detailed list of various activities and what they'll cost. For example:

- Dinner out: $5
- ✷ An *expensive* dinner out: $15
- ✷ A movie out: $3
- ✷ A movie in: $1
- ✷ I'll cook dinner: $12
- ✷ I'll bring dinner home: $1
- One backrub: $4
- ✷ Going shopping with you: $20
- ✷ Making love: $1
- ✷ Making love *(when I don't feel like it!)*: $98

Breakfast in Bed Coupon
Redeemable on any day of your choosing.
Never expires.

The Ultimate Bubble Bath Coupon
Complete with scented bath oils,
soft music, champagne & candles.

A Romantic Dinner Coupon
Gourmet dinner prepared by the
coupon issuer. Proper dress required.

The Saturday Night Date Coupon
Where? Wherever you want!
When? You decide.

How to Understand Each Other

954

There are several systems designed to help you understand yourself and others by utilizing a variety of "personality profile" techniques. Here are some recommended books:

❖ *Who Am I? Personality Types for Self-Discovery*, edited by R. Frager
❖ *16 Ways to Love Your Lover: Understanding the 16 Personality Types So You Can Create a Love That Lasts Forever*, by Otto Kroeger & Janet Thuesen
❖ *Please Understand Me: Character & Temperament Types*, by David Keirsey & Marilyn Bates

Also—

The Character Code, by Taylor Hartman

Who Do You Think You Are? by Keith Harary & Eileen Donahue

955

Have your handwriting analyzed together. You'll be amazed at what can be "read" in your writing.

"We all want, above all, to be heard—but not merely to be heard. We want to be understood—heard for what we think we are saying, for what we know we meant."

- DEBORAH TANNEN

956

Ten Quirky Questions to Help Couples Get Inside Each Other's Heads (and Hearts):

1. What three *nouns* best describe you?
2. What three *adjectives* best describe you?
3. If you could save time in a bottle, what would you do with it?
4. What do you want to be remembered for?
5. What are your prized possessions?
6. What did you want to be when you grew up?
7. Would you rather be rich or famous?
8. Would you rather live in the far future or the distant past?
9. If you had one more day to live, how would you spend that day?
10. If you were going to write a self-help book, what would you title it?

How to Bed & Breakfast

957

It has come to my attention that there are some guys out there who, having made reservations at a romantic bed and breakfast, have arrived there and proceeded to turn on the TV. Or, upon discovering that there *is* no TV in the room, have called the manager to complain. *No, no, no!*

- Set your VCR at home before you leave so you won't miss your favorite TV shows.
- Hide your watches in a drawer—go all weekend without bothering with the time.
- A little "afternoon delight."
- Ask your bed and breakfast hosts for suggestions. They always know their communities very well.
- Call ahead and make reservations at several recommended local restaurants.
- Enjoy a bubble bath or jacuzzi together.
- Bring some inspiring books to read.

No clocks.
No schedules.
No hassles.
No worries.
No interruptions.
No TV.
No mail.
No Email.
No phone.
No stress.
No kids.
No pager.
No computer.
No diet.

958

And here are some specific Bed and Breakfast resource books for you.

- *Bed & Breakfasts and Country Inns—Inspected, Rated and Approved.* These B&Bs visited personally and rated by the American Bed & Breakfast Association.
- *Bed and Breakfast U.S.A.*, by Betty Rundback. A huge guide, with over 1,200 listings! Includes favorite B&B recipes and a special section for travelers with disabilities.
- *Recommended Romantic Inns.* Chosen especially for their romantic qualities, these 140 B&Bs are described in detail by the authors, who have visited every site.

*Tip: Make bed and breakfast reservations for Valentine's Day a **year** in advance!*

Soundtrack to a Love Affair

959

Those romantic scenes in the movies wouldn't be *nearly* as romantic if they didn't enhance them with *music*. You could take some inspiration from Hollywood and create soundtracks for various romantic activities! I recommend these CDs for these romantic occasions:

❤ For a romantic candlelight dinner:
   ✳ *Crossroads*, by Nicholas Gunn
   ✳ *Picture This*, by Jim Brickman
   ✳ *Twin Sons of Different Mothers,* by Fogelberg & Weisberg

❤ For lounging by the fireplace:
   ✳ *Touch*, by John Klemmer
   ✳ *Watermark*, by Enya
   ✳ *Past Light*, by William Ackerman

❤ For a drive in the country:
   ✳ *Il Bacio*, by Paul Ventimiglia
   ✳ *Legends*, by Eric Tingstad & Nancy Rumbel
   ✳ *Crossroads*, by Nicholas Gunn

❤ For a Sunday afternoon picnic:
   ✳ *Picnic Suite,* by Jean-Pierre Rampal and Claude Bolling
   ✳ *Feels So Good,* by Chuck Mangione
   ✳ *Water Music,* by George Frideric Handel

❤ For lovemaking (romantic & gentle):
   ✳ *Canon in D (The Pachelbel Canon),* by Johann Pachelbel
   ✳ *Livin' Inside Your Love,* by George Benson
   ✳ *Winter Into Spring,* by George Winston

❤ For lovemaking (hot & sexy):
   ✳ *Enigma MCMXC a.D.*, by Enigma
   ✳ *Nine-1/2 Weeks* soundtrack
   ✳ *Midnight Love*, by Marvin Gaye

Make custom cassette tapes of romantic background music.

Make custom tapes of meaningful, romantic songs as gifts for her.

Make custom tapes of songs that were hits while you were dating.

Make tapes of your partner's favorite songs.

Guidelines for a Love Affair

960

The *Friends* of Love

- ▲ Faith
- ▲ Focus of attention
- ▲ Fun-loving attitude
- ▲ Stay in touch with your feelings
- ▲ Kindness
- ▲ Simplicity
- ▲ Clarity of your life's priorities
- ▲ Sense of adventure
- ▲ Creative attitude
- ▲ Patience
- ▲ Tenderness
- ▲ Empathy
- ▲ Goodwill
- ▲ Attentiveness
- ▲ Generosity
- ▲ Sense of Humor
- ▲ Commitment
- ▲ A good therapist/counselor/pastor
- ▲ Gifts that touch the heart
- ▲ Good role models
- ▲ Listening with your heart
- ▲ Appreciation for life
- ▲ Time—Quantity of time
- ▲ Time—Quality time
- ▲ Respect for your partner
- ▲ Presents that symbolize your love
- ▲ Playful attitude
- ▲ Eye contact

The *Enemies* of Love

- ▼ Emotional withdrawal
- ▼ Nagging
- ▼ Jealousy
- ▼ Complexity of modern life
- ▼ Arrogance
- ▼ Overly practical attitudes
- ▼ Impatience
- ▼ Guilt
- ▼ Stress
- ▼ Selfishness
- ▼ Lack of time
- ▼ Laziness
- ▼ Boredom
- ▼ Lack of respect
- ▼ Stereotyped attitudes
- ▼ Lack of role models
- ▼ Stinginess in general
- ▼ Stinginess with time
- ▼ Stinginess with money
- ▼ Rigid attitudes
- ▼ Apathy
- ▼ Fear
- ▼ Grudges
- ▼ Resentment
- ▼ Immaturity
- ▼ Thoughtlessness
- ▼ Superior attitude

*Have a love affair—**with your spouse!***

"It is only with the heart that one can see rightly; what is essential is invisible to the eye."

~ ANTOINE DE SAINT-EXUPERY

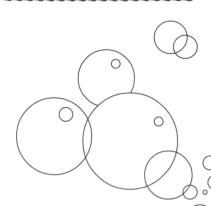

Bubble Baths (I)

961a

Start simple. Run her a bath. Steaming hot. Full of bubbles.

961b

Bath-and-Snack: Bubble bath plus grapes, cheese and crackers.

961c

Bath-and-Music: Bubble bath plus relaxing music. Featuring Enya's CD *Watermark* and George Winston's CD *Autumn*.

961d

Bath-and-Bubbly: Bubble bath plus champagne, two crystal champagne flutes and *you!*

961e

Bath-and-Book: Bubble bath plus a book by her favorite author.

961f

Steamy-Bath-and-Steamy-Eroticism: Bubble bath plus an erotic book—in which you've highlighted the "steamy" passages. This bath includes a follow-up lovemaking session.

961g

Bath-and-Relax: Bubble bath for one—plus two hours of peace and quiet (while you take the kids out to McDonald's).

Bubble Baths (II)

961h

Bath-for-Two: Watch the movie *Bull Durham*. Watch for the romantic bath scene. Use it for inspiration. (Hint: Candles. Lots and *lots* of candles.)

961i

Leaving-Work-Behind: Be waiting for him in the bathtub when he returns from work.

961j

Message-in-a-Bottle: Write her a love letter or a poem. Roll it up and stick it in a bottle. Cork it. Float the bottle in the bathtub.

961k

Bath-and-Sexual-Gymnastics: Test your agility—make love in the bathtub. If your tub is simply too small, spread towels on the floor and improvise!

961l

Bath-and-Products: Explore a wide variety of bath powders, lotions and potions. When you find one that she adores, get *lots* of it.

961m

For a touch of class: European soaps and other bath luxuries imported by Katherine March International. Call 800-87-MARCH; or write P.O. Box 1343, Osprey, Florida 34229; or visit www.KatherineMarch.com.

A Touch of Class

962

Be on the lookout for concepts and gifts that relate to your lover's interests. For example, if your partner loves *Romeo and Juliet*, or Shakespeare or theater in general, here's an unusual and cool gift idea: "One Page Books" are large, beautifully-designed prints that contain the complete, unabridged text of many Shakespearean plays and sonnets. Each one is a fine art print that measures 32-inches by 45-inches. When framed they are dramatic conversation pieces. These works are currently available:

- ✦ *Romeo and Juliet*
- ✦ *Macbeth*
- ✦ *Hamlet*
- ✦ *King Lear*
- ✦ *The Tempest*
- ✦ *Othello*
- ✦ *The Sonnets*
- ✦ *A Midsummer Night's Dream*
- ✦ *Much Ado About Nothing*
- ✦ *Love's Labors Lost*
- ✦ *Twelfth Night*
- ✦ *The Merchant of Venice*

Call the One Page Book Company at 972-714-0758, or visit them at www.OnePageBooks.com.

You *do* have an elegant fountain pen with which to write love notes and love letters, don't you?! A Mont Blanc pen will add an unparalleled touch of class to your act.

963

Attend an opera.

Wait! Don't skip to the next item yet! Give me a brief moment here. I *know* that most of you aren't very familiar with opera. To tell you the truth, I find opera to be somewhat intimidating. However, there are some very classic, very romantic arias that make the experience worth trying. (Watch the movie *Moonstruck* to see how profoundly opera can affect some regular folks like you and me.)

Attend a symphony. Get the program ahead of time, buy CDs of the symphonies to be performed, and listen to each of them *three* times. Even if you're not very familiar with classical music, this will greatly increase your enjoyment of the concert.

A Touch

964

✦ Take a massage class together. (Get a catalog from your local adult education center.)

✦ Give her a custom-made Love Coupon good for a professional massage. (Call local health clubs, chiropractor's offices, hotels, physical therapy clinics and spas for referrals.)

965

Hug. Cuddle. Caress. Touch. Pat. Tap. Brush. Graze. Stroke. Snuggle.

Ask your lover to tell you the most sensual thing you could do for him or her. *And then do it!*

966

Romantics are *sensuous* people. They understand the difference between sensuality and sexuality—and how they enhance one another. Here are fourteen specific ways to enhance the sensuality in your life together:

1. Run your fingers gently through your lover's hair.
2. Focus on one of the five senses at a time.
3. Create a romantic mood at home through soft lighting.
4. Have great music playing in the background all the time at home.
5. Keep three bouquets of fragrant flowers in the house.
6. Focus on touching a different part of your partner's body each day.
7. Prepare an extra-special taste treat for your lover.
8. Include more sensuality in your lovemaking.
9. Slow down, make time, relax.
10. Over the next five weeks, get five small gifts that focus on each of the five senses.
11. Focus on the present moment; appreciate the "now."
12. Buy ten scented candles.
13. Give him a great shoulder massage as he watches TV tonight.
14. Buy a basketful of scented bath oils.

A great resource: *Romantic Massage: Ten Unforgettable Massages for Special Occasions,* by Anne Kent Rush.

Chapter Theme Song:
"Touch," John Klemmer

Work

967

Make sure you find a way to do something romantic *during a time when you're the most busy at work!* A little planning will allow you to be romantic in the midst of your work day.

*It's **easy** to be romantic when you've got all the time in the world. The challenge is to keep expressing your love even during your busy and difficult times.*

968

Utilize your partner's secretary and staff as your allies. They can be *invaluable* in helping you spring surprises on him or her. They'll know her schedule; where he's having lunch; and whether he/she has had an especially rough day. All are crucial bits of information you should know.

969

A hot trend in business is TQM—"Total Quality Management." One romantic manager was inspired to create what he also calls TQM—but it stands for "Total Quality Marriage." (Good one!) "Basically, you apply the best business techniques to your marriage," he explains. For example:

❧ How would you give good customer service to your partner?
❧ How might you and your partner give each other yearly performance reviews?
❧ Are each of you being well compensated emotionally?
❧ Are you using good time management techniques to create more leisure time?

970

Create a "Gift & Card Drawer" in your desk at work. At all times your inventory should include: At least ten greeting cards, lots of Love Stamps, several "Trinket Gifts," a couple of *real* gifts, wrapping paper and bows.

Play

971

View romance as "adult play."

Some people (especially men) tend to view romance as a serious and difficult activity. Nothing could be further from the truth! True romance is *easy* because it's simply an expression of what's *already inside you:* Your feelings of love, caring and passion for your partner.

The concept of *adult play* is a reminder to loosen up, be creative, and remember the fun and passion you had early in your relationship. Adults need to *relearn* how to play—something that came naturally to all of us as children. Many ideas in this book are essentially exercises in *playing.*

Many couples have confided to me that this single concept has turned their "nice-but-boring" relationship into a fun and passionate love affair.

972

Send a taxi to pick him up after work. Have the taxi driver hand him a sealed envelope. The note inside says, "All work and no play makes you a dull boy—so come and play!" Pre-pay the cab fare (including tip!), and instruct the driver to take him to a local hotel. Have another sealed envelope waiting for him at the front desk. (*You* decide what kind of note to write!) Be waiting for him in the honeymoon suite with chilled champagne and a warm bed.

973

↔ Fingerpaint together.

↔ Fingerpaint *each other's bodies!*

"In our play we reveal what kind of people we are."

~ OVID

974

Use your kids' toys as romantic tools. Crayons are great for writing short notes. Play-Doh is great for sculpting messages and symbols. Legos are great for spelling out messages or leaving a trail through the house from the front door to your bedroom, where you're waiting for a little fun-and-games of your own.

"We don't stop playing because we grow old; we grow old because we stop playing."

~ GEORGE BERNARD SHAW

Sex Tips for Gals

975

More often.

Thousands of men in my Romance Classes have confided or complained that having their ladies wear lingerie more often is the one thing they want intensely that their women tend to resist.

Sex Tips for Guys

976

Make love to her *the way she wants to be made love to*.

The secret to being a World-Class Lover is contained in one little word, guys: Foreplay.

Romanti¢¢¢ Ideas

977

Buy camping equipment instead of going on an expensive vacation. A one-time outlay will assure you of years of inexpensive vacations. (You'll also be prepared for last-minute vacationing opportunities and quickie weekend get-aways.)

¢¢¢¢¢¢¢¢¢¢¢¢¢¢!!!!!!!!!!!!!!!!!!!!!!!!!!!!

978

Buy *season tickets* for shows and events that you attend. You'll save money in the long run, you'll get better seats, and you'll go out more! Box seats are great—whether they're at the ballgame or the ballet!

979

Many symphonies and theaters have discount tickets available on the day or evening of performances. If your partner doesn't mind a little uncertainty, this is a great way to save a few bucks and still enjoy an evening of culture and entertainment.

980

Where to get inexpensive flowers: Supermarkets. Street vendors. Meadows. Your own garden. Your neighbor's garden. Outdoor markets. The side of the road.

981

Discover your local community theaters. They're fun, inexpensive and entertaining. Many small cities and towns have truly *excellent* community theaters. Call them today for a schedule of upcoming shows. Don't forget to call a number of nearby towns, too!

Romantic Idea$$$

982

The single most expensive romantic concept I've found is the *three-week vacation trip around the world on the Concorde.* The trip is offered only once each year, with space limited to 96 people. The itinerary changes slightly from year to year, but usually includes two to three days in each of these cities: Sydney, Hong Kong, Dallas, London, Delhi, Nairobi and Cairo. Just $50,800 per person [1999 price].

The tour operator is INTRAV, a specialist in deluxe world travel. (They also run less expensive trips—averaging $3,400—to all seven continents.) Call 800-456-8100 or 314-655-6700, or write to INTRAV at 7711 Bonhomme Avenue, St. Louis, Missouri 63105; or visit www.intrav.com.

983

Other good ways of spending *lots* of money on your lover:

✦ Caviar
✦ A Mont Blanc fountain pen
✦ A Rolex watch
✦ A Harley-Davidson Fat Boy FLSTF
✦ A full-length mink coat
✦ A Porsche 911 Carrera Cabriolet

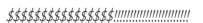

984

Dinner at The Wild Boar Restaurant, in Nashville, Tennessee. A wine list that fills a hundred pages and includes three thousand selections, with a total inventory of 12,000 bottles. Eighteen-karat gold table settings. And a $2 million art collection. Oh, and good food, too. Call 615-329-1313; or visit www.wboar.com.

Lawyers in Love

985

Romance tips for business executives:

- For lawyers in love: Treat your guy/gal like an equal partner in the "firm" of your relationship.

- For salesmen in love: Treat her better than your best customer.

- For VPs in love: Prepare a "Relationship Annual Report" for your mate.

- For advertising execs in love: Create an ad campaign that expresses your love.

- For stockbrokers in love: If there were a "Dow Jones Romance Average," how well are your "relationship stocks" doing?

- For PR execs in love: Create a love-related "PR stunt" for your partner.

- For managers in love: Are you managing your relationship as well as you're managing your career?

- For Regional Managers: If your partner were in charge of giving bonuses for your "performance" at home, how big would this quarter's bonus be?

- For Junior VPs: Are you practicing your relationship skills as diligently as you're practicing your golf skills?

- For CPAs in love: Conduct a cost-benefit analysis of love in your life.

- For engineers in love: Increase your expression of affection by twenty-three percent.

- For job hunters: Create a Relationship Resumé that lists your qualifications.

- For company presidents: Are you providing adequate leadership and inspiration at home?

Chapter Theme Song:

"Lawyers in Love," Jackson Browne

MBAs in Love

986

More romance tips for business executives:

❐ For CEOs in love: Are you keeping your most important "shareholder" happy?

❐ For Big Shot Board Members: Are your daily activities in sync with your "Mission Statement"?

❐ For CFOs in love: Review your emotional "investment" in your partner.

❐ For marketing managers: Identify and meet the Strategic Objectives of your relationship.

❐ For supervisors in love: Delegate more—and get home earlier.

❐ For manufacturing execs: Do you have your suppliers of romantic gifts lined-up?

❐ For bankers in love: You don't give cheap toasters to your most important customers, do you? *Well?*

❐ For sales managers in love: Focus 10 percent more effort on your most important customer—and watch your "bonus" increase proportionally.

❐ For computer programmers: Work the "bugs" out of your relationship.

❐ For Quality Assurance execs: Ensure the level of "quality time" spent at home.

❐ For Human Resources managers in love: Administer to yourself and your mate one of your corporate "Personality Profiles." Then use the results to improve your relationship.

❐ For entrepreneurs in love: You're creating something new and valuable. Go for it!

For workaholics in all fields: It's a cliché, but it's **true:** *No one, on his deathbed, ever said, "I wish I'd spent more time working."*

Chapter Theme Song:
"Takin' Care of Business," Bachman-Turner Overdrive

Hearts (#'s 1-32)

987a

1. Make a heart-shaped pizza.
2. Your initials in a heart—in skywriting.
3. Cut the kitchen sponges into heart shapes.
4. While out at a formal dinner, nonchalantly draw a heart on the back of his hand with a pen.
5. Have a heart-shaped pool built.
6. Your initials in a heart—on wet cement in a sidewalk.
7. Trace a heart shape in fogged-up windows.
8. Your initials in a twenty-foot heart in the snow.
9. A quilt with a heart motif.
10. Your initials in a heart—etched on a brick in your patio.
11. Place the pepperoni in the shape of a heart on the pizza.
12. Trace a fifty-foot heart in the sand on a beach.
13. Grill burgers in the shape of a heart.
14. Heart-shaped sandwiches.
15. For math nuts: $r = a\,(1 - \cos A)$.
16. Use heart-shaped stickers .
17. Band-Aids with heart designs.
18. Trace a thirty-foot heart on the ice when ice skating.
19. Heart-shaped place mats.
20. A silk tie with hearts on it.
21. A heart-shaped chunk of cheese.
22. A mug with hearts on it.
23. A heart-shaped mug.
24. A heart-shaped door mat.
25. Socks wih heart designs on them.
26. Heart-shaped doilies.
27. Heart-shaped eyeglasses.
28. A front-yard flag with hearts on it.
29. Poke holes in a heart-shape in the crust of a freshly baked pie.
30. Make heart-shaped chocolate chip cookies.
31. Heart-shaped confetti.
32. The classic heart-shaped box of chocolates.

Do you remember how to make **perfectly symmetrical hearts** *from grade school? (You fold the paper in half, then draw half a heart against the folded edge. Then cut it out and voilà!)*

Chapter Theme Song:

"Crazy on You," Heart

Hearts (#'s 33-65)

987b

33. Heart-shaped chocolate treats.
34. Carve a heart—with your initials in it—in a tree.
35. Get a heart-shaped tattoo with her initials in it.
36. Greeting cards with heart.
37. Fold the dinner napkins into heart shapes.
38. Silk boxer shorts with a heart motif.
39. Draw hearts on the bathroom mirror with lipstick.
40. Use only Love Stamps with heart shapes on them.
41. Find a wine with a heart motif on the label.
42. Heart-shaped rubber stamps.
43. Heart-shaped cakes.
44. Heart designs in icing on a cake.
45. Heart-shaped candles.
46. Heart-shaped appetizers.
47. Heart-shaped picture frames.
48. Heart-shaped wreaths.
49. Heart-shaped ice cubes.
50. A heart-shaped rug.
51. Find a heart-shaped Jell-O mold.
52. Cut banana slices into heart shapes and put them in Jell-O.
53. Shape pancakes into heart shapes.
54. Cut toast into heart shapes.
55. Cut a heart shape out of toast and fry an egg in the center.
56. Heart-shaped Rice Krispy Treats.
57. Slice strawberries into heart-shapes.
58. A heart-shaped pendant.
59. A heart-shaped pin.
60. Heart-shaped earrings.
61. Heart-shaped pasta.
62. Heart-shaped red balloons.
63. Heart-shaped cookie cutters.
64. Heart-shaped key rings.
65. Heart-shaped candy conversation hearts.

Bonus Hearts!

66. Cut the lawn into the shape of a giant heart.
67. Make a heart-shaped kite together.
68. Get a humongous heart-shaped box of Valentine candy.
69. Heart-shaped shrubbery/topiary.
70. A big, heart-shaped ice sculpture.
71. Send an envelope filled with heart-shaped glitter.
72. While tanning, place a small, heart-shaped piece of cardboard on your body.
73. Cut a piece of paper into a heart shape, then write a love letter on it.
74. Scrape the ice off his windshield—in the shape of a heart.
75. Heart-shaped beds (in the Poconos).

In My Humble Opinion

988

In my humble opinion . . . relationships start to go bad at the point when couples stop being romantic. Most couples allow their A+ Relationships to slide into mediocre C- Relationships.

How do you regain your A+ status? By taking creative action based on this wise observation:

"Sometimes progress is going back to where you first went wrong."

~ C.S. Lewis

989

In my humble opinion . . . every couple should, at some time in their life together:

Go skinny-dipping. Take a moonlit stroll on a beach in the Caribbean. Sing silly love songs to one another. Get giddy on champagne. Stay up all night talking and making love and talking and making love and eating and making love and watching old movies and making love and making love. Ride in a Tunnel of Love. Go gambling in Las Vegas. See your favorite singer live in concert. Make a baby. Watch falling stars.

Love without action is not love. At best it is a wish; at worst an imposter.

990

In my humble opinion . . . half of all love advice is erroneous at best, and harmful at worst; three-quarters of all relationship books are simplistic formulas dressed up in psychobabble to impress you.

I am a very positive, optimistic person, *but*—I'm very wary of big promises and simple answers. I don't believe you can turn a D-Relationship into an A+. (People just don't *work* that way.) You *can* turn a C- into a B+. You an turn a B- into a solid A. And that's *good enough*, don't you think?

My Personal Favorites

991

The Perpetual Bouquet—created by Tracey, during the writing of this book. She started bringing me one flower a day, and placed it in a vase on my desk. Each day she brought a *different* kind of flower. In a week I had a complete bouquet. She continued this for *three solid months*— every day removing one wilted flower and replacing it with a new one— so I had an ever-changing, always-fresh reminder of her love and support for me.

992

One of my rituals with Tracey is a changing-of-the-seasons ceremony which uses framed covers from *New Yorker* magazines. We have several covers for each season that hang in our living room. (FYI, we celebrate *five* seasons.)

At the start of each season we go through this little ritual: We set the mood with seasonal music; we fill two brandy snifters with Baileys Irish Cream for the seasonal toast; we bring out the ritual screwdrivers; we open each frame and slide in the new magazine cover; we rehang each frame; then sit back, toast one another, reminisce about the past season, and look forward to the coming season.

 Here are our current seasonal musical selections:

❤ Winter: *Antarctica* by Vangelis
❤ Spring: *A Winter's Solstice*, a Windham Hill collection
❤ Summer: *The Sacred Fire* by Nicholas Gunn
❤ Autumn: *Autumn* by George Winston
❤ Christmas: *A Charlie Brown Christmas*, by The Vince Guaraldi Trio

Sometimes, depending on our mood, we'll play the appropriate selection from Antonio Vivaldi's *The Four Seasons*.

My personal favorites . . .

Song: "I Won't Last a Day Without You," by Paul Williams

Rock group: The Moody Blues

Book: *Stranger in a Strange Land*, by Robert A. Heinlein

Story: "The Artist of the Beautiful," by Nathaniel Hawthorne

TV show: *Babylon 5*

Bed & breakfast: The Victorian Inn, Martha's Vinyard. 508-627-4784; www.TheVic.com.

Comic Strip: Calvin and Hobbes

Quote: *"We are each of us angels with only one wing. And we can only fly embracing each other."* ~ Luciano de Crescenzo

Woman: Tracey Ellen Godek

Best of the Best

993

- ✦ Best romantic gift: The gift of time
- ✦ Best romantic present: Your own presence
- ✦ Best romantic car: Triumph Spitfire
- ✦ Most romantic comic strip: Rose Is Rose
- ✦ Best romantic TV show: *Mad About You*
- ✦ Most romantic city (in the world): Verona, Italy
- ✦ Most romantic city (in the USA): San Francisco, California
- ✦ Best romantic color: Red/PMS #1795 CVU
- ✦ Most romantic Broadway musical: *Phantom of the Opera*
- ✦ Best romantic movie: *Casablanca*
- ✦ Best romantic actress: Greta Garbo
- ✦ Best romantic actor: Clark Gable
- ✦ Best romantic hotel: The Grand Hotel, Mackinac Island
- ✦ Best romantic voice (male): Barry White
- ✦ Best romantic voice (female): Sade
- ✦ Best romantic song: "You are So Beautiful (To Me)," by Joe Cocker

Do you agree? Disagree?
Voice your opinion at
www.1001WaysToBeRomantic.com

Best Brief Advice

994

Gals: You want more *romance?* Give him more *sex.* (Try having sex every night—night after night after night after night—until he *begs* you to stop! Just try it as a little experiment. It just might transform your ho-hum relationship into a raging love affair!)

No, I'm not joking.

995

Guys: You want more *sex?* Give her more *romance.* (Romance her like Don Juan. Like Romeo. Like Clark Gable. Romance her every day in every way. Romance her using every single idea in this book—and then think up one thousand and one *more* ways to be romantic. And she'll give you all the sex you could ever dream of.)

*Yo, guys, this **ain't** rocket science!*

996

Best way to create more time in your life: Shoot your TV.

997

Use gifts and presents to express love and appreciation. Don't use them to apologize after a fight or make up for some dumb thing you've done. This strategy eventually backfires.

998

✦ The unasked-for gift is most appreciated.
✦ The surprise gift is most cherished.

Top 10 Reasons to be Romantic

999a

1. You'll be happier.
2. Your *partner* will be happier.
3. You'll have sex more often.
4. You'll *enjoy* sex more.
5. You'll rise above mediocrity, and create an A+ Relationship.
6. You'll experience the spark of infatuation again.
7. You'll reduce the chance that your partner might cheat on you.
8. You'll increase the probability that you'll stay married.
9. You'll add depth and meaning to your relationship.
10. You will create a safe haven where you can really be yourself.

You may want to make a scroll of these reasons and present it to your partner.

Or jot one reason per day in his/her calendar.

999b

And a few *more* reasons to be romantic:

11. You will be truly heard and deeply understood by one other human being.
12. You'll save money by expressing your love in lots of little, creative ways.
13. Exercising your creativity will benefit you in *other* areas of your life.
14. You'll probably live longer.
15. You'll be better parents.
16. You'll be great role models for your children.
17. You'll be great role models for friends and neighbors.
18. Your children will understand love better than most kids.
19. Your children will experience what love is really all about.
20. Your children will have a better chance of choosing partners wisely.
21. Your children will be better able to create healthy love relationships.
22. You'll make the world a better place.
23. You'll come to appreciate your own uniqueness.

The Top 45 Reasons to be Romantic

999c

And still *more* reasons to be romantic:

24. You'll come to appreciate your partner's uniqueness.
25. You'll reduce or eliminate therapy bills!
26. You'll get more of what you want out of life.
27. You'll strengthen your self-esteem and self-confidence.
28. You'll never have to write to Dear Abby for love advice.
29. You'll be better able to live your faith (love is central to every religion).
30. You will have the quiet confidence that you've achieved something that few people accomplish.
31. You'll create a truly mature relationship.
32. You'll move beyond treating your partner like a stereotype.
33. You'll have more energy and focus for your career.
34. You'll surprise your skeptical in-laws!
35. You'll deepen your understanding of the opposite sex.
36. You'll reconnect with your creative, impulsive, spontaneous, childlike nature.
37. You'll live up to your true potential in life.
38. You'll never again be panic-stricken on Valentine's Day!
39. You'll never again have to feel guilty for having forgotten a birthday or anniversary.
40. You'll stay young at heart.
41. You'll keep the world spinning. (Love makes the world go 'round.)
42. You'll keep your love alive.
43. Your partner *wants* you to be romantic. What *more* reason do you need?
44. Why *not??*

#45: Life is simply too short **not** to be romantic!

The End

1000

Once upon a time . . . *they lived happily ever after.* The perfect ending to any story, wouldn't you say?

Your story—your personal story, the love story that the two of you are creating together—is somewhere in its middle chapters, I would guess. So how's it going? Is it turning out as you expected? If so, *marvelous!* If not, wrap up the current chapter of your story and create a *new* chapter. An exciting chapter. A fulfilling chapter. A *romantic* chapter.

Imagine that your life is a novel, and you and your lover are its co-authors. You have great artistic license to create a *love* story out of your *life* story. And if you need help in creating some romantic scenes, please use *1001 Ways To Be Romantic* as a resource. Take these ideas, give them a creative twist and the benefit of your unique personality, and they will truly become *your own.*

*"Work like you don't need the money.
Love like you've never been hurt.
Dance like there's nobody's watching."*

~ Anonymous

Chapter Theme Song:
"The End," The Beatles
(T.L.Y.T.I.E.T.T.L.Y.M.)

The Beginning

1001

In the beginning was the Word. And the word was Love.

Love. It is the single most important word in any language. It is the *defining* experience of what it means to be human. It is virtually the *first* (most welcoming!) word we hear when we are born; it is usually the *last* (most comforting) word we hear before we die; and it is the word we are obsessed with during every year in between.

Even though time passes and every couple creates a history together, love must still be re-created every day. If your yesterdays were great, they help make today even better. If your yesterdays weren't so hot, they help motivate you to make today *different*.

Yes, you *can* turn a C- Relationship into an A+ Relationship. I've helped many couples achieve this goal. *1001 Ways To Be Romantic* can help *you* achieve that goal, too. This isn't the end—it's just the *beginning* of your life as a happier, more loving and more loved person.

Love must be made real, brought alive in the world through action, thoughts and deeds. In a word, *romance*.

*When it comes to love, the secret is that there **is** no secret. Simply express love. There are at **least** 1001 ways to do it.*

About the Author

Gregory J.P. Godek is an author and researcher, speaker and performer, husband and father. He was romantic by inclination long before it became an avocation, then preoccupation—and finally—occupation. Greg has been teaching his acclaimed Romance Classes for twenty years.

This book was written at the request of thousands of romantically starved women and romantically impaired men. This book *works*. It's not a deep, theoretical book, and it's not another *cute* "love" book. It's a practical, inspirational (and occasionally humorous) book.

Greg burst upon the national scene with *1001 Ways To Be Romantic* in 1991 and became a national celebrity as his book became an instant classic. No one had ever before combined such a *huge* number of practical tips with just the *right* amount of psychology. Greg has since taught romance on *Oprah;* counseled troubled couples on *Donahue;* shared tips on *Montel;* and launched the biggest booksigning tour in the history of publishing by unveiling his custom-designed romance bus on *Good Morning America.*

1001 Ways To Be Romantic is a year-round bestseller with more than 1.5 million copies in print; it led to twelve additional books and a CD collection of romantic classical music; and it has been referenced by Jay Leno in his *Tonight Show* monologue. Greg has taught romance to the U.S. Army, to corporate groups and to audiences around the world.

Greg is a teacher and role model, not a therapist or theorist. He does not have a pet theory that he insists you accept. He is highly conscious of the diversity of human experience, of the infinite variability of human personality, of the uniqueness of every individual. Greg believes that romance is about expressing love in thousands of ways that reflect your creativity and your partner's specialness.

Greg has been working on this "Author's Annotated Edition" for *years.* Hundreds of new ideas and hundreds of his personal notes are included in this completely revised edition of *1001 Ways To Be Romantic.*

Greg is a rarity—a celebrity who actually practices what he preaches: He really *does* have a happy marriage.

---

*"Greg Godek is a **thirty**something Leo Buscaglia."*

~ Evening Magazine

Greg performs powerful and unique speeches and seminars on love and romance. Call 877-ROMANCE.

Theme Song:
"Good Old Fashioned Lover Boy," Queen

Index

*"Love creates an **us** without destroying a **me**."*

~ Leo Buscaglia

"People who are sensible about love are incapable of it."

~ Douglas Yates

D

E

*Couples who have A + Relationships know the secret of combining creativity and action to produce long-term monogamous love affairs. (In other words, they know the secret of **romance**.)*

*"By endowing the commonplace
  with a lofty magnificence,
  the ordinary with a mysterious aspect,
  the familiar with the merit of the unfamiliar,
  the finite with the appearance of infinity,
I am Romanticising."*

~ NOVALIS

"There isn't any formula or method. You learn to love by loving."

~ ALDOUS HUXLEY

L

Lady Chatterly's Lover 271
Lame excuses 78-81
Lewis, C.S. 340
Life Savers 114, 218
Limousines 149, 257
Lingerie 23, 67, 70, 98, 150,
    186, 218, 261, 320
Listening 30, 313
Lists 158
Little
    celebrations 42
    things 4, 40
Living happily ever after 3
Lobster 230
Long-term thinking 84
Lord of the Rings 223
Lottery tickets 86
Love 347
    advice 340
    coupons 23, 33, 47, 273, 318, 321
    letters 56, 57, 83, 241, 256, 328
    makes the world go 'round 195
    notes 4, 38, 39, 46, 56, 131, 229
    romance & sex 307
    sex & romance 295
    songs 164-175, 256, 262
    stamps 56, 106, 244
    stories 292, 293
Loveboat 186
Loveland, Colorado 244
LoveLetter newsletter 60
Lovemaking
    55, 101, 119, 138, 151, 190,
    201, 240, 296, 324
Lovesick 58

M

m&m's 218, 252
Mad about you 10, 279
Madonna 47
Madrid 297

Magazine gifts 192
Mail it 83, 98, 225, 244, 248, 281
Making love 87, 89, 119, 138, 151,
    190, 201, 260, 296
Making up after a fight 103
Male bashing (stopping) 104
Marriage 226
    magazine 186
    proposals 293
Married . . . with children 97, 273
Mars/Venus 130-133
Masculine & feminine 74
Massages 86, 88, 315, 329
Mathematics of romance 94
McDonald's 115, 135
Mementos 32
Memories 204, 259
Memorize this list 158
Men & Women 104, 130
Men only 261, 300
Merry Christmas 105, 133, 206
Metaphors of love 10, 128
Mickey Mouse 121
Microsoft 206
Mile High Club 151
Miller, Glenn 240
Miller, Henry 271
Mind-reading 304
Mindset of a romantic 29, 35, 40, 41,
    68, 83, 113, 115, 123, 131,
    134, 140, 198, 246, 247, 284, 285
Misconceptions about romance 129
Mobile phones 234
Modes of expression 42
Money 78, 91, 108, 281, 321
    makes the world go 'round 194
Month of romance 86, 87, 88, 89
Monty Python 311
Moody Blues 25
More power! 261
Most important lessons 10
Motivating him/her 287

Become an artist of your relationship.

Love does not—cannot—hurt.
*It's the **absence** of love that hurts.*

"The heart has its reasons which reason knows nothing of."

- BLAISE PASCAL

T

*"L'amour, l'amour fait tourner le monde." ***

~ A FRENCH FOLK SONG

* *"It's love, it's love that makes the world
go 'round."*

Romance is "adult play."

Romantic love. Anything else is a compromise.

~ GREGORY GODEK

*"Godek . . . is helping transform
men and women into modern
Romeos and Juliets."*

~ UPI